DIRECTIONS IN DEVELOPMENT

Safety Net Programs
and Poverty Reduction

Lessons from Cross-Country Experience

K. Subbarao
Aniruddha Bonnerjee
Jeanine Braithwaite
Soniya Carvalho
Kene Ezemenari
Carol Graham
Alan Thompson

The World Bank
Washington, D.C.

© 1997 The International Bank for Reconstruction
and Development/ THE WORLD BANK
1818 H Street, N.W.
Washington, D.C. 20433

The findings, interpretations, and conclusions expressed in this study are entirely those of the authors and should not be attributed in any manner to the World Bank, to its affiliated organizations, or to members of its Board of Executive Directors or the countries they represent.

K. Subbarao and Jeanine Braithwaite are principal economist and human resources economist, respectively, in the Poverty, Gender, and Public Sector Management Department of the World Bank. Aniruddha Bonnerjee, Soniya Carvalho, Kene Ezemenari, and Alan Thompson are consultants at the World Bank. Carol Graham is a fellow at the Brookings Institution, she was a visiting fellow at the World Bank when the study was written.

Cover photo: Curt Carnemark, The World Bank

Library of Congress Cataloging-in-Publication Data

  Safety net programs and poverty reduction : lessons from cross-country
experience / [prepared by] K. Subbarao ... [et al.].
      p.   cm.
  Includes bibliographical references.
  ISBN 0-8213-3890-0
  1. Income maintenance programs—Case studies.   2. Economic
assistance, Domestic—Case studies.   I. Subbarao, K.
HC79.I5S24   1997
362.5'82—dc21   97-3168
                                                                CIP

Contents

Foreword

There is now a widespread consensus on the need for safety nets as a key component of a poverty reduction strategy. Safety nets are basically income maintenance programs that protect a person or household against two adverse outcomes: a chronic incapacity to work and earn, and a decline in this capacity caused by imperfectly predictable life-cycle events (such as the sudden death of a bread-winner), sharp shortfalls in aggregate demand or expenditure shocks (through economic recession or transition), or very bad harvests. Safety net programs serve two important roles: redistribution (such as transfers to disadvantaged groups) and insurance (such as drought relief).

The ongoing structural adjustment programs and the unprecedented economic and political transition of countries of the former Soviet Union and Eastern Europe have given rise to a renewed interest in social safety net programs. Economic crisis—whatever its sources—is most likely to impinge harshly on vulnerable groups in the short run, underscoring the need for countervailing measures. Moreover, the role of these policies in specific countries depends on the way the economy distributes resources in the absence of safety net policies. A propoor development path will place less demands on safety net policies.

Over the past three decades several developing countries have embarked on a variety of programs, including cash transfers, subsidies in-kind, public works, and income-generation programs. Few studies have synthesized the lessons from widely differing country experiences. Moreover, there is little guidance on appropriate program design for countries and international donors supporting such safety net initiatives. This book fills the gap. It reviews the conceptual issues in the choice of programs, synthesizes cross-country experience, and analyzes how country- and region-specific constraints help explain why different approaches are successful in different countries.

It is hoped that World Bank staff, members of other international aid agencies, policymakers in client countries, and the academic community will benefit from this collaborative work of the Poverty and Social Policy Department.

Ishrat Husain
Director
Poverty and Social Policy Department
World Bank

Acknowledgments

This book was prepared by a team comprising K. Subbarao (team leader and main author), Aniruddha Bonnerjee, Jeanine Braithwaite, Soniya Carvalho, Kene Ezemenari, Carol Graham, and Alan Thompson. Nicholas Barr and Soonwon Kwon contributed background papers. The study was carried out under the overall direction of Oey Astra Meesook and Ishrat Husain, the former manager and the director, Poverty Analysis and Social Policy Department.

For helpful comments and suggestions, the authors wish to thank Petros Aklilu, Harold Alderman, Nicholas Barr, Bruce Fitzgerald, Louise Fox, Fredrick Golladay, Margaret Grosh, Ishrat Husain, Emmanuel Jimenez, Polly Jones, Steen Jorgensen, Shahid Khandker, Kathie Krumm, Soonwon Kwon, Peter Lanjouw, Samuel Lieberman, Kathy Lindert, William McGreevey, Oey Astra Meesook, Tawhid Nawaz, John Newman, Nick Prescott, Sandor Sipos, Elisabeth Stock, Dominique van de Walle, Jack van Holst Pellekaan, and Lawrence Wolff.

Michael Lipton, professor of economics at the University of Sussex, served as an external peer reviewer. The study benefited greatly from his valuable comments and suggestions.

Successive drafts of the paper were processed by Gay Santos and Maria Paz Felix. Ilyse Zable edited the book and Glenn McGrath laid it out.

Abbreviations

AGETIP	Agence d'Execution des Travaux d'Interet Public Contre le Sous-Emploi
AIDS	Acquired immune deficiency syndrome
AKRSP	Aga Khan Rural Support Project
APRA	American Popular Revolutionary Alliance
BKK	Badon Kredit Kecamatan
BRAC	Bangladesh Rural Advancement Committee
BRI	Bank Rakyat Indonesia
CDP	Community Development Program
DIRE	Délégation a l'Insertion et le Reinsertion a l'Emploi
EEP	Export Enhancement Program
ESF	Emergency Social Fund
FIS	Fondo de Inversión Social
GDP	Gross domestic product
GNP	Gross national product
ICDS	Integrated Child Development Services
ICM	Brazil's general value added tax
IFAD	International Fund for Agricultural Development
IFPRI	International Food Policy Research Institute
ILO	International Labour Organization
IMF	International Monetary Fund
IRDP	Integrated Rural Development Program
JRY	Jawahar Rojgar Yojuna
LAC	Latin America and the Caribbean
MCHN	Mother/child health and nutrition
MEGS	Maharashtra Employment Guarantee Scheme
MENPROSIF	Mendoza Provencial Program for Basic Social Infrastructure
MMD	Movement for Multi-Party Democracy
MPU	Microprojects Unit
MYRYDA	The Mysovre Resettlement and Development Agency
NGO	Nongovernmental organization
NIA	Philippines Communal Irrigation Project
NBU	National Bank of Ukraine

OECD	Organization for Economic Cooperation and Development
PAIT	Temporary Income Support Program
PAU	Urban Action Program
PEM	Minimum Employment Program
POJH	Occupational Program for Household Heads
PPP	Purchasing power parity
PRADAN	Professional Assistance for Development Action
PRI	Institutional Revolutionary Party
PRONASOL	National Solidarity Program
RMP	Rural Maintenance Program
SAPs	Social Action Programs
Sedesol	Secretariat of Social Development
SEWA	Self-Employed Women's Association
SF	Social fund
SPARC	Society for Promotion of Area Residence Centres
SRF	Social Recovery Fund
SRP	Social Recovery Project
TINP	Tamil Nadu Integrated Nutrition Project
UNICEF	United Nations Children's Fund
UNIP	United National Independence Party
USAID	United States Agency for International Development
WFP	World Food Program
WGTFI	Working Group in Targeted Food Interventions

1
Introduction

The current proliferation of structural adjustment programs and macroeconomic stabilization measures has given rise to a renewed interest in social safety net programs.[1] The economic and political transition of the countries of the former Soviet Union and Eastern Europe has contributed to this renewed interest as well. Countries in this region are restructuring their economic systems at the same time that they are attempting to liberalize prices and stabilize external balances, provide public services, and protect the well-being of their citizens. These countries have inherited systems of social protection that are no longer fiscally sustainable or able to protect economically and socially vulnerable groups. Public spending on social protection (social insurance and social assistance payments) as a share of gross domestic product (GDP) continues to be high, though many of the newly emerging working poor remain unprotected.[2] Evidence shows that poverty increased by as much as 100 percent between 1987 and 1993—the years immediately preceding and following transition. The unskilled laborer was most likely to experience worsening poverty during this period.

In low- and middle-income countries in the process of adjusting, formal safety nets and community and family support networks are increasingly unable to cope with the extent of need in the wake of events—such as the massive numbers of AIDS-orphaned children in Africa—unforeseen a decade ago.[3]

Regardless of a country's location, be it in Africa, Latin America, Asia, the former Soviet Union, or Eastern Europe, economic crisis and the adjustment or transition that follows have adverse short-term effects on the living standards of vulnerable groups. And shrinking budgets are severely restricting the amount of resources available for social assistance. There is clearly an acute need to protect the new poor and the chronically poor by introducing social assistance programs or restructuring existing ones in ways that make them fiscally, politically, and administratively sustainable.

Added to the urgent need to revisit safety net issues is the ongoing debate over the optimal policy mix between the indirect growth-oriented path to poverty reduction and the direct path of targeted transfers to the poor. Should all scarce resources be allocated so as to maximize economic growth, the benefits of which will eventually trickle down to the poor, or should a part of these resources be transferred to the poor to improve and maintain their living standards during the process of economic growth? A third option is to give the poor access to assets (such as land) that provide them with a source of economic growth based on their absolute advantage—that is, labor.

Although diverting scarce resources directly to the poor compromises economic growth in the short run, the forgone cost of not accounting for the poor may compromise economic growth in the long-run. In order to survive, the poor may seek to minimize income or consumption risks, resort to criminal or marginalized activities, or be forced to accept extreme insecurity and risk of death. Moreover, denying the poor access to economic and educational opportunities accentuates inequality—an outcome likely to retard economic growth (Lipton 1995). In democratic societies neglect of the poor, particularly during reform, can also lead to political instability.

Some conflict between direct poverty-targeted programs and growth-promoting activities is inevitable in most countries. But the dichotomy between the direct and indirect paths to poverty reduction may be minimized if a country adopts a growth-oriented adjustment program that is sufficiently broad-based to include all socioeconomic groups, particularly the poor, in productive activities. Finally, the path taken by a specific country, and the relative weight given to poverty-targeted programs, will depend on the level of institutional and administrative capacity, and on the quantity (and quality) of human capital. If the forgone cost of not including the poor—especially the accentuation of inequality in the short run—is a major consideration, then safety nets will need to be a strategic component of the path that is taken to poverty reduction.

What Constitutes a Safety Net?

Safety nets are programs that protect a person or household against two adverse outcomes: chronic incapacity to work and earn (*chronic poverty*) and a decline in this capacity from a marginal situation that provides minimal means for survival with few reserves (*transient poverty*). A chronic incapacity to work or earn will usually result from physical or mental disability, long-term illness, or old age. A decline in the capacity to work is usually caused by imperfectly predictable life-cycle events (such as the birth of twins or a sudden death of a bread-winner); a sharp fall in aggregate demand or expenditure shocks (through economic recession or transition, during unavoidable cutbacks in public spending, as a result of a decline in production in sectors from which workers are immobile); or poor harvests (due to drought, flood, or pests, especially when they affect prices and production over a wide area), which cause the rural poor to lose the usual sources of protection offered by informal transfers (see discussion below).

There is a broad range of mechanisms for protecting individuals from acute deprivation or inadvertent declines in income. In some societies informal or community-based arrangements (private safety nets) help mitigate the adverse outcomes in welfare. In addition, publicly supported social safety nets also help the vulnerable. These include social services (health and education in particular), social insurance programs such as pensions, all publicly funded transfers (cash transfers such as family allowances and in-kind transfers such as food subsidies), and income-generation programs targeted to the poor (such as public works). This book focuses on publicly funded transfers aimed at the poor and on income-generation programs. Although social insurance programs constitute the most dominant form of cash transfer in most countries of Eastern European and the former Soviet Union, and provide relief to the poor in the formal sectors, these programs are not addressed here because issues pertaining to pensions were the focus of a recent World Bank policy study (Fox 1994). Where necessary (as in the discussion on cash transfers in countries of the former Soviet Union), the study will make reference to the interface between social insurance and social assistance programs.

Who Needs Safety Nets?

In every society some individuals are able to take advantage of emerging opportunities better than others, in the same way that some individuals are more vulnerable to *chronic* or *transient* declines in income. Individuals are likely to be at a disadvantage in either situation if they are:
- Most prone to unpredictable, sharp falls in real spending power.
- Least resilient to a reduction in real spending power.
- Least likely to have formal insurance.
- Least likely to be attractive to informal insurance groups (such as reciprocal savings or insurance societies), which seek dependable co-contributors.

Thus the poor are most likely to be in need of safety nets. In the absence of publicly supported safety nets the poor are likely to turn their production and consumption behavior toward risk avoidance instead of toward income maximization. In other words, the poor often cannot afford to be entrepreneurial—and may remain underproductive and poor. In order to counteract this, cash and in-kind transfers, and poverty-targeted programs—the main focus of this study—should be examined in a broad developmental context, while ensuring that the poor also have access to the gains from economic growth.

Cash and In-Kind Transfers in a Developmental Context

Any cash or in-kind transfer requires real resources, and budgetary limitations imply that there are often difficult trade-offs between transfers and other programs supported by tax revenues. Therefore, it is important to coordinate transfer programs with broader developmental goals. These programs must be formulated in the context of a poverty-reduction strategy, comprising initiatives for labor-demanding growth and expanded access to social services for the poor. Targeted transfers to provide temporary relief to the poor should never replace development programs, such as irrigation, education, or infrastructure development, that enable long-term escape from poverty. In some countries or regions investments in drought-proofing or in activities such as village-to-market roads can significantly stabilize the poor's employment possibilities and incomes, dramatically reducing the need for short-term poverty relief (Ahmed and Donovan 1992; Binswanger, Khandker, and Rosenzweig 1993).

Thus the type and structure of demand for safety nets may vary with an economy's size, age structure, health, real average income, and type and extent of fluctuations in production, and may interact with other economic policies. A consequence is that as growth or redistribution increases a poor person's expected (average) annual real income, his or her capacity to save, insure, spread short-term risks, and meet both acute and chronic shocks without disaster also increases. In addition, governments opting for fast liberalization must factor in both the need for more spending on safety nets in the short to medium run and the likelihood that this spending will drop in the longer run. Well-distributed real income reduces the need for safety nets and increases an individual's ability to cope with distress. Also, policies that spend scarce resources on irrigation, control of infectious illness, labor-intensive production, and land redistributions—whatever their advantages or drawbacks—save resources by reducing the need for publicly provided safety nets. Therefore, under no circumstances should safety net policies be framed as alternatives to investments in labor-demanding growth activities.

Public Transfers and Private Safety Nets

Valuable empirical information is now available demonstrating the importance of personal reciprocity and informal safety nets in developing countries and in some economies in transition (table 1.1). Traditional coping mechanisms reduce economic insecurity.[4] Public transfers, therefore, should complement not only broader developmental activities, but also the prevailing traditional arrangements. The usefulness of public transfers for poverty relief is greatly reduced if public transfers induce reductions in private transfers (remittances, and so on) to the poor. But it is important not to exaggerate the role of private transfers in poverty reduction—as is commonly done by wealthy taxpayers to undermine public support for the poor. Private transfers could be minimal if an entire country or parts of a country are visited by a drought, or if transfers are made between groups that are poor.[5]

Cross-Country Patterns in Program Choice

Many countries have experimented with a wide array of social assistance and poverty-targeted programs. The choice and scope of instruments varied a great deal across countries, depending on circumstances. The degree of success in reaching the poor in a cost-effective way also varied with the extent and depth of poverty, the composition of target groups, the speed and sequencing of reforms, the availability of financing, administrative capacity, and political economy factors. Often, the same instrument produced quite different outcomes and effects on the poor in different countries and across regions in the same country.

The situation prevailing from the mid-1980s to the mid-1990s is the result of the historical evolution of programs (table 1.2). Four patterns are worth noting:

- Program choice was to some extent influenced by the nature and availability of food aid. Thus in the 1950s and 1960s food aid (particularly from the United States) led to the emergence of food-for-work programs, especially in South Asia. With the decline of food aid in the 1970s and 1980s, food-for-work programs also diminished in importance—now, only two countries have such programs.[6] During the 1980s availability of direct nonfood assistance by (bilateral) donors and an eagerness to channel such assistance through nongovernmental channels led to the emergence of social funds.
- A few countries sought to realize multiple objectives with one program. For example, public works programs that give staple food as wages seek to relieve poverty by ensuring that participants have access to food, are able to smooth their consumption, and build infrastructure—thus complementing economic growth.
- Countries varied in the pervasiveness of interventions: some relied on one major program (such as family assistance in the countries of

Table 1.1. The Importance of Private Transfers in Select Countries

Country and segment of the population	Year	National GNP per capita (1993 US dollars)
El Salvador (urban poor)	1976	1,320
Mexico (two villages)	1982	3,610
Peru	1985	1,490
India (rural)	1975-83	300
Indonesia (Java)	1982	740
Rural		
Urban		
Malaysia	1977–78	3,140
Philippines	1978	850
Kenya		
Rural	1974	
Urban	1974	
Urban (sample of recent migrants)	1968	270
Nairobi (urban poor)	1971	
Nationwide	1974	
Kyrgyz Republic	1993	850
Romania	1994	1,140
Rural	—	
Urban	—	
Russia	1992	2,340
United States	1979	24,740

— Data not available.
a. Number in parentheses denotes percentage for households in lowest income quintile.

the former Soviet Union), while others (such as India) experimented with a rich array of programs, including food subsidies, nutrition programs, public works, and credit-based livelihood programs.

- Labor-intensive public works (run either by governments or by private contractors) are more prevalent in Africa and Asia than elsewhere, whereas food transfers are prevalent in most regions. One difference between public works in South Asia and those in Africa is worth noting. In South Asia public works receive greater support, funding, and direct involvement of governments, while in Africa, works programs are driven largely by donors, and are short-lived.[7]

Within each program countries chose varying types of intervention. Food-related interventions ranged from open general food subsidies to more targeted programs, such as food stamps and feeding programs. The choice of a particular type of intervention is generally governed by the specific conditions in a country (such as its sociopolitical and economic history, its climate and agroecological zones, its limited administrative capacity, and so on) and the specific advantages in a country

Percentage of households		Average transfer amount (percentage of average income)		Source
Receiving	Giving	Receiving	Giving	
33		11		Kaufmann and Lindauer (1986)
		16–21		Stark, Taylor, and Yitzhaki (1988)
22	23	2	1	Cox and Jimenez (1989)
93		8		Behrman and Deolalikar (1987)
31	72	10	8	
44	45	20	3	
19–30	33–47	11(46)[a]		Butz and Stan (1982)
47		9		Kaufmann (1982)
	19	2	3	Rempell and Lobdall (1978)
	62	4	6	
	59		13	Johnson and Whitelaw (1974)
	89			
	27	3	4	Knowles and Anker (1981)
13	11	41	16	Cox, Jimenez, and Jordan (1994)
7	—	2		Subbarao and Mehra (1995)
5	—	1		
8	—	3		
24	24	31	12.9	Cox, Eser, and Jimenez (1995)
15	—	1		Cox (1987)

Source: Updated from Cox and Jimenez (1990). See the last column of the table for sources for different countries. The data for the Kyrgyz Republic, Romania, and Russia are taken from sources listed in the table. Data for GNP are taken from World Bank (1995m).

(such as the availability of private transfers). Thus in South Asia food rations emerged as a result of postwar shortages, but evolved into other schemes that continued to provide in-kind transfers for the poor long after food shortages had abated.

Variations in program choices and characteristics, total public spending as a share of GDP, and the amount of public spending on safety nets as a share of GDP across countries may be explained by variations in countries' objectives, historical circumstances, level of real purchasing power parity (PPP) GDP per capita, the inherent nature of constraints, and the degree of buoyancy of private transfers (Jimenez 1993). A broad, regional typology sets the high-income Organization for Economic Cooperation and Development (OECD) countries, where private transfers (as a fraction of average household income) are expected to be minimal,[8] and which typically can be regarded as "high public spenders," at one end of the spectrum (table 1.3). At the other end of the spectrum are the low-income countries of Asia and Africa, where private transfers (as a fraction of average

Table 1.2. Classification of Countries by Programs, Late 1980s to Mid-1990s

		Income distribution			
Country	GNP per capita (1993)	PPP GDP per capita (1993 int. $)	Poorest 20%	Richest 20%	Public works
Sub-Saharan Africa					
Botswana	2,790	—	—	—	x
Ethiopia	100	—	8.6	41.3	x
The Gambia	350	1,170	—	—	
Ghana	430	1,970	7.0	44.1	x
Kenya	270	1,290	3.4	61.8	x
Lesotho	650	1,620	2.9	60.0	x
Madagascar	220	670	—	—	
Malawi	200	690	—	—	x
Mali	270	520	—	—	
Mozambique	90	550	—	—	x
Nigeria	300	1,400	5.1	49.0	x
Senegal	750	1,650	3.5	42.8	x
Somalia	—	—	—	—	
Tanzania	90	580	2.4	62.7	x
Zambia	380	1,040	5.6	49.7	
Zimbabwe	520	2,000	4.0	62.3	
South Africa	2,980	—	3.3	63.3	
Middle East and North Africa					
Algeria	1,780	5,380	6.9	46.5	
Egypt	660	3,780	—	—	
Morocco	1,040	3,090	6.6	46.3	
Tunisia	1,720	4,780	5.9	46.3	
Jordan	—	4,100	6.5	47.7	
South Asia					
Bangladesh	220	1,290	9.5	38.6	x
India	200	1,220	8.8	41.3	x
Pakistan	430	2,170	8.4	39.7	
Sri Lanka	600	2,990	8.9	39.3	x
East Asia					
China	490	2,330	6.4	41.8	
Indonesia	740	3,150	8.7	42.3	
Philippines	850	2,670	6.5	47.8	x
Thailand	2,110	6,269	6.1	50.7	x

| | Program types | | | | |
Food transfers	Credit-based livelihood programs	Family assistance and/or cash social assistance	Energy subsidies	Housing subsidies	Others[a]
					SAP
x					SF
x					
x	x			x	SAP
x	x				
	x				SF/SAP
	x				SF
x	x				
	x				SF
x					SF
x	x			x	
x					SAP
x					
x	x				SF
x					
x					
x					
x	x				
x	x			x	
x					SAP
x					SF
					Regional
x	x		x		
x	x			x	

(Table continues on following page.)

Table 1.2 *(cont.)*

	Income distribution				
Country	*GNP per capita (1993)*	*PPP GDP per capita (1993 int. $)*	*Poorest 20%*	*Richest 20%*	*Public works*
Latin America and the Caribbean					
Bolivia	760	2,420	5.6	48.2	x
Brazil	2,930	5,370	2.1	67.5	
Chile	3,170	8,400	3.3	60.4	x
Colombia	1,400	5,490	3.6	55.8	
Costa Rica	2,150	5,520	4.0	50.8	
Ecuador	1,200	4,240	—	—	
Guatemala	1,100	3,350	2.1	63.0	
Guyana	—	—	—	—	
Haiti	600	2,990	—	—	
Honduras	600	1,910	2.7	63.5	x
Jamaica	1,440	3,000	6.0	48.4	
Mexico	3,610	6,810	4.1	55.9	
Nicaragua	340	1,900	4.2	55.3	x
Peru	1,490	3,220	4.9	51.4	
Uruguay	3,830	6,380	—	—	
Venezuela	2,840	8,130	4.8	49.5	
Europe and Central Asia					
Bulgaria	1,140	4,100	8.4	39.3	
Czech Republic	2,710	7,550	—	—	
Hungary	3,350	6,050	10.9	34.4	
Kyrgyz Republic	850	2,320	2.5	57.0	
Poland	2,260	5,000	9.2	36.1	
Romania	1,140	2,800	—	—	
Russia	2,340	5,050	4.2	48.0	
Ukraine	2,210	4,450	—	—	

— Data not available.
Note: Program types are based on cross-country reviews in World Bank (1995m); this is not an exhaustive classification of countries.

household income) are significant. Public spending is predictably lowest in these regions. In between fall the middle- and low-income economies in transition, all maintaining unsustainably high levels of public spending on safety nets.

As objectives, constraints, and country circumstances change, programs also change, though only rarely are programs discontinued entirely. Thus most countries in transition are attempting to curtail open-ended transfers that they can no longer afford. Various targeting options are being explored. In some countries a particular program may generate a constraint and induce its own change. For example, an expensive and untargeted program might lead to fiscal tightness, which, in turn, leads to a change in its design.

		Program type			
Food transfers	Credit-based livelihood programs	Family assistance and/or cash social assistance	Energy subsidies	Housing subsidies	Others[a]
	x				
x					
x				x	
x			x	x	
x					
	x			x	SF
	x				SF
	x				SF
	x				SF
x	x				SF
x				x	
x	x				SF
	x				SF
x	x				SF
x				x	
x	x		x	x	SF
		x	x		
		x	x		
		x	x	x	
		x	x		
		x	x		
x		x	x		
		x	x	x	
x		x	x		

a. SAP is Social Action Program. SF is Social Fund.
Source: World Bank (1995m).

Objectives and Outline of the Book

The main objectives of this book are to review the conceptual issues that arise when choosing among programs; analyze how country- and region-specific constraints help to explain why different approaches are successful in different countries and regions; synthesize the lessons learned from experience; and offer some promising best-practice examples.

The study's scope is limited to social assistance and poverty-targeted programs, of which there are two kinds: programs with and without work requirements. Programs with no work requirements include two principal cash transfers (prevalent especially in countries

Table 1.3. Regional Patterns in Safety Nets

Country type	Publicly supported social security (contributory pensions) + means-tested public housing and medicare to all in need
High-income OECD countries[a]	x
Middle-income countries in Latin America	
High/middle-income countries in East Asia	
Middle-income countries in transition	
Low-income countries in transition	
Low-income countries in Asia	
Low-income countries in Africa	

Country type	Food price subsidies, supported rations (other than subsidies)	Maternal and nutrition food stamps
High-income OECD countries[a]		
Middle-income countries in Latin America		x
High/middle-income countries in East Asia		
Middle-income countries in transition	x	
Low-income countries in transition		
Low-income countries in Asia	x	x
Low-income countries in Africa	x	x

a. The United States is the only OECD country to offer a food stamp program.
b. Data on private transfers are not available for OECD countries, but these are

in transition) and three in-kind transfers (prevalent in most developing countries and in countries in transition). Programs with a work requirement include public works and credit-based income-generation programs (prevalent in many developing countries). The selection of programs and countries to be included in this review is limited by the availability of rigorous evaluations. The programs and countries chosen do not constitute a representative sample in a statistical sense.

Chapter 2 outlines the issues pertaining to targeting and the accompanying trade-offs between cost and efficiency. Chapters 3, 4, and 5 discuss country experience with cash transfers, in-kind transfers, and income-generation programs. Three common issues are: how successfully the programs reached the poor (targeting and distributional efficiency), how cost-effectively they reached the poor, and whether or not the programs were able to avoid adverse incentives for work, labor supply, and private saving.[9]

Chapter 6 evaluates the design issues and delivery mechanisms generic to all programs, and develops a fourfold typology of program delivery. This chapter also examines how social funds—the most pop-

Publicly supported social security to formal sector employees only	Privately, fully-funded social security	Food stamps	Family assistance	Social assistance
		x	x	x
x		x		
	x			x
x			x	x
x			x	x

Credit-based livelihood programs	Public works, food for works	Region/country characteristics	
		Private transfers	Range of public spending (as percentage of GDP)
		Negligible[b]	10-15
x		Low	8-15
		Moderate	2-5
		Moderate	10-25
		Moderate	10-15
x	x	High	2-5
x	x	High	1-2

believed to be negligible.
Source: Authors' assessments.

ular institution in some countries—generate different outcomes depending on which delivery mechanism is chosen. Chapter 7 analyzes the issues involved in financing safety-net programs, reviewing the limited empirical information. Chapter 8 analyzes aspects of political economy through a country case-study approach. Countries studied include Bolivia, Chile, El Salvador, Ghana, Mexico, Peru, Poland, Senegal, Ukraine, and Zambia. Chapter 9 sums up the principle lessons from cross-country experience, and delineates the issues that should be borne in mind when choosing or designing programs.

Notes

1. Structural adjustment promotes incentive and regulatory reform, accompanied by a reduction in the role of the state. Macroeconomic stabilization is intended to ensure fiscal and monetary discipline.

2. Social insurance is defined as benefits provided by the state, most often through specified contributions, to cover specific risks. It includes unemployment benefits, sickness and maternity benefits, and retirement, invalidity, and survivors' pensions. Social assistance refers to a range of benefits in cash or in-kind intended to provide protection for the most needy in society. Family assistance refers to all benefits in cash or in-kind targeted directly to children or families with children.

3. Numerous case studies in the household-coping literature have examined how different shocks (environmental, economic, social, and political) affect, and at times undermine, traditional coping mechanisms based on community and family networks. This literature examines how households deal ex ante with anticipated shocks and what ex post coping strategies they apply following an adverse event. In particular, see Platteau (1991); Agarwal (1991); regarding the economic impact of AIDS, see Ainsworth and Over (1992); see Alderman and Paxson (1992) for a discussion of issues pertaining to risk sharing and consumption smoothing.

4. Private transfers may take various forms. In Sub-Saharan Africa community-level saving societies contribute to pooling and spreading of income risks. In Mali urban associations called "tontines" function as saving and insurance clubs, providing cash to members in difficult times (World Bank 1993a). There are similar groups in The Gambia and Burkina Faso (von Braun 1989; World Bank 1993b). Chapter 4 discusses the Islamic-based Zakat and Ushr system, which is a common form of safety net in parts of South Asia and some African countries. In Mongolia exchange of animals is a common form of private transfer (Subbarao and Ezemenari 1995).

5. Recent evidence from the Philippines illustrates this. Subbarao, Ahmed, and Teklu (1995) found that remittances from abroad were a significant source of household income in the relatively more developed regions of the country. In addition, within these regions a large proportion of the transfers went to upper-income groups. Domestic remittances, on the other hand, are predominant among the poorer income groups. The study concluded that foreign remittances accentuated income inequality among regions and households.

6. A food-for-work program, largely driven by P.L. 480 food aid from the United States, operated in India until the mid-1960s. The program was replaced by a regular employment program (now known as the Jawahar Rojgar Yojuna) with wages paid in cash rather than in-kind. As the composition of food aid changed from grains to infant formula, a program (introduced in the mid-1970s) aimed at improving child nutrition began to absorb the donor-supplied infant food.

7. A relatively lower emphasis in Africa than in Asia on labor-intensive public works programs, or other comparable programs for consumption smoothing, is probably the reason for the harsher impact of a drought in Africa than in South Asia. Thus a massive drought visited India in 1987, affecting nearly one-third of the population. Yet there was not a single drought-related mortality. This was because of the prevalence of consumption-smoothing public works programs, an administrative and institutional framework that is well-adapted (over time) to drought situations, and a free press. By contrast, a drought of much smaller magnitude in Ethiopia caused considerable distress and mortality in 1991. Moreover, rural infrastructure has remained in a very poor and neglected state in Africa— hurting the poor both as sellers (low product prices) and as buyers (high input prices).

8. As of now, no data exist on the share of private transfers in average household income for most OECD countries.

9. Not all of the issues could be addressed for each of the programs owing to paucity of data. In particular, data limitations narrowed the scope of chapter 3 (cash transfers).

2

Conceptual Issues in the Analysis of Social Assistance and Poverty-Targeted Programs

This chapter reviews the conceptual issues pertaining to public transfers and targeting, the impact of poverty-targeted programs on consumption decisions and labor market behavior, fiscal sustainability, and some political economy factors. The chapter suggests that the issue of whether to target or not depends on the costs and benefits of doing so. It then discusses how to target by describing the conceptual ideas behind the different targeting mechanisms. It concludes with a discussion of the trade-offs in delivering benefits in cash or in-kind.

The rationale for targeting is that the social returns for a given level of transfers are higher for individuals or households at the lower end of the income distribution than at the upper end.[1] To maximize the welfare effect of a transfer program, the appropriate target would be the population segment deemed poor according to some criterion. Thus the ability to measure poverty and identify the poor is essential for designing any targeted transfer program.

Targeting gains depend on initial country conditions and the type of targeting mechanism adopted. Targeting the poorest and most vulnerable saves budgetary resources by confining benefits initially to those who need them most, provided the administrative costs of identifying the poor are not high. Saving budgetary resources allows for greater benefits for the poor, greater expenditures on other programs—possibly income-generation programs—or the reduction in public revenue collection through potentially distortionary taxes.

Targeting Costs

Targeting is beneficial when it increases the efficiency of antipoverty programs, but it also entails costs. Four types of costs stand out: administrative, incentive (deadweight), stigma, and political.

15

Administrative Costs

Administrative costs are those associated with identifying, reaching, and monitoring the target population. Targeting requires some mechanism to distinguish the poor from the nonpoor so that the poor can avail themselves of benefits, and the nonpoor can be prevented from receiving benefits. Quantifying administrative costs by program is not easy, particularly if costs are shared across programs. Costs will also differ across program types. Following Besley and Kanbur (1993), the total revenue required to finance a program, R, can be broken down into three components: administrative costs, A, leakage to the nonpoor, L, and the effective transfer to the poor, P. Targeting efficiency is defined by the ratio $P/(L+P)$. The proportion of administrative costs to total revenue rises according to how meticulously the poor and the nonpoor are sorted, as measured by the ratio $P/(L+P)$. The trade-off between achieving finer targeting and curtailing administrative costs is often formulated in terms of type 1 (exclusion) and type 2 (inclusion) errors (table 2.1).

The numbers in table 2.1 represent the population covered by a given poverty-targeted program (disaggregated according to poverty status). If it is assumed that all individuals covered by the program receive one dollar of program benefits, then $P/(L+P) = 30/(20+30) = 0.6$. Leakage is defined as the total percentage of nonpoor covered divided by the total percentage of people covered by the program $(20/50=0.4)$; and coverage is defined as the percentage of the poor who are covered by the program divided by the total percentage of poor $(30/40=0.75)$. This is often referred to as the participation rate.

Lower levels of both inclusion errors and exclusion errors are preferable, though, as mentioned above, minimizing these errors can be costly. It is difficult to compare the trade-offs between type 1 and type 2 errors. The higher the priority given to raising the welfare of the poor, the greater the need to eliminate type 1 errors. Conversely, if more weight is given to saving budgetary resources, it is important to eliminate type 2 errors. Strict administration of a transfer program

Table 2.1. Program Leakage and Coverage
(percent)

	Covered	Not covered	Total population
Poor	Success 30	Type 1 (exclusion) error 10	40
Nonpoor	Type 2 (inclusion) error 20	Success 40	60

Source: Grosh (1994).

may exclude not only some of the nonpoor but also some of the poor. At times, it may be prudent to deliberately allow leakage so as not to exclude any of the poor.

Whether it is worth incurring the administrative costs to improve the targeting efficiency of a program depends not only on how well the targeting mechanism screens eligible persons but also on the value of the benefit delivered. Administrative costs are determined by the level of targeting (self-targeting is less costly than geographic targeting, and individual assessment is the most costly); the level of automation and information exchange (computers that hold data on all government programs reduce the cost of income testing an individual); the income/asset profile of the country (formal income is relatively easy to assess, whereas informal income and the value of land is difficult to assess); and the frequency of change in the benefit rate (the needs of a pensioner are likely to remain unchanged, whereas the needs of an unemployed family member could change frequently). A judgment must be made about the administrative costs of a benefit relative to the program costs. Grosh (1994) estimates (across various programs and countries) that targeted transfers cost about 3–8 percent more than a similar universal transfer.

Administrative costs also vary with the type of mechanism used, the level of existing information, the institutional capacity of a country, and the local costs of personnel and equipment needed to carry out the targeting.

Incentive Costs

Targeting schemes may foster both positive and negative incentive effects. Three negative incentive effects that may outweigh the beneficial impact of targeting are distortions in the labor-leisure choice, migration to advantaged areas, and the unproductive use of resources or time (moral hazard problems). Targeted programs can also foster positive incentives: a food subsidy targeted to parents whose children attend school encourages higher school enrollments.

The disincentive to work is one problem associated with programs targeted according to a means test (usually income). Agents may change their behavior by altering their labor supply and hence their income. For example, imagine a means test that proposes a monthly income of $350 as an eligibility threshold. Individuals with a monthly income less than $350 are eligible to receive $50 in benefits with no work requirement. Individuals with monthly incomes in the range $350–$399 (in the absence of the program) would be better off adjusting their labor supply to earn just less than $350, thus qualifying for the $50 income supplement. Their incomes would be higher than before, and they would be better off. But society as a whole would lose their output. Furthermore, program costs would go up since the number of claimants would go up.[2] Programs can also generate disincentive effects in the community—a generous food subsidy may lower community self-help efforts.

To the extent that marginal tax rates affect incentives to work, and thus income, income is an endogenous variable and depends on the tax rate implicit in the targeted program (Besley and Kanbur 1993). With a 100 percent marginal tax rate, no one with an income below the poverty threshold would have an incentive to work—they would instead choose to receive government payments to pull them out of poverty. But if all those with incomes below the poverty line chose not to work, the financial burden of the transfer would rise substantially, since each person below the poverty line would require a transfer equal to the full poverty gap. This result implies that the marginal tax rates on the rich would have to be higher to finance the program's increased costs. In turn, the rich would now have fewer incentives to work (since their incomes are being taxed away), meaning less revenue would be available for the intervention. Thus labor supply effects are important, though only some targeted programs have adverse effects.

Relocation is another potentially undesirable effect. If benefits are targeted geographically, people might have an incentive to migrate to areas covered by benefits. If the bulk of the movers are poor, then an increase in costs is justifiable, since more of the poor are being covered. But if better-off households also move, then program costs would increase without justification. If the relocation also causes problems, such as congestion in service delivery and a reduction in the number of benefits available per eligible person, the net costs to society could be large. The extent of the relocation effect depends on the size or amount of the benefits gained relative to the moving costs. If the rich have access to more efficient transportation and information networks, their unit costs of transportation may be low, and the relocation effect could be quite large.

Incentive compatibility problems also give rise to undesirable program effects. For example, in a child nutrition program rations given to children are planned according to what children were fed before they entered the program. Two kinds of incentive compatibility problems may arise. Mothers may feed children less (because they know they are being fed in nutrition programs) so that other members of the household can eat more (adverse incentive problem). Or, an inadvertent moral hazard problem may arise because the nutritional status of the children does not improve. Thus these children must stay in the program for a longer period.[3]

Dreze and Sen (1989) provide a rather drastic example of the adverse incentive problem. If food supplements in a nutrition program are based on children's nutritional status, mothers may have an incentive to gain eligibility by underfeeding their children before weighing them. Even though there is little empirical evidence to support this example, this type of behavior would generate a "deadweight" loss, since a wedge is created between private and social (collective) welfare.

Stigma Costs

Stigma is a possible negative consequence of means-tested government transfer programs. It arises from two main sources. First, recipients may lose their self-esteem because they regard themselves as failures who must rely on public support. In such cases needy people are unnecessarily screened out. Second, nonrecipients may have negative attitudes toward recipients, and recipients may be treated differently from nonrecipients by both program officials and the general public.[4] Individuals not wanting to be classified as needy could refuse subsidies and depress the take-up rate.

Stigma may not act as a deterrent to the nonpoor, particularly if the receipt of one transfer offers access to other transfers or privileges. Or, stigma may assist in targeting. Requiring welfare recipients to perform menial tasks may impose relatively smaller costs on the intended recipients who have very limited options anyway, while deterring impostors who may have other attractive options (Nichols and Zeckhauser 1982).[5]

Political Economy Costs

Targeting raises interesting political economy issues. First, any intervention creates losers as well as gainers. The goal is to transfer resources from the gainers to the losers so that the losers are just compensated for their losses, while the gainers are still better off than they would have been without the targeted intervention. But the distribution of political power in a country may not permit this goal to be realized. Second, the interests of the different players involved in administering the program will shape how it is eventually implemented. The poorest strata of society are often the most difficult and costly to reach, and therefore intervention efforts tend to focus on the most vocal and organized groups, which are not necessarily poor. Third, very fine targeting may sometimes run counter to the interests of the poor. If a program is well-targeted and the poor are relatively disenfranchised, the program may have scant political support and be allotted a small budget. In contrast, a broadly targeted program may elicit greater political support and a larger budget.[6]

Good targeting should increase take-up rates among intended beneficiaries and reduce leakage. It should minimize distortions, reduce program costs, and distribute scarce public resources fairly and efficiently. These objectives invariably imply difficult trade-offs. Leakage is minimized only at the expense of higher administrative costs. Finer targeting carries some benefits, but it also imposes costs and distortions, and may lead to loss of political support. The decision to target more finely, therefore, hinges on the balance between these benefits and costs, which vary from country to country depending on the economic, political, and social fabric of specific economies. These considerations imply that targeting mechanisms should provide incentives for the target group (and no others) to seek the subsidy.

Targeting Mechanisms

The mechanisms used to identify the poor can be classified according to three broad categories: individual targeting, geographic or indicator targeting, and self-targeting. Any of these types of targeting could be applied to the individual or the group. This flexibility is important because some of the information and incentive problems that seem daunting at the individual level may not be so at the group level.

An example of an individual assessment is a means test that ascertains whether household income is below the cutoff point. The test uses either income, nutritional status, or type of dwelling (with or without electricity, toilet, and so on) as a criterion. If it is possible to conduct a "perfect" means test, cash transfers dominate other forms of interventions because they carry only an income effect and do not distort private consumption decisions at the margin. But because of the informational and administrative constraints, means testing may not be perfect and may induce costly leakages and create adverse incentives.[7]

These considerations have led to a variety of schemes for indicator targeting, whereby transfers are made contingent on some correlates of poverty. Geographic and indicator targeting mechanisms grant eligibility to groups of individuals on the basis of an easily identifiable shared characteristic. The idea is to find an indicator that is less costly to identify (than income) but is sufficiently correlated with income to be useful for identifying the poor (Besley and Kanbur 1993). Although some leakage is inevitable, the cost of leakage can be offset in part by reduced administrative costs. The indicators used for targeting should not be easily manipulable during the course of the intervention since adverse incentive effects could result. For example, individuals might fake attributes that would qualify them for assistance (such as ownership of land or other durable assets) or change their behavior to legitimately acquire such attributes. Indicators that are good predictors of income are land ownership, house (floor area) or other durable asset ownership, number of children, level of education, and so on. Most of these indicators are easy to observe and difficult to manipulate in the short run. But if the number of indicators increases, the situation may degenerate to one in which every individual is "tagged" separately, enhancing administrative costs.[8] Geographic targeting allocates resources to states, municipalities, or neighborhoods based on their average welfare level. The headcount index is commonly used to establish a geographic ranking of poverty.

Alternatively, combinations of region, residence, and household characteristics could be used, as in Colombia, where areas of poverty were first identified as part of the national development plan. Food subsidies were then targeted to households with children under five, or to pregnant or lactating mothers. Prospects for reaching the poor through regional and indicator targeting depend on a number of factors, including local administrative infrastructure, the incentives facing local administrators, their social relations with the poor, and the extent of political representation of the poor.

Self-targeting occurs when a program is ostensibly available to all but is designed to discourage the nonpoor from participating. For example, participants can be required to work, as in public employment programs. Alternatively, a low-quality product could be subsidized, inducing the nonpoor to stay away from the program. If individuals are heterogeneous with respect to ability and tastes, then in-kind transfers of goods or services preferred by the target group may help ward off impostors (Nichols and Zeckhauser 1982). For example, subsidies on coarse flour in Egypt accrued disproportionately to lower-income groups. It is not always easy, though, to obtain accurate information about the preference structure of individuals. Nevertheless, an important advantage of self-targeted programs is that they are less vulnerable to administrative corruption and bureaucratic manipulation.

One problem with all targeted approaches is that along with the nonpoor, some of the very poor may also be screened out. Self-targeted approaches are no exception. For instance, self-selection methods of targeting used in public employment schemes by lowering wage rates do screen out the nonpoor, but some of the poor may also be screened out in the process. The aged, the infirm, or the physically handicapped do not participate in such schemes. Thus countries depending largely on self-targeted public works programs must develop other programs to protect vulnerable groups that are unable to work.

The Choice between Cash and In-Kind Transfers

In theory, cash transfers are preferable to in-kind transfers because they do not distort individual consumption or production choices at the margin. But only rarely would actual country conditions allow this proposition to be true. Less-than-ideal circumstances (such as the costs involved in conducting means tests) often tilt the choice in favor of in-kind subsidies.

There are situations when in-kind transfers are equivalent to cash transfers. For example, a ration of commodity x at a unit price r (where $r < p$ is the price to the target group, and p is the market price) is equivalent to a lump-sum transfer of m dollars—that is, $m = (p - r)x$. This equivalence holds providing there are no restrictions on (or exorbitant costs to) the resale of the subsidized commodity. Even if the subsidized commodity cannot be physically resold (as in the case of education and health services), there may still be an equivalence to a lump-sum transfer under specific conditions. This equivalence can arise if households prefer as much or more of the free commodity (inframarginal transfer), in which case the composition of consumption is not affected (Gill, Jimenez, and Shalitz 1991).

Where means tests are imperfect and costly, in-kind transfers may be preferable to cash transfers. When information is less than perfect, governments must develop mechanisms that enable members of the target group to select a consumption bundle different from the one offered to the nontarget group. Since governments cannot distinguish between individuals, the provision of subsidies with a self-selection mechanism will weed out impostors and constrain program costs (such as subsidizing coarse grains consumed only by the poor). While such in-kind subsidies may cause distortions at the margin, these deadweight losses may be outweighed by the decline in leakage. And in some countries with high levels of inflation in-kind transfers have higher real denominations than nonindexed cash transfers. This difference occurs only because the program provider absorbs the cost of inflation when making an in-kind transfer, while, without indexation, the recipient absorbs that cost. For that reason governments may think they have greater control over the cost of cash transfers. In countries with weak institutional and administrative capacities it may be easier to implement in-kind subsidies than cash transfers. In-kind transfers can also be used to reduce intrahousehold discrimination against women or children. Thus information gaps, inflationary conditions, and the need to realize specific policy goals (household food security, nutrition to children) may induce governments to opt for in-kind transfers.[9]

When in-kind subsidies are chosen, one question that arises immediately is which commodity to subsidize? In theory, the government should try to find commodities that form a significant part of the poor's (but not the nonpoor's) food expenditures. The chosen goods do not have to be inferior goods, but they must be goods that are consumed disproportionately by the poor when their prices drop. If these commodities are consumed only by households below the poverty line, leakage will be eliminated. But because it is difficult to isolate commodities that only the poor consume, errors of exclusion may still arise.

Conclusion

Poverty-targeted interventions could be provided to the entire population or aimed at only certain individuals. Because of information gaps, perfect targeting is rarely achieved. The decisions of whether or not to target, which targeting mechanism to use, and how to target depend on the economic and opportunity costs of targeting, negative incentive effects, the size of the target group relative to the total population, the prevailing differences in consumption patterns between the poor and the nonpoor, the characteristics of the commodity or services selected for targeting (including the size of demand and income elasticities), and administrative capability and political economy considerations. In particular, minimizing leakage and reducing costs simultaneously may involve trade-offs. It is important to be aware of these limitations, even if it is not possible to estimate the leakage and costs associated with targeted programs.

Notes

1. This chapter draws from Barr (1995), Besley and Kanbur (1993), Lipton and Ravallion (1995), and Gill, Jimenez, and Shalitz (1991).

2. For a thorough treatment of the incentive effects on labor supply see Besley and Kanbur (1988) and Kanbur, Keen, and Tuomala (1994).

3. Kennedy and Alderman (1987) discuss the conceptual issues and empirical evidence associated with program leakage of this kind. Pinstrup-Andersen (1988a) provides estimates of this type of leakage.

4. See Besley and Coate (1991) for additional details regarding the ramifications of stigma associated with targeting.

5. While the problem of stigma is much referred to in the literature on transfer programs, there is very little empirical evidence on this issue. Ranney and Kushman (1987) examine this problem in the context of food stamps in the United States.

6. The history of food subsidies in Sri Lanka since 1977 is a case in point. With the introduction of targeting the poor lost the support of the middle class, and the real value of food stamps was allowed to depreciate. Similarly, a food subsidy directed to the poor in Colombia was so tightly targeted that it lacked an effective political constituency and was dropped subsequently with a change of government. A broadly targeted program may foster links between the middle class and the poor, though at a higher budgetary cost.

7. An interesting counterexample of a successful means test based on community identification is provided by the Antyodaya Program in Rajasthan, India, where the village elders decide which are the poorest ten families in the village.

8. Ravallion and Chao (1989) illustrate the intuitive proposition that the percentage gains from targeting using indicators are greater when budgetary resources are smaller. See also Glewwe and Kannan (1989) and Grosh and Baker (1995).

9. Basu (1996) argues that in-kind transfers also insulate nonrecipients against supply pressures that cash transfers may create.

3
Cross-Country Patterns
of Cash Transfers

This chapter reviews cross-country experience with providing cash transfers for poverty reduction, and explains differences in the type and scale of programs adopted among regions.[1] The review highlights issues most relevant to the design and implementation of cash transfers. Cash benefit programs are frequently designed to help individuals and families with incomes just below the poverty line. Often, the programs require that only small amounts of assistance go to the individual or family. A dearth of reliable household data limits the scope for determining how effectively cash transfer programs meet their objectives. Nevertheless, wherever possible, the implications of various programs and targeting mechanisms for reducing poverty are discussed.

Common cash transfer programs include social assistance programs and family assistance programs. Social assistance refers to a range of benefits given in cash or in-kind intended to protect the most needy persons in society. Family assistance refers to all benefits given in cash or in-kind targeted directly to children or families with children. These programs are found in various forms in different countries. All have the same primary objective: poverty relief. But the secondary objectives vary widely. Social assistance has the greatest impact when it is targeted to the poorest and most vulnerable. In most countries children greatly outnumber adults in households with incomes that are below the poverty level. Thus family assistance will help reduce poverty even when provided to all children.

Family assistance and social assistance often have very different objectives. Consequently, seemingly similar programs can have different outcomes. It is possible to draw conclusions about the effectiveness of one scheme compared with another in terms of costs and effects on poverty—but it is wrong to attempt to rank the outcome indicators because of differing objectives. This point is important to many countries of Eastern Europe and the former Soviet Union that seek to emulate Western European models without determining the best model for their specific situation and the best time scale for moving from one model to another.

A cross-country comparison suggests that social assistance and family assistance are used in two different ways. OECD countries use social and family assistance as part of a broader social safety net program, which often features a social insurance program. Developing economies in Africa, South Asia (and part of India), and parts of Latin America rely more on social and family assistance as the primary transfer mechanism in their social safety net.

Countries of Eastern Europe and the former Soviet Union are in a confused position because their inherited social safety nets were built around a social insurance program. Their starting point was therefore more akin to the OECD model. But the changes during transition have been great: loss of secure incomes, steeply rising unemployment, increasing inability to fund social insurance programs, and rising numbers of poor spread throughout society rather than in isolated and identifiable groups. Such changes have forced these countries to cut back on social insurance programs and rely more on social and family assistance programs. Because they now rely so much on social and family assistance, their position is more akin to that of developing countries.

Designing the best system for the countries of Eastern European and the former Soviet Union is difficult because their economies are in transition. The problems of poverty are emerging in different sections of the community and are changing at different rates. Also, the inherited family assistance and social assistance schemes had different objectives. These countries will require a variety of long-term cash transfer systems for the poor. The type of system will depend on the speed of transition and on the emphasis given to different aspects of transition. The policy context of the chosen system will depend on the long-term prognosis for the economy in general and the social welfare system in particular. It would be helpful, therefore, in designing systems for economies in transition, to compare objectives and outcomes in developed economies with those in developing or emerging market economies.

Family Assistance

Family assistance programs are usually tied to the number of children in a household. Family assistance can have two main financial objectives: to smooth consumption over the life cycle by maintaining per capita household income with each additional child or to maintain a level of income that allows one parent to care for the children full-time.

In some economies family assistance also has other pronatal objectives. For example, given the aging populations and acute labor shortages, in the former Soviet Union, family assistance was employed to promote high fertility rates (Sipos 1994).

Several mid- to high-income countries (such as Argentina, Brazil, Chile, and Uruguay) in Latin America have adopted family assistance programs. They usually help people covered by social insurance, mainly the nonpoor. Family assistance in Latin America accounted for between 3 and 14 percent of total social security spending in 1988 (Mesa-Lago 1990).[2]

In Latin America family assistance is intended primarily for consumption smoothing over the life cycle for households covered under social insurance. But spending on family assistance in these countries declined during the early 1980s (table 3.1). In some Latin American countries costs were pushed to intolerable levels by slack entitlement conditions and high benefits, combined with leakage and inequalities in benefits for different segments of the population. Also, in the 1980s economic crisis, followed by adjustment, eroded the level and quality of benefits. Mesa-Lago (1994:51) indicates, however, that expenditure levels may now be increasing.

The Western European Model of Family Assistance

Economies in transition are emulating the family assistance model of Western Europe. Thus it is important to understand this model's background. Family assistance was introduced in Western Europe between the late 1930s and mid-1940s. All countries in the region offered some form of benefit by the mid-1950s. The initial intention was to provide easily targeted assistance to families (with children) who were most likely to be among the poorest groups in the post–depression and war years (Kamerman and Kahn 1988:370). Program design varied by country. Some countries paid a flat rate for each child. Others paid a

Table 3.1. Family Allowance Expenditures in Latin America, 1961–86
(percentage of total social security)

Country	1961	1965	1970	1975	1983	1986
Argentina	—	—	—	27.0	14.3	22.4
Bolivia	30.9	—	—	—	3.8	2.2
Brazil	—	—	9.2	—	3.3	3.7
Chile	—	45.9	—	—	10.3	7.0
Uruguay	—	—	—	16.9	10.7	6.7

— Data not available.
Note: Social security expenditure includes that for sickness, maternity, pensions, employment injury, family allowance, and unemployment.
Source: ILO (1991) as cited in Mesa-Lago (1994).

**Box 3.1. Evolution of Family Assistance
in the United Kingdom**

Family assistance was introduced in 1945 as a universal benefit designed
to reach all families with more than one child. Assistance was given at a
flat rate for the second child and subsequent children. These payments
were intended to meet the needs of growing family expenditures, rather
than to guarantee income when one adult was out of the labor market.
That need changed as families became able to command two incomes;
relative poverty became much more concentrated on single-parent families, which increased sharply as a proportion of all families. Thus while
family assistance remained in place, its real value fell, and a one-parent
benefit was added to improve targeting. But during the 1980s the real
value of family assistance declined. Increasing the level of assistance
would have resulted in large cash transfers to the nonpoor, so a family
credit was introduced, in which a family with low earnings could have
its income supplemented up to a predetermined level.

Family assistance in the United Kingdom has always been given
without regard to income. And as such, it provides a continuing income
source for the poor even if family income improves. Thus it creates an
incentive to become self-sufficient, while also smoothing out potential
poverty traps. The United Kingdom has gone from offering a simple universal benefit aimed at supporting larger families to a complex group of
benefits with a number of different secondary policy intentions, all with
the aim of providing cash transfers to families with children. These benefits are increasingly targeted to the poorest group (single parents)—the
poorest identified by a simple income test.

Note: Family assistance is only one small part of the comprehensive social safety
net in the United Kingdom, and this illustration should not be seen as an example of best practice.

---

variable rate for the second and subsequent child. But they all had the
same objective: protecting people in poverty. In time, the objective of
family assistance changed to reflect changes in the nature of family
poverty. These programs have worked well to reduce poverty (table
3.2). Moreover, these programs are only a small part of a much bigger
social safety net system. Thus they should not be viewed in isolation
from other social insurance programs. For example, family assistance
in the United Kingdom must be judged by how it affects social assistance and general tax legislation (box 3.1). It is a mistake for any country trying to develop family assistance to copy another country's
model without considering the broader national social safety net program and its fiscal implications, particularly how revenues are raised
to finance a program.

Table 3.2. The Role of Public Transfers in Reducing the Poverty Gap among OECD Families, Mid-1970s to Mid-1980s
(percentage of family poverty reduced)

	Families with children			Single-parent families		
	Social insurance	Means-tested programs	Child allowances	Social insurance	Means-tested programs	Child allowances
Australia	n.a.	87	13	n.a.	88	12
Canada	38	48	14	19	69	12
Germany, Fed. Rep. of	68	11	21	67	16	18
Norway	86	3	11	83	4	13
Sweden	52	37	11	45	45	10
Switzerland	93	7	n.a.	92	8	n.a.
United Kingdom	38	38	24	15	63	22
United States	29	71	n.a.	7	93	n.a.

n.a. Not applicable.
Source: Smeeding, Torrey, and Rein (1988), tables 5.2 and 5.11.

Except for Italy, all countries in Western Europe pay family assistance as a universal benefit without regard to income. But they all have separate systems with variable rates, depending on age or number of children. All countries, except for Denmark, have improved targeting and reduced expenditures as a percentage of GDP between 1980 and 1990 (table 3.3). Western Europe's family assistance benefits are much larger relative to GNP in the north (Belgium, Denmark, and France) than in the south (Greece, Spain, and Portugal), which has higher levels of poverty. This difference reflects the north's higher income levels, its better ability to provide transfers, and a greater willingness of the extended family to support assistance socially and politically. Note that a higher share of GNP need not imply higher benefits per person at risk.

Table 3.3. Family Assistance Expenditures
(percentage of GDP)

Country	1980	1990
Belgium	3.1	2.2
Denmark	2.7	2.9
France	2.6	2.2
Greece	0.4	0.2
Italy	1.0	0.6
Netherlands	2.6	1.7
Portugal	0.9	0.8
Spain	0.5	0.1
United Kingdom	2.3	2.0

Source: Eurostat (1993).

Family Assistance in Economies in Transition

Prior to the transition the objective of family assistance programs in Eastern Europe and the former Soviet Union was to maintain a level of per capita income as family size increased. Assistance was also provided as a supplement to wages. Take-up of the allowance was almost universal; administration was handled by the enterprise. If both parents worked or if one parent worked for more than one employer, duplicate payments were common. Family assistance now accounts for 2–4 percent of GDP among countries in the former Soviet bloc, and up to 7 percent of household expenditures in the Kyrgyz Republic (table 3.4).

After the transition many governments modified their near-universal coverage (box 3.2). The Kyrgyz Republic discontinued family assistance to children older than age eighteen. It also introduced income testing for family assistance. In Moldova universal coverage was withdrawn, and family assistance was income tested. All countries now support families with children if either parent is out of work or if families become too large to support themselves on two incomes.

Over the course of the transition expenditures on family assistance (as a percentage of GDP) have varied among countries (table 3.4). Countries can be divided into three groups according to spending trends. In the first group of countries expenditures have either been maintained or increased. In the second group expenditures have been reduced to preindependence levels (figure 3.1). And in the third group (Belarus, Georgia, Lithuania, and Russia) expenditures increased until 1991–92, then decreased thereafter. In the latter two groups countries appeared to protect social insurance (pensions) to the detriment of social and family assistance, as fiscal constraints tightened. Moreover, linking family assistance to nonindexed minimum wages led to a

---

Box 3.2. The Evolution of Family Assistance in Poland

Poland inherited a program of family assistance that was paid by the enterprise as a part of compensation. In four years the benefit has changed from being available to all workers, regardless of income, to being available to only the poorest families in and out of work. The program was still in existence in 1991–92, and the value of assistance was increased in line with rising wages. At that time only families with at least one employer received benefits. In 1993 entitlement was extended to the unemployed, and the benefit was paid at a flat rate and not increased in line with either price or wage increases. In 1994 income testing was introduced, and only families with a low per capita income became eligible.

Source: Transmonee data set.

steady decline in expenditures. At the same time, poverty has increased among countries in this region. Generally, rural areas have been adversely affected.[3] Hardest hit were individuals, such as young children and adults, the working poor and the unemployed, the disabled, and the aged without family support (Sipos 1994; Milanovic 1995a).[4] In most countries with hyperinflation family assistance has not been indexed to inflation. Because the poor suffer most from inflation, family assistance has not adequately protected the people in greatest need. Data are lacking that will help to determine the impact

Figure 3.1. Share of Expenditures on Family Allowance in Selected Countries in Transition, 1989–94
(percentage of GDP)

Those that maintained and/or increased

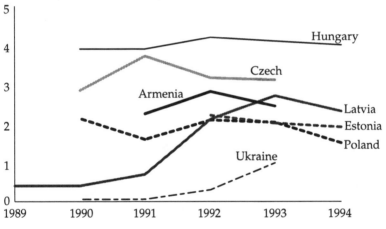

Systemic decline

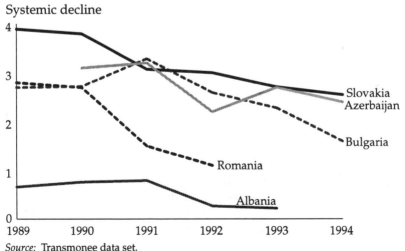

Source: Transmonee data set.

**Table 3.4. Indicators of Poverty and Expenditures on Family
Assistance in the Transition Economies**

Region and country	Headcount ratio		Total fertility rates (most recent estimate)	
	Pretransition (1987-88)	Posttransition (1993-94)	1980-85	1988-93
Balkans and Poland	5	23[a]		
Bulgaria	2[b]	17[a,c]	2.0	1.5
Poland	6	20[a,c]	2.3	1.9
Romania	6[b]	32[a]	2.2	1.5
Central Europe	0.5	1		
Czech Republic	0	<1	2.0	1.9
Hungary	<1[b]	2	1.8	1.7
Slovak Republic	0	1[c]		
Slovenia	0	0	2.3	1.9
Yugoslavia	17	24	2.3	2.0
Baltics	1	36		
Estonia	1	33[d]	2.1	1.6
Latvia	1	19[a]	2.0	1.6
Lithuania	1	49	2.0	1.8
Slavic countries and Moldova	2	40		
Belarus	1	11	2.1	1.7
Moldova	4	65	2.5	2.1
Russia	2	43[a]	2.0	1.5
Ukraine	2	41	2.0	1.6
Central Asia	15	43		
Kazakstan	5	50	3.0	2.5
Kyrgyz Republic	12	76	4.1	3.6
Turkmenistan	12	48	4.8	3.9
Uzbekistan	24	29	4.7	3.8
China		9[c]	2.2	2.0

Note: Regional headcount ratios are population weighed averages and are taken from
Milanovic (1995a, table 2). Headcount ratios are the percentage of the population
below the poverty line, which is based on $120 per capita per month at 1990
purchasing power parity.
a. Expenditure-based.
b. 1989.
c. 1992.
d. 1995.

of family assistance on poverty in these countries. But the importance
of family assistance may be deduced from the high correlation
between family size and poverty.

This correlation is particularly pronounced in the poorer Central
Asian republics. For example, in Uzbekistan two-thirds of all children
are from poor families. This trend is likely to continue, given the high
population growth rate in this country. Family assistance thus has an
essential role in poverty reduction. But this is not true of all countries

Family assistance (percentage of GDP)		Real spending on family benefits 1992-93 (1987=100)	Family assistance as percentage of household expenditure/income
Pretransition 1987-88	Posttransition 1992-93		
2.5	2.4	83	
2.6	2.3	46	2.3
1.4	1.8	107	9.2 (poor)
			2.9 (nonpoor)
5.1	1.8	26	27
2.5	2.4	83	4.3
2.0	1.8	71	5.6
2.7	4.5	137	6
2.7	3.2	81	
1.4	2.0	151	
2.3	2.0	47	4.0
0.4	2.4	341	
1.5	2.0	64	
1.0	1.2	108	
1.7	0.4	17	
0.4	1.1	199	
2.4	3.3	146	
2.3	4.1	182	6.9 (poor)
			0.9 (nonpoor)
2.5	2.5	111	

Sources: Poverty ratio is from Milanovic (1995a and 1992a); World Bank (1995k); data on family assistance as a portion of household income for Romania, Central Europe, and Estonia taken from Transmonee data set; poverty data for Yugoslavia and China are from Sipos (1994) and are not comparable to other countries reported in the table; data for Kyrgyz Republic are from World Bank (1995b); data on family assistance as proportion of household income are from various World Bank poverty assessments and country studies.

of Eastern European and the former Soviet Union. For example, in Bulgaria, where family size is not correlated with poverty, family assistance has had a regressive effect on poverty (Krumm, Milanovic, and Walton 1995).

The incidence of poverty is also crucial in determining how much of the family assistance transfer reaches the poor. In Poland, where less than 20 percent of the population is poor, family assistance has reached a significant percentage of poor households. But this transfer has occurred with high leakage rates. In Poland 46 percent of the nonpoor receive family assistance (table 3.5). Given the low incidence of poverty there, this figure translates into 74 percent of the total transfer accruing to the nonpoor. Contrast this distribution with that of Kyrgyz Republic, where poverty is more widespread and the distribution of family transfers is more progressive. Thus in countries where the incidence of poverty is low, means testing of family assistance is crucial to minimizing costs.

In some countries the level of benefits and the duration of coverage are high. For example, in Poland family assistance is payable up to age twenty for individuals engaged in full-time education. In Kyrgyz Republic 80 percent of families with children qualified for family assistance (World Bank 1995b). In such cases total available resources are spread thinly among a large number of families, thus reducing the program's potential impact on poverty.

To better target limited resources, all countries are now concentrating on how to use family assistance to reduce poverty. Those countries with a high correlation between family size and poverty recognize the advantages of retaining their family assistance programs. In these countries program administration is simple and the take-up rate is likely to be high. Thus payment per child to all families has the potential to reduce poverty at an administrative cost much lower than means testing. But in countries where the correlation is less pronounced, family assistance remains an ongoing program, largely because of the political difficulty of withdrawing it. In these countries or in countries where the objective is to maintain the income of one parent while caring for children, means testing or some form of indicator targeting may be the best method for identifying potential beneficiaries.

The total fertility rate has not increased since family assistance programs have been in place (see table 3.4). Influences in addition to assistance programs contribute to low fertility rates. One factor may be the

Table 3.5. Incidence of Family Assistance in Select Transition Economies, 1992–94

Country	Percentage of poor households receiving transfer	Percentage of nonpoor households receiving transfer
Kyrgyz Republic	51	50
Romania	75	10–12
Poland	64	46
Hungary	46	22
Bulgaria	—	—

— Data not available.
Note: The categories poor and nonpoor are based on relative poverty lines, thus they are not comparable across countries.

high rates of female education in the region coupled with high rates of female labor participation (compared with other regions). These influences tend to increase the opportunity cost of women's time and therefore dampen any effects family assistance may have on fertility rates. Still, evidence suggests that family assistance—although not increasing fertility—prevented further declines in fertility in this region.[5]

Social Assistance

Social assistance is given according to a household's (or individual's) income level or ability to earn income. These (cash transfer) programs have much greater coverage in countries where they form part of a safety net that includes a comprehensive social insurance program. So far, they have had limited coverage and offered a limited amount per family in the countries of Eastern Europe and the former Soviet Union. Programs are available to only the aged and disabled who have no one to care for them. There are a few sparse examples of cash social assistance programs in Asia and virtually none in Latin America and Africa. For example, the Fiji Islands introduced a pension system in 1975. It transfers a monthly payment that enables heads of households with very low incomes to consume a minimum number of calories. Jordan established a National Assistance Fund in 1987 to give cash transfers to poor households and unemployable individuals. Also, Pakistan and Jordan established the Zakat and Ushr system—taxes on wealth and agricultural produce—as a way to transfer income to the poor and the needy.

Social assistance cash transfers work best in countries with relatively little poverty. In Asia these transfers account for less than 1 percent of GDP. In Latin America and Africa they are negligible. Across all regions, social assistance is given predominantly in the form of in-kind transfers. The objective of these schemes is to identify the poorest people and provide a series of cash transfers, often aimed at specific consumption goods, such as food, clothing, housing, and energy.

Percentage of transfer going to		Average household size	
Poor	Nonpoor	Poor	Nonpoor
58	42	5	4
44	56	4	3
26	74	4	3
—	—	—	—
19	81	3	3

Source: Subbarao and Mehra (1995); Grootaert (1995, tables 15 and 22); various World Bank poverty assessments and country studies.

For example, the Zakat and Ushr system in Pakistan accounts for 0.3 percent of GDP. This program, however, has a limited impact in reducing poverty for several reasons. First, although most recipients of Zakat and Ushr are poor, the program reaches only 2 to 11 percent of the poor.[6] Second, the method of selection is broad with no standard criteria; selection is at the discretion of local Zakat committee members. In fact, selection appears to be strongly related to familiarity with Zakat committee members. Also, the status of beneficiaries is not kept up to date; beneficiaries may continue to receive support for years after their initial entry into the program, regardless of their current status. Third, the amounts received are small and erratic. For example, in Karachi and Dhaka transfers account for only an estimated 1 to 2 percent of monthly household spending.

In India only Kerala state has an old-age pension scheme. It targets extremely needy destitutes. Yet only 20 percent of the extremely needy and destitute receive transfers from this scheme. Also, men benefit more than women. The reason for this bias lies in the method of targeting, which is based on individual application as opposed to village-level participatory decisionmaking. The application procedure limits access of the poor: proof of age, residency, and limited sources of income are required. Individuals in targeted age groups are often unable to provide proof of age. Proof of residency is difficult for the poorest and homeless people to furnish, especially in urban areas. Finally, procedures related to providing proof of limited income sources put a stigma on beneficiaries. A pension for widows has recently been introduced in Kerala, however, which corrects for the gender bias of old-age pensions (Dreze 1990).

In China, the Republic of Korea, and Thailand public spending on social assistance is low relative to countries with similar per capita incomes (those in Latin America, Europe, and Central Asia). This pattern stems from a tradition of holding social goals in high regard, even at the cost of private objectives (Kwon 1995). This tradition puts the onus of social assistance on the family and community, rather than the government. Mutual help is encouraged through voluntary efforts of clans, charitable groups, and religious organizations (Ahmad and Hussain 1991; Kwon 1995). For example, spending on social assistance in the Republic of Korea and China reflects an important Confucian ethic that emphasizes close solidarity within the family—which is an important form of safety net. Thus the level of public social assistance (both in-kind and cash) is quite low.[7] A similar emphasis on the clan or community is also found in Africa and South Asia.

Like the economies in transition, China based its social assistance in the urban formal sector on enterprises. In China's rural areas there is a system for the vulnerable (widows, orphans, and the elderly without family or kin support) called *wu bao* (translated, "the five guarantees"). This system puts more emphasis on preventing the nonpoor from getting relief than on ensuring that all the eligible poor are covered. In addition, severe social stigma restricts take-up rates and maintains the elderly's reliance on sons (Ahmad and Hussain 1991).

Social Assistance Objectives

As with family assistance, social assistance programs in different countries have different objectives. Small programs not linked to social insurance programs aim to ease poverty by identifying the poorest people and providing either a single or continuing cash payment. The success of these programs is directly related to the level of objectivity in the selection process and the level and duration of support given.

Social assistance coupled with a strong social insurance scheme attempts to ensure that the income of an individual (or family) does not fall below a predetermined level (that is, a country-specific poverty line). To succeed, these programs require a sophisticated administration capable of identifying and tracking the income of each individual or family on a daily, weekly, or monthly basis. These are the schemes most prevalent in Western European–style economies. The development and cost of social assistance programs have grown as the level of coverage and the real value of the associated social insurance scheme have fallen. These patterns are evident among the OECD countries (see table 3.2). In countries where the social insurance program plays a large role in poverty reduction (for example, Germany, Norway, and Switzerland), social assistance programs play a smaller role (type "A" countries as defined by Sipos 1994). Their primary objective is to ensure that no one falls below the poverty line. Similarly, those countries that ascribe a smaller role to social insurance in poverty reduction (for example, Australia and the United States) rely more on social assistance to reduce poverty (type "B" countries as defined by Sipos 1994).

Social Assistance in Eastern Europe
and the Countries of the Former Soviet Union

As a percentage of GDP, cash transfers for social assistance are negligible in all of the former centralized economies. There, social assistance has a limited effect in reducing poverty. In Poland 9.6 percent of poor households receive cash transfers compared with 2.5 percent of nonpoor households; in Hungary 20.8 percent of the poorest decile of households receive social assistance compared with 5.2 percent of the wealthiest decile.

The way social assistance developed in these countries explains the limited effect of cash transfers. Before the transition cash social assistance was a small budget item. It was narrowly targeted to the physically handicapped and the aged, and it was paid at the discretion of the social worker without means testing because near-guaranteed employment protected people of working age, while pensions with high replacement rates protected people who were out of the work force. Also, eligibility for social assistance was not related to any real measure of a minimum consumption basket or social policy; instead, it was based on perceived poverty. As a result, people in poverty tended to be outside of accepted social norms (nonworking alcoholics, people with long prison records and limited work records). They were the unacceptable poor in society, and their financial security was at the discretion of the social worker (Ferge 1991; Sipos 1994).

Economic transition worsened poverty. The contraction of enterprises forced large numbers of people into open unemployment or, where jobs have been artificially maintained, very low earnings have generated a working poor. Generous social insurance benefits linked more to earnings than to years of work cannot continue to be paid at the prevailing high levels. In addition, the withdrawal of subsidies on items such as heating, housing, and food hurts most people with low fixed incomes. These changes have increased the number of people in poverty and the spread of poverty across different parts of society. Most countries have reacted by changing their policy design—first, to increase provisions to cope with the increased depth of poverty and second, to increase coverage to cope with the greater breadth of poverty, improve targeting and efficiency, and reduce costs. This approach has proved difficult and confusing for the poor because the legislation has been changed frequently. But changing the policy design is a simple process compared with changing political and public attitudes toward the new poor. The acceptance of unemployment and poverty in working families is a slow process, and is just beginning to show. Adopting a more structured approach to identify the poor requires an institutional capacity not yet in place.

Social assistance is not a static problem, particularly in Eastern Europe and the former Soviet Union. It is closely related to changes in social insurance. Since 1990 the old ideals of universal coverage with some form of social insurance protection have been revised. The new movement is toward restricting the coverage of universal benefits while attempting to target limited resources to the poorest people. This trend follows a similar pattern in Western Europe. The northern European countries in the 1940s and 1950s intended to provide universal social insurance without means testing. This practice gave way in the 1970s and 1980s to restricted social insurance benefits and a greater reliance on means testing.

A similar pattern has been emerging in all Eastern European and former Soviet Union economies since 1990.[8] These countries hoped to retain their comprehensive pay-as-you-go pension system and still provide a high replacement rate at a low pension age. Rising numbers of pensioners and falling numbers of workers made this objective unattainable. Consequently, the scheme began to change to the more targeted approach of social assistance. The first change was to scale back social insurance benefits, placing greater reliance on social assistance provided as in-kind benefits. Now, a number of countries are replacing their in-kind programs with cash transfer programs.

Such changes are driven more by the need to contain expenditures than by a desire to reach the poor. Thus the focus is often on keeping individuals off the benefit system rather than ensuring full coverage of the target population. Such a strategy often reduces the effectiveness of the program. The task of reaching all the poor becomes even harder in transition economies, which have a growing gray-black economy and a legacy of distrusting government.

Cash Transfers in Eastern Europe and Countries of the Former Soviet Union

Economies in transition handle family assistance differently than other countries because of the cash transfer structure inherited from the previous regime. Were it not for their political history, the current social and economic structure of some transition countries would suggest a cash transfer program aimed directly at the poorest people. Their political history, however, makes it difficult to enforce such narrow targeting.

Rising Expenditures

Expenditures on total cash transfers increased significantly from 1987–88 to 1993 in transition economies (table 3.6). In Poland the increase has been as high as 9.1 percent of GDP. None of the countries has reduced total spending, however, many have increased their spending on pensions, crowding out the ability to increase spending on family and social assistance. For example, in Romania expenditures on pensions rose by 2.9 percent of GDP, and overall cash transfers fell by 0.4 percent of GDP, while social assistance expenditures fell by 3.2 percent of GDP. By 1993 total expenditures on cash transfers were greater than 10 percent of GDP in twelve countries in this region and greater than 15 percent of GDP in four. This rise in expenditures has forced governments to review their assistance policies and attempt to target better, reduce spending, and make more effective use of limited resources.

Table 3.6. Pensions and Total Cash Social Transfers in Transition Economies
(percentage of GDP)

Country	Pensions		Total cash transfers	
	1987–88	1993	1987–88	1993
Europe	7.4	10.3	10.9	13.5
Bulgaria	7.7	9.6	11.3	10.4
Czech Republic	8.0	8.0	11.2	10.7
Hungary	9.0	10.4	13.1	17.5
Poland	7.1	14.8	8.7	17.8
Romania	3.9	6.8	9.4	9.0
Slovak Republic	7.4	9.6	11.3	11.7
Slovenia	8.7	13.0	11.1	16.3
Baltic states	6.5	7.3	8.8	11.0
Estonia	6.9	5.6	10.8	9.8
Latvia	5.9	9.6	7.4	12.3
Lithuania	6.6	6.8	8.3	10.8
Slavic countries and Moldova	6.7	6.6	7.7	8.0
Belarus	5.7	5.5	5.7[a]	6.9
Moldova	7.1	5.9	7.9	6.2[c]
Russia	6.2	7.2	7.9	8.9
Ukraine	7.9	7.1	9.5	8.2
Central Asia	5.5	5.4	7.4	8.5
Kazakstan	5.7	4.5	5.7[a]	4.7[b]
Kyrgyz Republic	6.8	7.2	10.0	16.2
Turkmenistan	4.0	4.6	4.4	4.6[a]
Uzbekistan	5.4	9.2	9.3	12.5

Note: Regional means are unweighted averages. Total cash transfers include pensions, various family benefits, leave benefits (including maternity leave), and unemployment allowances.
a. Includes only pensions.
b. Includes only pensions and unemployment benefits.
c. Includes only pensions and sick leave benefits.
Source: World Bank PRDTE data files as cited in Milanovic (1995a).

For example, in Poland the poor received 59 percent of social assistance transfers (although 15 percent was "overflow," raising the income of the poor above the poverty line), and 41 percent was leaked to the nonpoor. Consequently, of the 15.3 percent of the population living in poverty before the transfer, 14.4 percent remained there after the transfer. The pretransfer average poverty gap was $10.5 and the posttransfer average poverty gap was $9.2: in effect, social assistance reduced the deficit by 18 percent.[9]

Poland's current system would be inefficient if the country's sole objective were to reduce poverty. But the overflow of 15 percent would be largely acceptable in an OECD-type model. It offers great incentives to the poor to become self-sufficient. The 41 percent leakage to the nonpoor is inefficient in any system, but it may be seen as acceptable to ensure that 100 percent of the poor receive benefits (as with universal family assistance in the United Kingdom).[10]

Because of fiscal constraints, poverty reduction must be the short- to medium-term objective in Eastern Europe and the former Soviet Union. Countries there have taken Western European–style social safety net systems as their models, but their effectiveness and efficiency can be tested only against basic objectives of poverty reduction. Tested against Western European systems, Poland is moving toward an effective system, but tested against the sole objective of poverty reduction, it fails in both effectiveness and efficiency.

Focusing on Poverty Reduction

Constant changes in cash transfer legislation keep policy moving in directions that are not always clear. What is clear is that the objectives must be understood before the cash transfer program is designed. Cross-country experience concludes that, given fiscal constraints, cash transfer systems will be effective and efficient only if the objective is poverty reduction. Family assistance and targeted social assistance are effective tools for short-term poverty reduction. Countries vary in how much social assistance they can use to reduce poverty in the short term. Thus in countries where posttransition poverty is widespread (that is, headcount ratios are exceptionally high, as in the Kyrgyz Republic;[11] see also table 3.4), the role of transfers is limited: there is no alternative to quick resumption of the growth process. In such economies income-generating programs and public works seem more relevant than transfer programs.

In countries where poverty ratios have not risen to high levels, targeting social assistance is critical. The appropriate targeting mechanism will depend on the country situation, type of program, and size of the target population relative to the nontarget population. Targeting mechanisms should be as simple as possible. One simple indicator is family size. Family size is often negatively correlated with household income, and the poverty rate among single-parent households can be high in some countries. But one should use caution in employing these as the sole indicators of poverty. Data from Russia show that less than 8 percent of the very poor are from female-headed households, and only 9 percent of very poor households have more than three children (see World Bank 1995f). Unless most of the poor are found among these households, targeting based on family characteristics may not reach a significant proportion of the poor. Thus the particular method of targeting adopted can either raise or reduce errors and costs.

The basic problem for many countries in transition is that while general economic policy pushes individuals to become self-sufficient, some may not be able to become so. While attempting to move away from central control, the state must decide how involved it should be in smoothing out income variations by providing cash transfers to those in need. At the same time the state needs to address issues of education, improved access to markets, insurance, and information.

The natural tendency is to try to ensure equality. But widening wage distributions makes this objective impossible. Protection of the poorest people requires greater transfers from wealthier people, however, the institutional capacity is not in place to ensure that only the better off contribute or only the poorest benefit. In a few countries poverty is so widespread that the scope for redistributive taxation is limited.

Addressing these issues, many countries of Eastern Europe and the former Soviet Union are copying Western Europe's model of social assistance. But they run into a number of problems when trying to target the poorest people with limited resources.

- Combining state social insurance and private provisions, the social safety net policy in Western European countries minimizes the need for social assistance. Without these inputs the costs would be too great, requiring a much more restrictive program.
- As reliance on social assistance increases, the ability to become self-sufficient decreases. Also, the need to design more mechanisms that discourage disincentives to work reduces programs' cost-effectiveness by increasing real economic costs.
- To be effective, social assistance should not be given based on whether the beneficiary is among the new or old poor. This requirement often conflicts with the subjective approach to poverty, which gives better treatment to the aged and disabled (the "acceptable" poor) than to the unemployed and single parents (the "unacceptable" poor).[12]
- Western European–style programs have dealt with these problems through a series of incremental changes over fifty years. Economies in transition are forced to adapt their programs to rapidly changing situations over a much shorter period. Financially, countries cannot afford the old universal coverage, and, politically, countries find it hard to cut back on existing programs (see chapter 8). Yet there appears to be no alternative to concentrating benefits on the poorest if economic and social costs of transition are to be minimized.

Notes

1. Special thanks are due to Sandor Sipos, who provided the authors with unlimited access to the Transmonee dataset. Transmonee is a stand-alone statistical database application developed by the Central and Eastern Europe in Transition Monitoring Public Policies and Social Conditions' project, undertaken by the Economic and Social Policies

Research Program of the UNICEF International Child Development Centre, Florence, Italy.

2. Family assistance was promised only to those formal sector employees who were covered under pension schemes. Thus the source of funding for social assistance came from social insurance funds. Social security includes social insurance and social assistance.

3. Rural areas suffered more than urban areas, presumably because of larger family sizes. Armenia, however, is an exception. There, land was privatized so that larger families secured more land. As the return on the land improved, it contributed to generally lower poverty rates in rural areas. Armenia's experience with land privatization stands in sharp contrast to that of livestock privatization in Mongolia, where families with young children (often headed by women) were given fewer animals (compared to those with relatively more adults) because it was felt that adults were necessary for managing livestock. Rural poverty and inequality increased dramatically as a consequence (Subbarao and Ezemenari 1995).

4. Milanovic (1995a:13) reports that in 1993 both heads of household worked in one of seven poor households in Poland. In addition, in Bulgaria, Hungary, and Poland, the poverty rates for households with at least one member who was unemployed were 2.5 to 4 times greater than the country average.

5. See also Andorka (1990a). He argues that family assistance in Hungary helped stop the already declining trend in fertility rates, although it did not succeed in increasing fertility rates to the same level as the population replacement rate. Andorka (1990b) further argues that the higher education rate for women has had a dampening effect on fertility rates in Hungary.

6. World Bank (1990b) reported that in 1984–85, 73 percent of Zakat and Ushr recipients were not working. Of this number 27 percent were children (0–9 years of age), 10 percent were elderly or disabled, and the remaining 36 percent were either housewives, students, or the unemployed. Roughly 12 percent were widowed, and of those working, 54 percent were self-employed, with the rest divided between unpaid family workers and the self-employed.

7. In-kind benefits are based primarily on food subsidies and a funeral grant.

8. A reference to social insurance reform in this and other paragraphs is necessary, though pension-related issues are beyond the scope of this paper. In some countries social assistance and insurance payments are made from the same source; thus if insurance payments increase, social assistance gets crowded out. This pattern can be seen in table 3.2 for OECD countries. The need for social assistance in transition economies is at least partly determined by the insurance systems that are being reformed. For comprehensive treatment of issues in social insurance, see Fox (1994).

9. See World Bank (1995n). The deficit mentioned here is used to distinguish the total amount of the shortfall from the average shortfall or gap. This distinction is necessary because the average varies with the reduction in the deficit and with the resulting reduction in the number of poor (the denominator).

10. Acceptable is used in the context of a known outcome that is either allowed to happen or is dealt with in some other program.

11. Using a poverty line of Som 1,048 per year per individual, estimates are that 40 percent of the population is poor. This estimated poverty line is substantially below the "official" poverty line, according to which more than 50 percent of the population is poor (World Bank 1995b).

12. The "old acceptable poor" refers to the old socialist definition of the needy, that is, primarily orphans, invalids, the aged, and others in institutions with no family. The "new unacceptable poor" refers to the working poor whose ranks have grown since the transition.

4
Cross-Country Patterns of In-Kind Transfers

Although cash transfers are preferred to in-kind transfers for minimizing distortions in the economy, the choice may tilt in favor of in-kind transfers if the objective is to encourage the consumption of a particular commodity, if the objective is to encourage the modification of behavior, and if there are political objectives that are better served through in-kind transfers. Also, taxpayers may object less if an in-kind subsidy program is targeted to such vulnerable groups as children in school feeding programs. In addition, in-kind transfers lend themselves more easily to self-selection than cash transfers, enable better targeting, and hold their real value during periods of inflation.

In-kind subsidies can be administered in various ways. For example, governments can raise the quantity of commodities and services consumed disproportionately by the poor (for example, increase the production of low-cost bread); provide direct subsidies (for example, food rations); provide cash compensation or cash equivalents (for example, food stamps); or resort to price controls (for example, legally control the consumer price of bread). Each of these interventions has different implications for producer and consumer incentives.

Three in-kind transfers are evaluated in this chapter: food subsidies, housing subsidies, and energy subsidies.[1] Because better targeting is the main purpose of in-kind transfers, attention is devoted to targeting and distributional incidence. The implications for economic efficiency and incentives are also analyzed. Where possible, cost effectiveness and budgetary implications are reviewed.

Food Subsidies

Food subsidies have existed for more than four decades in some Asian countries. Three programs are used: open general subsidies, quantity rationing, and food stamps. In addition, some programs have addressed the nutritional deficiencies of specific groups, such as children and pregnant women. Among the programs involving subsidies, food stamp programs may enhance welfare more than price subsidies or quantity rations. Food stamps are the least distortionary program in that they allow the consumer the widest choice of commodities.

But in some countries wider consumer choice may perpetuate intrahousehold discrimination. Food stamps allow adults to make food choices that may not raise children's welfare. Thus quantity rations on food staples with high transaction costs might be more beneficial to children than food stamps. Moreover, if transport costs or local monopolies prevent isolated regions from operating competitive markets in food staples, then public distribution may be necessary, and food stamps may be irrelevant for addressing basic food needs.

Regional Patterns in Program Choice

Some regional patterns are worth noting. Quantity rationing is the preferred form of intervention in South Asia, food with work requirements in Latin America and the Caribbean, and open general price subsidies (often with heavy involvement of parastatals) in some African and Middle East and North African countries (table 4.1).[2] There are nutrition and school feeding programs in all regions, though predominately in Latin American countries. Why do countries differ in their choice of programs? Broad patterns suggest that the administrative and physical infrastructure required to implement programs such as food stamps is lacking in Africa compared with South Asia or Latin America. Food-for-work programs are prevalent in only a few countries that have a low level of infrastructural development and a high headcount poverty ratio (for example, Bangladesh and Ethiopia). Conversely, there are food stamp programs in countries that have more developed infrastructure and a lower incidence of poverty.[3]

Political economy and administrative considerations also determine program choice: it is politically infeasible and administratively difficult to run finely targeted programs in countries where the incidence of poverty is high and households in need are difficult to separate from those that are not.[4]

Changes in the character or coverage of programs over time have been driven by fiscal tightness (Sri Lanka and Tunisia), poor cost-effectiveness (the Philippines and India), or high inclusion and exclusion errors (Egypt and Brazil). Most countries introduced a food-based intervention (not necessarily targeted to the poor) in response to shocks that disrupted household food security. They remained with

Table 4.1. Regional Patterns of Food Transfer Programs, 1970s–90s

Region and country	General price subsidy	Quantity rationing	Food stamps	Feeding programs	Food with work requirement
Sub-Saharan Africa					
Ethiopia	x				x
Gambia				x	
Tanzania				x	
Zimbabwe				x	
Middle East and North Africa					
Algeria	x				
Tunisia	x				
Morocco	x			x	
Egypt	x	x			
Jordan	x[a]		x[b]		
South Asia					
Bangladesh		x			x
India		x		x	x
Pakistan	x	x		x	
Sri Lanka		x	x		
East Asia					
Philippines		x		x	
Indonesia				x	
Latin America and the Caribbean					
Brazil	x				x
Chile				x	x
Colombia				x	x
Costa Rica					x
Honduras			x	x	
Jamaica			x	x	x
Haiti					x
Peru					x
Uruguay					x
Mexico		x			
Eastern Europe and Central Asia					
Romania	x				
Ukraine	x				
Bulgaria	x				
Uzbekistan	x			x	

Note: This classification is by no means exhaustive. Rather, the table gives a flavor of programs reviewed in this document.
a. Until 1992.
b. After 1993.
Source: This table is derived from World Bank poverty assessments.

the chosen intervention until one of the above-mentioned considerations dictated a change in the program. The pattern of change depended on political economy considerations. Some governments responded by modifying the existing program, some by replacing it with a new program, and some by eliminating it altogether. In some countries attempts to totally eliminate a program resulted in riots, eventually forcing governments to resort to a much less targeted program than had been planned. Bangladesh, Egypt, India, Pakistan, and Sri Lanka all initiated universal ration programs in the early 1940s (Ahmed 1988; Alderman 1988, 1991; Edirisinghe 1987; Subbarao 1989).

Almost all of these countries are restructuring their programs. For example, in Sri Lanka the universal ration program in operation prior to 1979 cost the government up to 5 percent of GDP. The unsustainably high cost drove the government to institute food stamp programs. The move cut costs to 1.3 percent of GDP.[5] Tunisia also cut costs from 4 percent to 2 percent of GDP by moving from a universal price subsidy to a more targeted program. Other countries that have switched from universal to targeted programs and have lowered costs include Bangladesh, Honduras, Jamaica, Jordan, and Mexico.

India is slowly reforming its expensive and poorly targeted nationwide program, the Public Distribution System. Some programs run by states, such as the program that sells a kilogram of rice for 2 rupees (6 cents) in Andhra Pradesh, are proving to be extremely expensive and wasteful.[6] But India also has some innovative and better-targeted programs, such as the Integrated Child Development Services and the Tamil Nadu Nutrition Program. At the state level Kerala's record in reaching the poor with subsidized food is much better.

Many countries operate food supplement and nutrition interventions for women and children. These programs operate as temporary safety nets for poor families and as direct measures to improve the nutritional status of vulnerable individuals. Three types of programs can be distinguished: general maternal and child nutrition programs, covering all pregnant and lactating mothers, and preschool children (MCHN programs); targeted nutrition programs, aimed only at mothers and children who are at nutritional risk, in combination with nutrition education and growth monitoring; and school feeding programs.

In terms of program outcomes, three questions are relevant: How well were the poor reached? Were programs cost-effective? Have there been any disincentive effects for food and labor supply? The answers to these questions may differ among important subgroups, such as the ultrapoor (those in extreme poverty), poor women, the poor in remote areas, the urban poor, the transient poor, and the chronic poor (those who are ill or elderly).

Targeting Efficiency

Whether or not a program reaches the poor depends on how effectively the program is targeted. Leakage is measured as the amount of transfers going to the nonpoor as a percentage of the total transfer. Generally, the proportion of leakage is higher under price subsidies and quantity rationing, modest under food stamps, and lowest under programs involving food with work requirements (table 4.2).[7] Maternal and child nutrition programs appear to be better targeted than most other programs, presumably because targeting women and children requires less administrative effort. But targeting efficiency is tied not only to the type of food program adopted, but also to its design. For example, Tunisia was able to greatly improve the targeting efficiency of a universal price subsidy by subsidizing only those foods consumed by the poor (World Bank 1995j). In Bangladesh leakage to the nonpoor from the ration program was greatly reduced by tying distribution to primary school attendance (Ahmed and Billah 1994). In the case of food stamps targeting was improved in Honduras and Jamaica by linking stamp delivery to health clinics (Subbarao, Ahmed, and Teklu 1995).[8] Thus cross-country and cross-program experience suggest that leakage can be prevented mainly by innovative delivery systems.

Program Costs

Program costs include administrative costs and food costs. The usual measures adopted for program costs are cost per beneficiary, cost as a percentage of GDP, or cost per unit of nutrient (calories) transferred. Total costs for general price subsidies and quantity rations, as a percentage of GDP, are typically higher than they are under more targeted programs, such as school feeding (table 4.3).[9] Costs vary across programs according to the administrative requirements of each program and the amount of food transferred. Transferring calories to only the poor is more expensive, because the narrower is the targeting of the program, the more expensive is it to administer. In some instances the savings on food costs by better targeting are more than offset by additional administrative costs. In most countries and programs the cost of leakage can be extremely high (figure 4.1). Also, studies on Latin America show that food costs contribute more to total costs than do administrative costs (Grosh 1994; World Bank 1991c). Typically, programs that have work requirements or other obligations (such as sending children to school) have proved to be much more cost-effective than food rations.

Universal maternal and child nutrition programs, and targeted nutrition programs aimed at mothers and children at nutritional risk are much more cost-effective, efficient, and nutritionally beneficial

Table 4.2. Targeting and Transfer Efficiency of Selected Food Programs, 1980s and early 1990s

Country	Program	Targeting	Date
Bangladesh	Ration	Geographic	1991
Bangladesh	Food-for-work	Self-selection	1991
Bangladesh	Food-for-education	Individual assessment and child enrollment	1994
Brazil	Feeding	Geographic	1980
Brazil	Subsidy	Universal	1974
Colombia	Feeding	Geographic	1982
Colombia	Ration	Geographic	1981
Dominican Republic	Feeding	—	1982
Egypt	Ration	Universal	1982
Honduras	Stamps	Health center	1991
Honduras	Stamps	Schools	1991
Mexico	Ration	Universal	1982
Mexico	Subsidy	Milk	1986
Pakistan	Feeding	Self-selection	1982
Sri Lanka	Stamps	Means test	1982

— Data not available.
a. Calculated as cost per beneficiary per day (assuming 365 feeding days), multiplied by 1000 and divided by the calorie transfer.
b. Accounts for leakage to the nonpoor—cost to transfer 1,000 calories times (1 + the percentage of leakage to the nonpoor).
c. Although leakage to the nonpoor is low, leakage out of the program has been estimated to be high (that is, 45.9 percent for Colombia Feeding, 85.8 percent for

than school feeding programs. Still, in most countries the total spending on maternal and child nutrition programs is less than 0.5 percent of GDP. External donor support (including World Bank support) has been substantial. Results have differed greatly among countries spending about the same amounts. In general, targeted nutrition programs backed by nutrition education and growth monitoring have been highly cost-effective in combating malnutrition.[10] In food stamp and nutrition programs design appears to be crucial for targeting and cost-effectiveness. Thus clinic-based programs that combine health inputs with nutrition supplements operate with lower administrative costs than school-based programs (World Bank 1991c:23).[11]

Economic Costs and Disincentives for Work

Examining only program costs is not enough to assess program effectiveness. Economic costs of reduced work effort are also important. Economic costs by their very nature are difficult to quantify, though they can be significant. For example, a recent study of the generous

Leakage to nonpoor (percentage of total transfer)	Cost to transfer 1,000 calories per day (1987 US$)[a]	Cost to transfer 1,000 calories to the poor per day (1987 US$)[b]	Cost (percentage of GDP)
74	1.21	2.11	—
31	—	—	—
7	—	—	—
—	0.36	—	0.11
81	0.46	0.84	—
Low[c]	0.46	0.67	—
—	0.41	0.41	—
Low[c]	0.24	0.45	—
66	0.22	0.36	15.0
Negligible	0.13	0.13	0.2
Negligible	—	0.20	—
77	1.29	2.29	n.a.
0.49	—	—	0.2
Low[c]	0.44	0.69	—
31	0.20	0.32	1.3

Dominican Republic Feeding, and 56 percent for Pakistan Feeding). This arises mainly from leakage to other household members and through the substitution of program food for food normally consumed in the household.
Source: Calculated from IFPRI (1994); Musgrove (1989, 1991); Serageldin and Landell-Mills (1994); World Bank (1995d); Pfefferman and Griffin (1989); Mateus (1984); Pinstrup-Anderson (1998a, b); Edirisinghe (1987); Grosh (1994); Ahmed and Billah (1994); and Garcia and Pinstrup-Anderson (1987).

Figure 4.1. Administrative Cost and Cost of Leakage of Food Subsidies per Rupee of Income Transfered, India
(rupees)

Centrally administered public distribution system

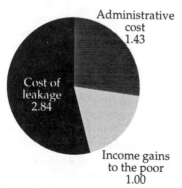

Two rupees per kilo scheme administered by Andhra Pradesh state government: cost per rupee of income transfer

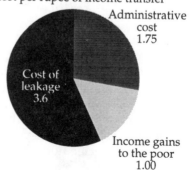

Source: Radhakrishna and others (1996).

Table 4.3. Cost-Effectiveness of Targeted Income Transfer Programs in Bangladesh, 1993–94
(dollars per ton of grain)

	Rural rationing (rice)	Vulnerable group development (wheat)	RMP[a] (cash)
Costs			
Grain purchase cost[b]	272	129	129
Sales receipts	207		
Net cost per ton	65		
Net government contribution			16
Administration			
DG Food	60	54	27
CARE/WFP	1	13	13
Ministries	2	1	1
Total cost per ton	125	186	170

	Ideal IFPRI	Actual IFPRI	Ideal WFP	Actual IFPRI	Ideal CARE	Actual IFPRI
Income transfer						
Leakage (percent)	0	70	0	14	8	0
Income transferred per ton if monetized at world price (dollars)	73	19	129	111	119	129
Cost/income transferred	1.73	6.55	1.44	1.68	1.56	1.32

Note: RMP is Rural Maintenance Program, WFP is World Food Program, and IFPRI is International Food Policy Research Institute. "Actual" refers to the current situation. "Ideal" refers to the situation (simulated) with zero leakage to the nonpoor. Vulnerable households include those at risk of malnutrition and poverty. They constituted about 55 percent of the population in 1991–92.
a. The Rural Maintenance Program pays cash wages to its workers for maintaining rural roads. But the cash is generated by monetizing wheat at the official ration price.

food stamp program in Sri Lanka found a substantial reduction in work effort by individuals receiving food stamps.[12]

Political Economy Aspects

Political economy aspects are analyzed for many transfer programs, though empirically validated political economy studies are available only for food subsidies.[13] These studies have contributed to a greater understanding of the constraining influence of pressure groups on program adoption, program expansion or contraction, and the changes in program design and implementation that led to the reallocation of benefits between the poor and the nonpoor.

Presumably, targeted nutrition programs are least likely to generate disincentive effects. Another advantage of some nutrition programs is their ability to combat intrahousehold discrimination. Programs that

Food-for-work CARE (wheat)		Food-for-work WFP (wheat)		Food-for-education (wheat)	
129		129		129	
54		54		54	
1					
8		8			
233		192		191	
Ideal IFPRI	Actual	Ideal	Actual	Ideal	Actual
0	0	36	0	28	0
129	129	83	129	93	129
1.32	1.64	2.81	1.49	2.06	1.48

Therefore, the purchase price of wheat, handling, and monetization costs are included in cost calculations.
b. IFPRI (1994) estimated the cost-effectiveness of targeted programs at the then prevailing world price of $195 per ton of wheat. Currently, Bangladesh imports wheat under the U.S. Export Enhancement Program (EEP) and pays a CIF price of $129 per ton of wheat. This report uses the current EEP wheat price.
Source: Ahmed and Billah (1994).

successfully combat leakage and intrahousehold fungibility are few and far between.

The effects of alternative food subsidy interventions on different social groups are shown in three studies: Binswanger and Quizon (1984); de Janvry and Subbarao (1986), for India; and Kouwenaar (1988), for Ecuador. De Janvry, Fargeiz, and Sadoulet (1992) also present an interesting approach. They construct a political feasibility index for a variety of antipoverty programs, including consumer food subsidies that took into account alternative financing possibilities. Thirteen policies were then ranked in terms of their political feasibility; the rankings were validated with ex-post experience from India and Ecuador. Three policies underscore the interplay of political coalitions and food subsidies.
• Policies that benefit all groups (except the rural rich) and raise GNP. An example is food subsidies based on aid-funded (P.L. 480) imports. The rural rich are not an effective coalition in this set of

policies. Political feasibility is the highest, 13, for this intervention (validated with the experience of India and Bangladesh; such aid-funded intervention lasts as long as food aid lasts).

- Policies that confer exceptional benefits to the rural poor from a base of domestic supply and taxation of the rural rich. Attempts were made to form a coalition of the rural poor and the rural rich. But the political feasibility rank was the lowest, 1 (validated by India's experience). India tried a "producer levy" during the mid-1970s. Most large farmers evaded the levy and protested, and the levy was withdrawn after 18 months (Subbarao 1993).
- Policies that benefit both the urban poor and the rural rich. These are food subsidies for the urban poor and production subsidies for all farmers in theory, but in practice a disproportionate share goes to rich farmers. A political coalition of the urban poor and the rural rich is feasible (as is clear from the experiences of India and Ecuador). Political feasibility ranks for such policies are 7, 8, and 9. This ranking is validated by country experience. This set of policies prevailed for the longest period in India and Ecuador. The most visible symptom of such political distortion is the urban bias that food subsidy programs have displayed for so long in Bangladesh, India, and Pakistan. Such policies benefit the politically vocal urban population, who are not at nutritional risk. They also hurt the rural poor (the landless in particular), who face food prices that are both higher and more unstable in the absence of government procurement and food subsidies (de Janvry and Subbarao 1986).

Transfer policies benefiting both the poor and the rich require heavy subsidies. As programs expand in response to the demands of political coalitions for rents from the state,[14] explicit trade-offs emerge between spending on safety net programs and investments for growth. The resulting fiscal drain and macroeconomic disequilibrium set in motion the difficult political process of scaling down. In addition to India, Bangladesh, Egypt, Morocco, Pakistan, Sri Lanka, and Tunisia are in various stages of scaling down to better target food subsidy programs.[15]

Political economy issues seem to prevail even in programs aimed at the welfare and protection of children. Growth monitoring and targeted food supplements for children under three years of age, and for pregnant and lactating women have proven to be cost-effective and nutritionally beneficial. Despite such proof, the less-effective school feeding programs are often used purely for political economy reasons. An example is India. The ruling party suffered many reverses in the 1995 interim elections in states that introduced populist transfer programs, including expensive and notoriously untargeted food subsidies. The ruling party, with an eye to the general elections in 1996, announced a nationwide program of school feeding—at an enormous cost. Yet research in India points to the ineffectiveness of school feeding as a nutrition intervention, especially since malnutrition is prevalent among preschoolers (Subbarao 1989). School feeding is being used in this case for political mobilization rather than as a nutrition intervention.

Housing Subsidies

The countries in transition have historically given massive subsidies for housing.[16] In the former Soviet Union, for example, heavily subsidized housing was provided free of charge through employers or local authorities. Private expenditures on housing have been low: Russian households spent less than 0.5 percent of all expenditures on housing in 1991. In Poland households spent about 3 percent of all expenditures on housing, but 11 to 15 percent on alcohol and tobacco in 1991. In Poland and Russia housing subsidies accounted for 25 to 35 percent of government expenditures during 1991–93. In South Asia and Sub-Saharan Africa housing subsidies were less than 0.005 percent of government (budget) expenditures (table 4.4). Although prevalent in many countries, housing subsidies pose a serious budget problem only in the former centrally planned economies of Eastern Europe and the former Soviet Union.

Housing subsidies are of two kinds. On-budget subsidies take the form of direct grants for public housing construction and free maintenance of public housing. In several countries outside of Europe and Central Asia some direct subsidies go to upgrading slums and paying housing allowances for government employees or workers in parastatals. Off-budget subsidies include subsidized or negative interest rates, high default rates, or complete forgiveness of loans, tax exemptions, and rent control. On-budget subsidies are easier to quantify than off-budget subsidies. In transition economies on-budget subsidies are the predominant form of housing subsidies.

Table 4.4. Housing Subsidies, Early 1990s
(percentage of government budget)

Region	Budget share
Sub-Saharan Africa	0.005
South Asia	0.00
East Asia	0.01
Latin America and the Caribbean	0.06
Europe, Middle East, and North Africa	0.08
Industrialized countries	0.07

Source: Persaud (1992).

Evidence is overwhelming that housing subsidies are regressive (World Bank 1993c): they benefit few at the expense of many. Thus in the former Soviet Union, while a family currently occupying subsidized housing pays little rent to the government, the number of households waiting for such subsidized accommodation has risen. A reduction in house building and a relaxation of housing standards increased the list of people waiting for housing to 16 million in 1994. Some people on this housing list are among the nonpoor who have adequate housing, but are waiting to be upgraded to better units. These nonpoor households receive a non-means-tested subsidy, while some of the poor reside in inadequate accommodations. The mean percentage of reported housing that is allocated to households below the median of the income distribution (for all regions) was 31 percent. In poor countries of South Asia and Africa the proportion of subsidy reaching the fraction of the population below the median income distribution was even lower (20 percent), but it was higher (50 percent) in the industrialized countries (table 4.5). Among the formerly centrally planned economies, evidence suggests that while the proportion of government budgets devoted to housing subsidies is higher than that of noncentrally planned countries with similar income levels, the degree of targeting to low-income households is lower (Persaud 1992). Within each region, however, there are intercountry differences. Thus in Latin America and the Caribbean subsidies have benefited 6 percent of households below the median income distribution in Ecuador, 20 percent in Jamaica, 16 percent in Venezuela, and 50 percent in Chile.

The distributional incidence has also been unequal in countries that resorted to off-budget subsidies. Thus in Uruguay subsidized loans from the Mortgage Bank of Uruguay have been highly regressive. Moreover, the highest reported arrear rates on mortgages (about 20 percent) are found in Latin American and the Caribbean.

The adoption of means tests did not prevent the nonpoor from gaining access to subsidies and did not ensure that the poor received a proportionate share of subsidies (table 4.6). In El Salvador, for example, only 6 percent of the bottom quartile received a housing subsidy, even

Table 4.5. Percentage of Housing Subsidies Reaching Households that Fall Below the Median Income, Early 1990s

Region	Budget share
Sub-Saharan Africa	0.18
South Asia	0.10
East Asia	0.31
Latin America and the Caribbean	0.18
Europe, Middle East, and North Africa	0.28
Industrialized countries	0.50

Source: Persaud (1992).

after a means test. Colombia fared much better: means tests substantially improved the share of subsidies going to the bottom decile.

Public subsidies for housing sectors that have the character of public goods (slum upgrading) can be justified in theory. But in practice programs' potential to reach the poor has been very limited.

In contrast to government efforts to provide low-cost housing to the poor, the efforts of nongovernmental agencies have been impressive. Thus the Self-Employed Women's Association (SEWA) in Gujarat extended its operations to provide collateral-free loans to poor women for making repairs, improving roofs, or adding home-based workplaces. Similar efforts were made by the Society for Promotion of Area Residence Centres (SPARC) for rehabilitating homeless women in Bombay. A seminar on state-level experience with public housing for the poor in India noted various reasons why the benefits did not reach the poor. Among those were poor accountability and monitoring by public agencies. Most slums failed because a public-private partnership was not ensured, and communities and voluntary organizations were not involved. One consequence of the unequal distribution of

Table 4.6. Distributional Incidence of Housing Subsidies

Country	Date	Targeting mechanism	Quartile (percent)			
			I	II	III	IV
Distribution of beneficiaries						
El Salvador	1976	Means test	11	32	38	19
El Salvador	1977	Means test	6	38	37	19
Zambia	1978	Means test	18	38	14	30
Zambia	1980	Means test	28	26	16	30
Upgrading						
Philippines	1979	Means test	27	24	23	26
Zambia	1976	Means test	38	22	17	23

			Quintile (percent)				
			I	II	III	IV	V
Distribution of housing subsidy							
Colombia	1991	Means test	35.0	25.4	25.0	11.0	1.6
Colombia	1991	Without means test	14.5	24.3	26.9	26.1	8.1
Uruguay	1989	Without means test	5.4	9.4	11	15.1	13.8

Country	Date	Targeting mechanism	Bottom 50 percent	Top 50 percent
Colombia	early 1990s	Proxy means test	0	100
Jamaica	early 1990s	—	20	80
Brazil	early 1990s	—	48	42
Venezuela	early 1990s	—	16	84
Chile	early 1990s	Indicator targeting	50	50
Ecuador	early 1990s	Geographic	6	94

— Data not available.
Source: Keare and Parris (1982) for distribution of beneficiaries; World Bank (1994b:113) for Colombia data with and without means test; World Bank (1993k) for Uruguay; Persaud (1992, table 1) for remaining data from distribution of housing subsidy.

housing subsidies is the relatively high private expenditures incurred
by the poor, even in economies in transition. In Russia very poor
households spent 2.1 percent of their expenditures on housing, whereas nonpoor households spent only 0.2 percent.

Housing Subsidies, Efficiency Losses, and the Labor Market

The worst efficiency loss from housing subsidies in Eastern Europe
and the former Soviet Union comes from the labor market. A change of
job, which may involve giving up an advanced position in one housing queue and entering another, simply reduces labor mobility, labor
market efficiency, and impedes the adjustment process.

Where governments have provided an alternative—heavily subsidized accommodation to the population living in urban slums (for
example, in India)—the results have not been entirely sanguine.
Because families received housing at a price much lower than the free-
market price, they were prone to dispose a part of or the entire house
for a profit. Thus slum dwellers in cities who had been rehabilitated
with subsidized housing again returned to the slums after selling their
houses at a profit—a financial gain to specific families but not to the
government. Even when beneficiaries had been carefully screened and
monitored, estimates suggest that after five to six years, a third or half
of the accommodations were sold or leased by the beneficiary
households.

In principle there is nothing wrong with the beneficiaries renting a
part of their subsidized housing, but there is no willingness to meet
repayment obligations, notwithstanding the heavily subsidized price
of the units. Most of the occupants of shelter homes were able to repay,
but they were unwilling to do so because they knew they would not be
evicted for nonpayment. Evidence also suggests that despite chronic
arrears on highly subsidized units, governments—democratic and
nondemocratic—have never resorted to eviction.

Housing subsidies also distort housing prices that nonrecipients
confront. Such adverse effects are strong when subsidies take the form
of less-than-market interest rates. For example, in Malaysia in the early
1980s subsidized mortgage loans were made available to civil servants
at 4 percent (compared with 11 percent for the general public). This
program caused subsidized mortgage lending as a percentage of total
mortgage lending to increase from 0 to about 40 percent in barely five
years. There was considerable upward pressure on housing prices and
a drop in demand by nonrecipients (World Bank 1993c:126).

Rent controls are the most common off-budget subsidy in many
developing countries. Where this form of subsidy was adopted, private investment in rental housing was reduced drastically because

owners of rent controlled houses could not obtain adequate returns on their investments.

Reform of Housing Subsidies

In all of the countries of Eastern Europe and the former Soviet Union the housing sector is undergoing a major reform. At the core of the reform are privatization, easing of restrictions on rentals and exchanges, and a revised rent control system. These changes are bound to increase labor mobility, apart from reducing the fiscal burden. In moving toward a liberalized housing market, it is important to protect the poor from sharply increased costs for dwellings and utilities.

In Russia reform is proceeding along two tracks: privatization and improved cost recovery through increased rentals. Privatization transferred about a third of Russia's total housing stock to its occupants by the close of 1994. A major problem with "housing giveaways" is the priority extended to existing tenants, thus perpetuating past inequities. One solution would be to design a mechanism that allows people on the waiting list who have not yet received any housing unit to be compensated by tenants who have. Housing giveaways, however, are not always inappropriate. Where current tenants are poor, housing giveaways are probably the best immediate safety net because of the economywide gains in labor mobility. But the first round of rapid privatization was taken advantage of by rich and better-located tenants, who quickly made substantial profits. Relatively poorer tenants owning apartments of only moderate value are still waiting because of their inability to pay higher fees for maintenance, utilities, and property taxes (Struyk and Daniell 1995).

Some of the housing stock has been transferred to local authorities, along with the responsibility for housing services. Because local governments have not explored revenue-raising possibilities and because they are strapped for resources, transfer of the housing stock generated enormous incentives to jack up sales prices well beyond the means of ordinary citizens. Thus reform, including privatization, proceeded slowly. It is more expedient politically to sell the acquired housing stock at high prices than to raise revenues through redistributive taxation.

The second track of reform deals with enhancing rentals on public housing. To mitigate the impact of increased housing (and utilities) costs on poor families, some local governments in Russia have introduced "housing allowances," administered by separate offices after means testing. Relatively simple procedures have been established for means testing. But the take-up rate in the housing allowance program has been very low (about 10 percent). Because the scheme is new, lack of information could be one problem. It is not clear how well the poor living in poorer localities (mostly rural) are being protected. Evidence suggests that the cost of administering the program averaged about 1.5 percent of the incremental rent collected—thus increased rental revenues contributed to local budgets and to improved maintenance and repair of houses. The demands on the program will grow as the real costs of housing and utilities rise further and take-up rates increase.

Reform should aim at enabling individuals to build and own houses and use their housing assets to increase their incomes. Such a development is possible only when housing finance systems are in place. Russia is still far from setting up mortgage lending institutions. But Hungary is not. Housing subsidy reform in Hungary has progressed rapidly. Interest rate subsidies, which accounted for as much as 3 percent of GDP, have been eliminated. In place of the earlier complex and inequitable system of subsidies, a targeted housing allowance was introduced. Only low-income households (identified after careful means testing) are eligible for housing allowances. Rents were brought up to market levels. Hungary has proposed to privatize its entire housing stock. Hungary clearly has an edge over Russia in housing reform. One important factor that contributed to Hungary's speedy reform was the existence of well-functioning, local-level social assistance offices that successfully identified the poor.

In Africa, Asia, and Latin America off-budget subsidies dominate, and reform has been slow and implementation ineffective. For example, in Chile the government moved from poorly targeted credit subsidies to direct, explicit, one-time subsidies that allowed households to purchase housing on the private market. But Chile permitted high levels of arrears without loan foreclosures, and many of the advantages of the reformed subsidy system (such as transparency) were lost. In other countries, such as India and Ghana, rent control has proved an inefficient way to protect the poor; yet reform has been slow in coming.

Energy Subsidies

Energy use by the poor follows distinct regional patterns. In the transition economies of Eastern Europe and the former Soviet Union the poor (particularly the urban poor) use such nontraditional fuels as coal-fired steam heating plants, district heat, gas, and electricity.[17] By contrast, the poor in much of Africa, Asia, and Latin America use traditional fuels, wood, charcoal, animal dung, and agricultural residue. Moreover, in all regions traditional fuels are consumed by the rural poor. Further, in Africa, Asia, and Latin America (more than in Europe and Central Asia) the urban poor spend a higher percentage of their total expenditures on energy than the nonpoor (Barnes and others

1994). But in Europe and Central Asia the middle- and high-income consumers spend more of their budget on energy than low-income consumers (Freund and Wallich 1995).

Because of the varying patterns of energy consumption by the poor and the nonpoor, tax and subsidy policies may generate unintended consequences (beneficial or adverse) for the poor. Thus a tax in Asia or Africa on nontraditional fuels consumed by the nonpoor may encourage the substitution of traditional fuels. In such a case traditional fuel prices may increase, causing the poor to suffer real income losses. In Europe and Central Asia a subsidy on nontraditional fuels will benefit the poor, but the nonpoor will benefit more than the poor. Moreover, owing to variations in consumption, energy subsidies help accentuate already prevalent inequality in rural and urban living standards. In general, energy subsidies on nontraditional fuels (with few exceptions, such as kerosene) have benefited the urban poor and nonpoor more than rural dwellers.

Energy Subsidies and the Budget

In Europe and Central Asia and most other developing countries the energy sector is dominated by public sector enterprises. Prices are generally set by governments. Depending on how well the administered prices cover the economic cost of producing the energy, government subsidies vary among regions and among countries within regions. In Europe and Central Asia, prior to the transition, real or perceived distribution problems were sought to be solved by underpricing or inefficient pricing of energy (as much as for housing, food, transport, and several other services). The reluctance to raise the average price stems from the (misplaced) fear of contributing to inflation (and wage pressure). In reality, subsidization may actually increase the potential for inflation—because subsidies eventually feed into budget deficits. If the resulting budget deficits are financed by inflation—which is most likely to be the case—keeping energy prices low may actually contribute to inflation.[18]

The problem now facing countries in Europe and Central Asia is how to manage the change from subsidizing energy to charging an economic price. The problem is compounded because energy is centrally controlled; many families are unable to control their individual consumption and therefore cannot reduce their costs by lowering their consumption. Removing all subsidies overnight would leave many families unable to pay their energy costs. Countries are approaching this problem with a mixture of continuing subsidies, lifeline rates, and targeted cash transfers. The important issue is to ensure that the poor continue to have access to energy, particularly in areas where the climate is harsh. Whatever program is adopted, it should offer the greatest incentive for the individual to conserve energy.

Targeting and Distributional Implications

The benefit to the poor from energy price subsidies (or the loss sustained by removing or reducing energy subsidies) depends on the poor's share of energy expenditures, the responsiveness of energy demand to prices, and the possibility of replacing subsidized fuel with nonsubsidized fuels.

In Africa, Asia, and Latin America it is not clear whether energy subsidies actually benefit poor people. The fuels consumed by the poor for heating (such as coal or firewood) or for transportation are not necessarily the ones that are subsidized. Thus gasoline subsidies—pervasive in low-income developing countries—are not necessarily directly beneficial to the poor, because motor vehicles are owned by the nonpoor. If gasoline subsidies are intended to keep public transportation costs low and keep benefits from leaking to nontarget groups, subsidizing public transportation fares may be more efficient than subsidizing gasoline.[19] Because the poor use kerosene for lighting and cooking in many low-income countries, a subsidy on kerosene may be justified. But even so, the urban poor (whose average incomes tend to be higher than those of the rural poor) benefit disproportionately. Moreover, where kerosene is supplied under rationing schemes (for example, in India), the requirement of a permanent residence has precluded the ultrapoor (who live in urban slums) from using the subsidy.

Because of the asymmetry between energy subsidies and the poor's pattern of energy consumption, the distributional effects of energy subsidies in Africa, Asia, and Latin America have not been propoor. In Colombia 81 percent of the lowest quintile had access to electricity in 1992, compared with 98 percent of the highest quintile. Households in the lowest quintile received a smaller share of the subsidy than the richest quintile. In Ecuador energy subsidies (mostly for liquified petroleum gas) benefited the top quintile disproportionately. In Venezuela petroleum and electricity subsidies in the late 1980s and early 1990s benefited the nonpoor more than the poor. In Indonesia the poorest 40 percent of the population received 22 percent of the energy subsidy, whereas the top 60 percent received 78 percent. The main reason for the regressive incidence in Indonesia was the preponderance of subsidies on automotive diesel rather than kerosene, the main fuel consumed by the urban poor.

In all transition economies of Eastern Europe and the former Soviet Union subsidizing energy prices is common practice. An analysis shows that this policy is regressive. While it does help the poor by providing lower cost energy, it is more useful to the rich, who consume more energy (Freund and Wallich 1995). It is not even clear whether all the poor benefit from energy subsidies in this region. Evidence from the Russia Longitudinal Monitoring Survey shows that only 48 percent of the poor had access to gas and 61 percent had access to central heating. According to that survey the current structure of consumption of housing utilities prevents the subsidy from reaching many poor households, particularly those in rural areas and small towns. In Kyrgyz Republic the heavily subsidized district heating and natural gas are available only in urban areas. A universal subsidy on district heating is clearly inequitable (apart from being inefficient).

Bearing in mind consumption and country differences between the transition economies and developing countries in Africa, Asia, and Latin America, the conclusion is overwhelming: the impact of energy subsidies has been regressive. If energy subsidies are prominent in a country's budget, the main reason is political economy. When it comes to energy pricing, many governments are concerned not so much with the poor, but with the more vocal, broad (and growing, in countries like India) urban middle class.

Energy Subsidy Reform

In recent years some countries in Europe, Central Asia, and the former Soviet Union have raised energy utility prices to cover average financial costs, but not economic costs. Moreover, in many countries governments have maintained the old structure of prices, subsidizing the residential consumer more than the industrial and commercial user. Policy changes on energy pricing are still evolving. Thus only the implications of alternative policies under consideration can be assessed.

The options under consideration, following a reduction or removal of energy subsidies, focus on four sets of compensation policies: lifeline rates, vouchers, targeted cash compensations to the poor, and targeted in-kind payments (Freund and Wallich 1995).

Lifeline rates involve charging a discounted rate for a small block of energy consumed. If not targeted, every person—the rich and the poor—benefits from a low tariff. It is not clear if targeting for the purpose of block pricing is cost-effective, given that means tests are expensive and unreliable in transition economies. The amount of leakage depends on how successfully beneficiaries are screened. Administering a lifeline pricing system would pose problems because there is no metering system. There is no evidence on the correlation of dwelling size and income level (Freund and Wallich 1995).[20] Thus the distributional impact of lifeline pricing, based on square meters of floor space rather than actual consumption, is difficult to assess. Lifeline pricing may also exclude some of the most needy people in rural areas, who do not have access to district housing. But one advantage of block pricing must be recognized: when the subsidy is paid out of the budget, the utility and the industry are not burdened with distortions. Despite its disadvantages, lifeline pricing may have merits for electricity pricing.

Vouchers are like food rations. Following a price increase, the eligible poor are protected with a voucher that enables them to buy a certain amount of energy at a fixed price. Unlike lifeline pricing, vouchers can reflect differences in household size and composition. But vouchers do not create incentives for energy conservation: every consumer will consume the entire quantity allowed. If consumers are able to trade in vouchers, the system amounts to the poor receiving cash grants, however, in the process some of the benefits leak to the nonpoor. How many of the poor (versus the nonpoor) benefit depends on the transaction costs in voucher trading. Vouchers are clearly very difficult to administer.

Targeted cash compensations following an increase in energy prices is the third option. Since energy prices are not manipulated, the resulting allocation of resources will be more efficient. But desired results depend on the ability to identify households according to their welfare position, which then determines the cash payment. Bulgaria is already using this system. Households are grouped into three categories by income, and a predetermined subsidy (transfer) is paid to each group. The transfer falls as income goes up. Households in the poorest group are fully compensated. The main advantage of the system is that it encourages more efficient energy use. It would have been more appropriate, however, to use income (consumption) per person, or per adult equivalent, rather than per household.

Cash compensations can work if local social assistance offices are already reasonably efficient, and the poor are already being identified. Such is the case in Hungary. In other countries, where mechanisms for targeting social assistance at the grass roots level are not in place or are not efficient, cash compensation can lead to gross abuses.

Some countries are aiming to provide social assistance based on a "minimum income guarantee" (for example, Romania). In such cases it would be wise to include cash compensation for energy price rises. Such a strategy would avoid a proliferation of offices administering various types of assistance.

Tied cash transfers may be politically more acceptable in some countries than in others. Under this system, once the social assistance office identifies a poor person or household, the office pays the consumer's heating and power bill directly to the heating or utility company.

Whether paid in cash or in-kind, the critical factors determining the success of such programs are data availability, and institutions and practices that can track new information (on the income and welfare position of households including household size), which can then be fed into the system to weed out ineligible households and to include new households. Many countries neglect the need to include new households (especially if they are immigrants, refugees, or ethnic groups). Obviously, the preferred approach depends on the situation of the individual country.

Conclusion

Almost every country that adopted open-ended food price subsidies to protect the poor has found the policy fiscally unsustainable, and distortionary to the agricultural sector.[21] Many countries have resorted to targeted approaches. No particular targeted method has been found to be perfect; yet programs that are imperfectly targeted have been better at reaching the poor and keeping costs down than those with no targeting at all. Moreover, leakage appears to be lowest in programs that selected beneficiaries not on income-based means tests but on beneficiaries' (or their children's) participation in primary schools or clinics.[22] Tying beneficiary participation (or time contribution) to food transfers not only reduces leakage, it may also lower economic costs associated with work disincentives.

The cost of transferring income to the poor is lower for food stamps and targeted food and nutrition programs than for quantity rations or general subsidies. Nevertheless, it is difficult to rank the targeted programs in terms of their cost effectiveness and incentive costs because of the significant variation across countries and programs. Also, evidence on incentive costs is unavailable in many countries. The cost-effectiveness of a program depends greatly on the choice of a particular targeting method and the design and delivery of the program. That choice, in turn, depends on the needs of beneficiaries and on country-specific constraints. Generous coverage leads to incentive costs and adverse effects on labor supply.

Finally, political economy considerations are a major country-specific constraint in designing sustainable food transfer programs. In particular, too much fine tuning in targeting may erode political support for food transfers.[23]

As for housing subsidies, on-budget and off-budget subsidies rarely ever reached the poor. In Africa, Asia, and Latin America the urban middle class benefited most from public housing programs. Vast numbers of rural poor did not benefit at all. Off-budget subsidies do not appear to be a good instrument for protecting the poor, least of all the rural poor. The urban poor are protected best by increasing and encouraging low-cost housing production and upgrading slums (by providing sanitary facilities). Such help appears more desirable than off-budget, nontransparent subsidies, which are generally captured by the nonpoor. In Europe and Central Asia housing reform is taking place, and major subsidies must be removed to achieve fiscal balance. Thus a targeted housing allowance must form an important component of the overall safety net. Perhaps the best way to achieve this objective is to institute a targeted housing allowance that would preceed freeing up rents, establishing housing finance institutions, and privatizing the housing stock. In this effort the danger of passing on all the benefits to owners of supply-inelastic urban land is very real; where such benefits accrued, the scope for mopping up tax revenues may have to be explored. The resources thus raised could be used for targeting benefits to the poor. The exact mechanism for targeting to protect the poor will vary among countries, depending on the administrative competence of local social assistance offices.

Like housing subsidies, energy subsidies have also been regressive. But in Europe and Central Asia reduction or elimination of energy subsidies is bound to hurt the urban poor in the short run. Many approaches are being floated for compensating the poor in countries of Eastern Europe and the former Soviet Union. These options include lifeline rates, vouchers, cash compensations, and in-kind transfers. Lifeline pricing has definite merits for electricity pricing. For other sources of energy, vouchers or cash compensations can work only in countries where local social assistance offices are already efficient. Current domestic energy consumption is much higher in Europe and Central Asia than in Western countries, and any new system adopted should include incentives that lead to energy conservation.

Notes

1. Credit subsidies for the poor are prevalent in many countries, but these subsidies do not fall into the same category as food, energy, and housing subsidies. Unlike these latter subsidies, credit subsidies involve some obligation to work, and recipients have to repay at least a part of their loans. Credit subsidies are assessed in chapter 5.

2. The objective of protecting the consumer and the belief that private marketing channels are exploitative led to the creation of parastatals throughout Africa. The adverse impact of administered price regimes implemented by the parastatals for producer and consumer welfare and equity is well-known. Reform and reduction (if not elimination) of parastatals is an important component of the ongoing adjustment policy framework of many African countries.

3. This does not imply that food-for-work programs are easier to organize and target cost-effectively than food stamp programs.

4. This is not to argue that a generalized price subsidy that lowers staple food prices for all consumers is the best way of approaching the problem. Indeed, such a policy had the

opposite effect in some African countries: by enforcing lower farm prices and blunting incentives to producers, it exacerbated supply responses and aggravated the food problem.

5. The program in Sri Lanka could be better targeted, and its costs could be further reduced—nearly half of the country's population has access to food stamps, whereas the incidence of poverty is less than 30 percent. Sahn and Alderman (1995) have estimated potential adverse effects on labor supply from what appears to still be a generous transfer program.

6. These two programs were so expensive that other critical expenditures have had to be cut. See Subbarao (1989) and Radhakrishna and others (1996).

7. Different national poverty lines and systems of measurement make comparison across countries difficult.

8. In most voucher and stamp schemes leakage (defined as the value of vouchers and stamps going to the nonpoor) is low. But vouchers and stamps are tradable, and the real test is how much of their value reaches the poor.

9. One might argue that primary schooling is so important that school feeding may be necessary to encourage attendance. School feeding, therefore, might be a good idea even if it is expensive. It may be important for political reasons as well.

10. India's Tamil Nadu Integrated Nutrition Project program confirms this finding—mothers who brought their first child into the program and who were given "nutrition education" absorbed the lessons. This result was evident in that they brought their second child and subsequent children into the program (Shekar 1994).

11. But school feeding programs may achieve other objectives, such as promoting school enrollments, particularly of girls, or improving the learning abilities of students. If this is the case then school feeding programs should be assessed not as nutrition interventions but as programs meant to realize other social objectives.

12. Sahn and Alderman (1995) found that in the rural areas of Sri Lanka, the reduction in work effort had a value of 50 percent (for males) and 40 percent (for females) of the value of the subsidy.

13. This section draws heavily from de Janvry, Fargeiz, and Sadoulet (1992) and de Janvry and Subbarao (1986).

14. An example is the substantial improvement in the coverage of food subsidies in rural India following severe criticisms of urban bias.

15. It is difficult to speculate on what configuration of political forces will eventually bring about the desired change. In economic markets the equilibria between demand and supply are derived from consumers maximizing profits. Presumably, in political markets equilibria are reached when neither supporters nor opponents of a program, nor politicians, are willing to alter the form or intensity of government interventions. A change in government intervention away from this equilibrium would lead potential losers to at least partially compensate potential gainers, while gainers would be willing to offer up to a certain amount to secure the intervention. In the case of food subsidies in developing countries the potential losers of a more targeted program are usually the nonpoor, while the potential gainers are the poor. Obviously, if all markets are perfect and there is no cost to acquiring information and forming coalitions, the amount offered by potential losers (the nonpoor) to oppose the change would always exceed the amount offered by the potential gainers (the poor). As a result, country experiences show that redistributive government interventions usually occur in favor of the groups that are politically more effective at managing this transformation. For programs such as food subsidies, again, the demands of the most malnourished will rarely have the same political clout as the demands of the better organized, who usually constitute the nonpoor (de Janvry and Subramanian 1985).

16. This section draws heavily on World Bank (1993c) and other recent papers and sector reports on housing issues in countries in transition.

17. District heat refers to an arrangement whereby apartment complexes receive steam heat through a district heating grid, which also provides hot water. District

heating has been found to be highly energy efficient. It is the typical heating system in many cities of the former Soviet Union.

18. It is worth stressing that this conclusion is valid only for the posttransition period, which witnessed a complete breakdown of fiscal discipline. With a balanced budget, a policy of subsidizing wage goods could be disinflationary, assuming labor markets are functioning normally.

19. In some countries subsidies on diesel fuel have led to inefficient dieselization of industrial equipment and automobiles, and leakage of benefits to unintended groups and sectors.

20. Freund and Wallich (1995) do not refer to correlation between household size and income level, in addition to mere household size.

21. Although not discussed here, some of these policies that tax agriculture have had deleterious effects on production, particularly in Sub-Saharan Africa.

22. The reference here is not to school feeding, but to programs such as food rations that are given subject to the household's willingness to send children to schools.

23. Gelback and Pritchett (1995) argue that too much indictor-based targeting may result in expenditure cuts that offset the benefits of better targeting. Self-targeting may survive politically more than other forms of targeting, because the politician can say the individual decided to participate or not to participate. It was not a government decision.

5
Income Generation Programs

Unlike cash and in-kind transfers, income generation programs obligate the recipient to exchange labor time for an income transfer. Two programs have been used widely: labor-intensive public works and credit-based self-employment (livelihood) programs. While public works can be used as a temporary measure for consumption smoothing during economic or natural shocks (such as a drought), or as year-long poverty reduction programs, credit-based livelihood programs aim to raise the average real income of the poor in the long term. Public works provide immediate income; credit programs aim to generate medium-term income streams. Both of these programs involve subsidies of varying degrees.

Public Works

Public works have been an important countercyclical intervention in industrial and developing countries.[1] These programs were used in some Western countries during the depression years of the 1930s and also during the mid-1950s (especially in Germany). Public works originated in India in the nineteenth century as massive antifamine interventions, though the works consisted of useless excavating-type programs (Dreze 1989). India's programs had their origin in England's workhouses under the 1834 Poor Law Amendment Act (Besley and Coate 1991). Prior to the formal launching of public works by governments, Kenya had a tradition of voluntary labor contributions to build schools, known as *harambee* (schoolbuilding) and other community infrastructure. India tried *shramadan* (donation of labor), pioneered by social worker Vinoba Bhave. But these earlier experiments were not income generation programs—they were more like community self-help programs.

While the argument for public works in nineteenth century England and India centered around the ethic of work (often long and nasty work), their relevance for developing countries is in using labor for production and to build infrastructure. The scale of public works operations (in terms of employment generated) was as high as 21 percent of the labor force in Botswana in 1985–86, 13 percent in Chile in 1983, and 5 percent in Honduras in 1990–93. In terms of number of workers employed (or person-days of employment created) the programs in Bangladesh and India are probably the largest in the world. During the mid-1980s the Maharashtra Employment Guarantee Scheme (MEGS) in India created about 150–170 person-days of employment per person per year (Dev 1995b). Employment in India's massive Jawahar Rojgar Yojuna (JRY) program reached 1 billion workdays by 1995, covering 123 underdeveloped districts of the country's 350 districts (India, Ministry of Rural Development). In 1992 JRY generated about 20 person-days of employment per person, or 62 person-days of employment per family (India, Ministry of Rural Development).

There are several variants of public works programs in different countries. They can be distinguished by the mode of payment, duration and timing of employment (whether or not there is a guarantee of employment), and extent of private sector involvement. Thus in the 1950s and 1960s availability of bilateral food aid (mostly wheat under U.S. P.L. 480) facilitated the emergence of the food-for-work program in South Asia, where wages were paid in food and the program was oriented toward road construction. These programs were also a major policy response to severe droughts and floods that visited parts of India and Bangladesh. In the 1980s the food-for-work program diminished in importance in Asia. But the program continues in a few African countries largely with multilateral food aid from the World Food Program. Independently of food aid, some countries pay part of wages in-kind and part in cash. Their motivation is to ensure food security at the household level. But now most countries pay wages in cash.

Unlike credit-based self-employment schemes, public works provide mainly current benefits. They are not meant to function as a permanent escape route from poverty. In fact, most countries offer only temporary employment during off-seasons, when agricultural work is limited. Thus programs are expected to offer only stabilization benefits (consumption-smoothing in poor households), not transfer long-run benefits. Moreover, sudden and unanticipated declines in farm activity during bad agricultural years offer greater scope for consumption smoothing than do anticipated declines during slack seasons. The MEGS in India differs from others in that it makes employment available year-round within 5 kilometers of an individual's residence, and employment at the worksite is guaranteed.[2] Whether or not employment is guaranteed, public work programs in South Asia are massive and offer employment for a long period—often more than 100 person-days of employment per person in some provinces—and during exceptionally bad agricultural years (Subbarao 1997). The source of funding also affected the duration of employment. In most African countries bilateral donors funded many public works. Programs lasted only as long as donor support, and they offered only short-term employment. In countries where public works are domestically funded, either partially (as in Bangladesh) or entirely (as in India), programs have operated for much longer periods. Thus depending on historical circumstances and sources of financing, there is much cross-country variation in the scale of operation of public works (table 5.1).

Public works are implemented by governments directly (through line ministries), the private sector (contractors), or nongovernmental organizations (NGOs).[3] The exact nature of the institutional framework and implementing agencies differ a great deal across countries (table 5.2). In some countries in Africa and Latin America public works are funded by social funds, but executed by private contractors.

The central issues in the management of public works are:
- How to implement programs cost effectively.
- How to target programs to the poor.
- How to strengthen the secondary benefits from assets, and how to share these benefits between the poor and the nonpoor.
- How to design the program so as to minimize transaction costs to the poor, exploit potential complementarities with other developmental projects, and encourage private sector involvement and NGO participation.

Cost per Job Created

Many countries have explicitly stated that the objective of public works is to create temporary jobs. But few countries have actually paid attention to keeping the costs of such job creation low. The most critical factor governing the cost per job created is the share of wages in total cost. In general, countries in which the ratio of wage cost to total cost is 0.5 or higher have a lower cost per job created (table 5.1). But there is much cross-country variation—from as low as $1 per person-day of employment created in Bangladesh to $8 in Bolivia and $11 in Niger. To place cross-country comparisons in perspective, table 5.1 also shows mean consumption per person per month. The main finding is that not all countries managed to create jobs at low cost; cost per job created is low in Asia, but with few exceptions, high in Africa.[4]

There are, however, similarities. Low-income developing countries in Asia and Africa—Bangladesh, India, Botswana, and Tanzania—have incurred a cost per person-day in the (modest) range of $1–$2.

Table 5.1. Public Works: Scale of Operations, Costs, and Benefits for Selected Countries

Country	Program type	Year	Source of financing	Scale of operation (annual)
Asia				
Bangladesh	Food for work	1982–83	90 percent external external CARE WFP	400 million person-days
	Food for work	1991–92	90 percent external	15 million person-days
	Cash for work	1991–92		
India	Cash for work (National JRY)	1991–92	Entirely domestic	830-850 million person-days
	Cash for work (MEGS)	1991–92	Entirely domestic— via a special employment tax	100-180 million person-days
Pakistan[c]	Cash for work (IGPRA I-III)	1984–95	Largely external	23 million person-days
	Cash for work (IGPRA I)	1984–87	Largely external person-days	5.9 million
	Cash for work (IGPRA II)	1984–87	Largely external person-days	11.97 million
	Cash for work (IGPRA III)	1992	Largely external person-days	5.15 million
Philippines	Food for work	1986–87	External (World Food Program)	NA
	Cash for work	1990	ILO/IBRD	300,000 person-days
Africa				
Botswana	Cash for work	1982–87	70 percent external	4.6 million person-days annually
		1992–93	Unknown	About 7 million person-days annually

Total cost (wage + nonwage) per person-day of employment created[a]	Ratio of wage cost to total cost (percent)	Mean consumption per month per person[b] (US$)	Program wage/remarks
1.1–1.5	0.4	52.70 (1985)	Program wage was less than the prevailing agricultural wage.
1.6	0.5		
	0.6	46.85 (1990)	Program wage was less than the prevailing agricultural wage.
1.3	0.5–0.6	28.40 (1990)	Program wage was equal to the statutory minimum wage.
1.2	0.51		Program wage was less than both the market and minimum wage until 1987; program was raised to the minimum wage thereafter. Female participation was high.
2.7	0.51	61.40 (1985)	Program wage was lower than the prevailing (local) market wage for unskilled labor.
2.5	0.34		
3.7	0.59		
2.8	0.6		
—	—	61.00 (1988)	Total (food+cost) wage rate was higher than the market wage; program poorly targeted.
3.2	0.5		Program wage was about 25 percent higher than agriculture market wage; poorly targeted.
—	—	77.4 (1985–86)	No details available.
1.7	0.63		Program wage was set at 70 percent of the lowest statutory minimum wage, but the program wage was nevertheless more attractive than rural market wages; excess demand for works; jobs were rationed; poor targeting.

(Table continues on following page.)

Table 5.1 *(cont.)*

Country	Program type	Year	Source of financing	Scale of operation (annual)
Africa				
Ethiopia	Food for work	1982	50 percent external	27 million person-days (mid-1980s)
Ghana	Cash for work	1988–91	External	0.5 million person-days
Kenya	Cash for work	1992–93	100 percent external	0.6 million person-days
Mali	Cash for work	1991–92	IDA/AGETIP	537,000 person-days
Niger	Cash for work	1993	IDA/AGETIP	800,000 person-days
Senegal	Cash for work	1988-91	External	2.1 million person-days
Tanzania	Food for work	1980–86	90 percent external	2.1 million person-days
	Cash for work	1987–90	90 percent external	0.17 million person-days
Latin America				
Bolivia	Cash for work	1987–90	External (85 percent) through social fund	8–9 million person-days
Chile	Cash for work	1987	External and domestic	40–45 million person-days
Honduras	Cash for work	1990–91	External through social fund	2.5 million person-days
Costa Rica	Cash for work	1991–94		8.9 million person-days
Middle East				
Egypt	Cash for work		ESP	27-30 million person-days

— Data not available.

a. Costs include wage and nonwage costs. Where donor food was used, opportunity costs of that food was used (that is, how much would the government have spent if the food were to be bought in the open market and used as wages in food for work programs).

b. Mean per capita consumption per person per month are PPP corrected numbers. Data are for years listed in parentheses.

Total cost (wage + nonwage) per person-day of employment created[a]	Ratio of wage cost to total cost (percent)	Mean consumption per month per person[b] (US$)	Program wage/remarks
—	—		No details available.
3.4	0.2	73.00 (1988–89)	Program was administered through private contractors; market wage was paid.
3.0	0.3–0.4	58.60 (1992)	Program wage was equal to the statutory minimum wage, but much higher than the reservation wage of the poor.
2.7	0.25	—	
11	0.29	—	Primarily urban-oriented; poorly targeted.
3.0	0.20	45.8 (1991–92)	
1.4	0.6		Program wage was equal to the minimum wage. Wages were set uniformly regardless of variables such as location, type of work.
—	—	72.8 (1991)	
8.0	0.4	86.2 (1990)	Implemented by private contractors and social funds; low female participation; program poorly targeted overall.
0.5	—	131.40 (1990)	Jobs were provided at very low wages often at equivalent of one-fourth of minimum wage. About 25 percent were female, highly self-targeted.
1.0	0.4	42.80 (1990)	Implemented through private contractors.
4.0	—	99.70 (1990)	
4.2	—	—	

c. The Income Generation Program for Refugee Areas (IGPRA) was funded by UN agencies. For this program, the data in the sixth column refer to 1987 (constant) prices.
Source: Ahsan and Khandker (1995); India, Ministry of Rural Development, Annual Progress Reports on Anti-poverty Programs; Dev (1992, 1995b); Gaiha (1995a, b; 1993); Ravallion (1991); Ravallion, Datt, and Chaudhri (1993);
Teklu (1994a, b; 1995a, b); Subbarao and Rudra (1996); Mesa-Lago (1994); Stewart and van der Geest (1994); World Bank (1994h, o, p); World Bank (1996).

Table 5.2. Selected Public Work Programs

Country	Program	Government	Social fund/ social investment fund	Nongovernmental organizations	Other
Bangladesh	Food for work	x			
	Cash for wage[a]				x
Bolivia	Cash for work[b]		x		
Botswana	Cash for work	x			
Burkina Faso	Food for work/ Cash for work	x			
Cameroon	Food for work	x			
Chile	Food for cash	x			
Ethiopia	Food for work/ Cash for work	x			
Ghana	Cash for work[c]		x		
Honduras	Cash for work		x		
India	Cash for work	x			
Kenya	Cash for work	x			
Nepal	Food for work	x			
Niger	Cash for work[c]	x			
Peru	Cash for work[c]		x		
Rwanda	Food for work/ Cash for work[c]	x			
Senegal	Cash for wage[d]				
Tanzania	Cash for wage[d]	x		x	
Tanzania	Food for work/ Cash for work	x			

a. Banks were implementing agencies.
b. Some NGO, private contractor, and governmental participation.
c. Some government involvement.
d. Some government involvement and private contractor involvement.
Source: Various World Bank Poverty Assessments.

Honduras and Chile in Latin America have incurred a lower cost per job created than others in the region. The variations in the cost per job created seem to widen when evaluated in PPP exchange rates (table 5.3). The cost when evaluated at PPP exchange rates appears to be much too high for Senegal and Ghana. Various factors influence cost per job created, including the mix of locals and expatriates involved in the implementation of subprojects; the delivery mechanism selected, particularly the modalities of hiring private contractors; the wage rate; the capital intensity of operations; and countries' general and administrative capacity. Disaggregated information on the above factors is hard to come by, so it is difficult to disentangle the variations in cost shown in tables 5.1 and 5.3. A recent study has shown that labor-based methods in road construction cost $12,035 per kilometer, while equip-

Table 5.3. Annual Cost of Job Creation in Public Works
(US$ per job)

Country	Cost per job at market exchange rates	Cost per job at PPP exchange rates
Egypt	1,401	7,212
Honduras	2,120	9,759
Nicaragua	2,580	14,302
Madagascar	786	3,620
Bolivia	2,700	9,388
Senegal	5,445	12,100
Ghana	2,122	10,610

Source: Bank staff estimates, as cited in World Bank (1995k).

ment-based methods cost $19,463 per kilometer (Stock and de Veen 1996). Few studies have analyzed the data on costs disaggregated by type of work, methods of production, and by location. Unfortunately, Stock and de Veen (1996) do not provide information on cost per job created.

Wage Rates and Targeting

The best way to ensure that the program reaches the poor is to maintain the program wage at a level no higher than the ruling market wage for unskilled labor. This practice helps keep costs down. The poor can be attracted to the program even at a wage slightly lower than the market rate if other incentives are offered, such as employment a short distance from home. Moreover, in addition to keeping wages at ruling market levels, the program could have other features that might render it unattractive to many. For example, payment of 50 percent of wages in-kind (food stamps) may attract more women than men (as it did in Zambia and Lesotho).

The wage rate is a key element determining the distributional outcomes of the program. In most countries governments set the minimum wage for unskilled labor. Though minimum wages are legally binding, their enforcement varies, especially within large countries. Thus in India minimum wages are enforced in Kerala and are believed to be lax in other states. Whether the minimum wage is higher or lower than the ruling market wage and whether or not it is enforced are empirical questions. Even in the same country the relationship between the two might vary over time and across regions (in large countries). In countries where the market wage is less than the minimum wage, the poor may self-select into the program. But political and legal constraints may make it difficult to maintain the program wage at levels less than the minimum wage. Not surprisingly, there is much cross-country variation. The program wage rate was 70 percent of the minimum wage in Chile, about 25 percent higher than agricultural market wages in the Philippines, and equal to the statutory minimum wage in Kenya and Tanzania (see table 5.1, column 9). In India's MEGS, until 1988, the wage rate was equal to the minimum wage, but lower than prevailing peak season agricultural market wage for unskilled labor. In 1988 the minimum wage and the MEGS wage were doubled, and both wage rates exceeded the market wage rate for unskilled labor. The wage hike reduced the program's self-targeting ability; person-days of employment also dropped (Subbarao 1993).

Maintaining a low program wage ensures that participation rates are low, attracting only the poorest to work sites. In the well-researched MEGS Datt and Ravillion (1994) reconfirm Subbarao's (1993) finding—that the upward revision of the wage rate contributed to rationing, thereby eroding the guarantee of employment expected of the program. It is worth stressing, however, that even though the transfer benefits of the program were reduced following the wage hike in 1988, MEGS continued to offer stabilization benefits (Subbarao 1997). Both before (1981) and after the wage hike (1991), the program operated intensively in slack sessions.

In Tanzania and Botswana, as well, jobs had to be rationed—particularly during droughts, when the need for public works was the greatest—because the program wage rate was maintained at a level higher than the market wage for comparable unskilled activities (Teklu 1994a). The program wage in Kenya was also higher than the market wage for unskilled labor. As a result substantial numbers of nonpoor were attracted to the program (Teklu 1994b). In Burkina Faso and Senegal program wages were generally lower than market wages, enabling high participation rates by the poor. In Sri Lanka public works under the Janasaviya Program were generally well-targeted, since program wage rates were below ruling market wage rates. In the Philippines the total wage rate (food plus cash) in the food-for-work program was maintained at levels higher than the market wage. The higher level not only limited the scope for self-targeting, but also attracted many nonpoor to the program.

In Chile public works were an important safety net during the mid-1980s. Nearly 13 percent of the labor force participated. Wage rates were kept low to make the program unattractive to the nonpoor. In the Republic of Korea a public works program was used effectively to reduce poverty in the 1960s. The program worked as long as there was an excess supply of labor. As the Korean economy entered its boom period in the 1970s and 1980s, wages for manual labor soared. As a result only old and less-active workers participated in public works. Thus the program's effectiveness diminished, and in the late 1980s it was abandoned (Kwon 1995). In terms of introducing and abandoning the program, Korea's timing was perfect.

While a lower program wage is most likely to make a program self-targeted, other features, such as careful timing (so as to synchronize work with the agricultural slack season) might also help in targeting. India's most important safety net has been the JRY, the nationwide program of public works. This program has been generating more than 800–850 million person-days of employment annually, with 55 million people employed in the agricultural off-season. In the JRY the program wage has always equaled the minimum wage. The duration of employment offered was generally lower than under the MEGS. Nevertheless, the program operated intensively during the agricultural off-season. A recent evaluation shows that the benefits of the program were reasonably well-targeted to the poor—more than 70 percent of the person-days were used by people living below the poverty line, and more than half by people belonging to socially deprived communities (the scheduled castes and tribes) and the landless. Because of the timing of the program, consumption-smoothing benefits were considerable. Yet the disadvantages are worth noting. Transfer benefits tend to be low, and the program attracts some of the nonpoor. In Kenya and Tanzania not only are program wage rates higher, but the timing of public works is synchronized with the busy agricultural season, thereby significantly diminishing the stabilization benefits to the poor (Teklu 1994a,b). In Bangladesh the food-for-work program was poorly synchronized with seasonal work and food needs.

It is never easy to perfectly predict seasonal food needs in any country. It is reasonable, however, to expect even poor people to anticipate seasonal shortfalls and plan in advance. Even assuming that the poor anticipate off-season distress, they may not be able to protect themselves fully, owing to a fall in their purchasing power and hence effective demand. Therefore, the expectation is that in off-seasons work programs may provide much-needed purchasing power to the poor and protect them from seasonal undernutrition.

Timing public works is very difficult in countries where these programs are executed by private sector contractors. When the private sector is involved, the government must schedule works, prepare contract documents, and tender works during the lean agricultural season. This has been very difficult for most countries. This timing is also very closely related to government financing. The ministry administering the program is at the mercy of the funding body (treasury or donors) in terms of being able to pay contractors or having resources available to draw up a contract. In Ghana the Department of Feeder Roads often has no money (from the Treasury) during the lean agricultural seasons. Thus the financial management of works programs also determine the extent to which programs can be synchronized with lean season (Stock and de Veen 1996).

Share of Wages in Total Costs

In most programs the share of wages in total program costs varied between 30 and 60 percent. While a higher share is desirable in that higher transfer benefits are conferred on the poor, many factors determine this ratio, including the nature of the asset to be created, the duration and timing of the works, and, most importantly, the availability of technically and economically feasible labor-based methods of production. In most road construction activities the share of wages in total costs ranged from 40 to 50 percent. Where the work has been entrusted to private contractors, the share of wages in total costs is often unpredictable.

It is not clear whether labor-based methods are readily adopted by private entrepreneurs. Evidence from Ghana suggests that timely availability of project funds is often a critical factor for the adoption of labor-based methods. For example, where the project is financed by bilateral donors and funds are available without delays, contractors have shown a willingness to adopt labor-based methods. Where project funds originated from government departments, enormous delays were experienced in the receipt of funds, with corresponding delays in payment of wages. Fearing strikes and agitation by laborers, contractors opted for machine-based methods (Stock 1996). Thus the institutional delivery mechanisms and the efficiency with which projects are financed are often critical determinants of the extent of labor use in public works programs.

Use and Maintenance of Created Assets

Two sets of issues are relevant: how to improve the quality of output of public works, including better maintenance of the assets created, and how to share the secondary benefits from the created assets between the poor and the nonpoor. Where the proportion of capital inputs was maintained at extremely low levels (to expand labor use), the quality of assets created suffered. This shortcoming is being corrected in many countries, and now nearly 60 percent of the total expenditure on a typical activity (such as road construction) constitutes capital inputs. Even then, quality of work can be improved with better supervision, and with possible incentives for field officers.

Whether or not the created assets confer long-term benefits on the poor is an important issue. India's two leading programs—the JRY and the MEGS—have both sought to create minor irrigation infrastructure on small farms. These assets are bound to increase labor use and incomes of small farmers. The MEGS also focused on drought-proofing infrastructure. This effort included soil conservation and afforestation, which are most likely to benefit relatively poor dry-land farmers, although, recently, road building has dominated (Dev 1992). In Bolivia and Honduras many public works focused on health and education infrastructure (construction of primary health clinics and schools). But the choice of assets is fraught with potential conflicts of interest. If only the poor benefit from the created assets, the rich may not (fiscally) support employment schemes. If assets that serve the rich are also created, and if these activities involve a high proportion of capital inputs, benefits to the poor may be reduced (since the wage component will be low).

Maintaining created assets is extremely important. Few countries have actually made any financial allocations for maintenance. Poor maintenance has resulted in the erosion of economywide benefits from public works (Teklu 1994a, b).

Impact on Incomes, Poverty, and Social Life

Evaluations of works programs in general, and the MEGS in particular, suggest significant income gains. Thus the annual wage incomes of MEGS households were found to be higher than those of non-MEGS households (Acharya and others 1988). Numerous microeconomic studies have shown that 60 to 70 percent of the participants of both the nationwide program and the MEGS belonged to poor households. The immediate net income gain from works programs as a percentage of total gross earnings is high. For example, the severity (not the incidence) of poverty has fallen from 5.0 percent to 3.2 percent because of participation in the MEGS (Datt and Ravallion 1992). But simulations by Datt and Ravallion suggest that the effect on poverty of additional income earned from the program is no more than could be achieved through a uniform allocation of the same gross program budget across *all* rural households. This result stems from losses associated with forgone income and administrative and other nonwage costs. Nevertheless, significant (though unquantifiable) social gains are attributable to the MEGS. Dev (1992) notes that the MEGS has "made considerable impact on the social life of the workers. Concentrating large numbers of workers in one place in similar conditions and increasing their interaction helps to break down social differences. This has resulted in increasing social understanding of workers belonging to various castes. The MEGS also discourages sexual barriers and inequality. Emergence of women on works in large numbers has created confidence among them. Women now dress better and their economic power has given them a better status in their families" (p. 54).

Even if the wage rate is low and self-targeting is promoted, it is not immediately obvious that public works constitute the most cost-effective option for transferring benefits (income) to the poor. Much depends on whether or not participants forego income (and how much) from alternative activities while participating in public works programs. Evidence on this issue is difficult to find. Evidence for the MEGS shows that the foregone income is small—the opportunity cost of participation for the poor was typically quite low (Datt and Ravallion 1994).

It is possible to reduce the potential cost of foregone income by designing public works appropriately. Thus projects where piecework was adopted attracted women because participation did not crowd out their other activities (that is, women were better able to dovetail wage work and household work). Correspondingly, the danger of foregoing income from other sources was diminished. In a village survey in Tanzania women expressed a preference for working for payment on specific tasks in road projects because task-based payment enabled them to work whenever they had leisure time, without crowding out other activities. Flexibility in timing can enhance women's participation in public works and reduce the potential for forgone earnings.

Providing work close to homes and villages is another way to promote higher female participation. The MEGS has been a pioneer in providing employment within 5 kilometers of a person's village. This convenience is another reason why female participation is much higher in the MEGS than in the nationwide JRY.[5] In determining program design, it useful to ask: how is the opportunity cost of participants' time in general and women's time in particular affected by the scheme's timing?

Another way to reduce potential foregone income is to make the program available in rural areas during the agricultural slack season. Such timing would also maximize income-smoothing benefits. How this scheme is likely to affect transfer benefits depends on the relationship between the public works' seasonal operation and the agricultural wage rate in the peak season. If public works operating in the slack season raise the peak season wage rate, transfer benefits are improved. But this outcome is unlikely. It is more reasonable to expect peak season work programs to raise peak season wage rates in the private sector. Given the overall scarcity of resources, it may be difficult to provide significant transfer benefits by timing public works in peak seasons. Not surprisingly, some countries (especially those in semiarid zones prone to greater weather and agricultural production variability) modestly aim for the provision of income-smoothing benefits to the poor during slack seasons, with the possibility of second-round benefits from the infrastructure created.

The poor who participate in public works may have to pay part of their wages to officials, contractors, or politicians; incur transportation costs; or bear other related transaction costs that may potentially reduce program benefits. Appropriately designed public works programs should be able to reduce such transaction costs. For example, offering a guarantee of employment at a low wage will substantially reduce leakage. Involving NGOs is critical for organizing participants into pressure groups, through which they can articulate their grievances with work managers (Lipton 1995). Piece-rates, if properly supervised and enforced, can also reduce the scope for corruption. Provisions for tendering contracts to private contractors (on a competitive bidding basis) can also reduce transaction costs, but the procedures may be time-consuming and may not always prevent abuse.[6] Encouraging grass roots participation can prevent abuse in public works as much as in other transfer programs.

The Political Economy of Public Works

Since public works are usually highly visible and always must be implemented locally (in villages), political factors are likely to be important in shaping their design (the wage rate offered, the choice of project, the timing of activities, and the overall size of the program). Three interest groups are usually involved in the design and execution of public works: the politicians and bureaucrats who influence the size and design of the program, the poor who benefit from the program, and others who may or may not benefit from the program—such as large farmers or private contractors—but who wield considerable political and social power in many societies. Each of these groups perceives the advantages and disadvantages of public works differently. While the poor who participate in a program may favor the positive impact on the peak season's agricultural wage rate, large farmers who hire laborers may oppose any such program. Politicians may see the program as an opportunity to reward existing political supporters, while bureaucrats may fear losing control of the program to another agency (such as a social fund). The target group—the poor—may resist low wage rates, even though a low wage may encourage self-targeting and render the program propoor.

Although it is difficult to empirically establish the precise influence of each of these political factors, evidence is overwhelming that new public works programs have usually been introduced before elections (such as in Bangladesh, India, Indonesia, Pakistan, and the Philippines). In some countries public works are introduced to fulfill election promises immediately after a new government has been formed (as in Jamaica). Civil disturbances also triggered the emergence of public works programs in India and Tunisia.

The potential for absorbing labor in road construction and rehabilitation public works is substantial. Comparative studies of labor-based versus equipment-based approaches in feeder road construction and rehabilitation carried out in Rwanda (Martens 1989), Ghana (Bentall 1990; Stock 1996), and Botswana (ILO 1991) showed the cost-effectiveness of labor-based construction methods. These approaches proved to be 10 to 30 percent less costly than equipment-based methods, reduced foreign exchange expenditures by 50 to 60 percent, and created 240 to 320 percent more employment—particularly benefiting unskilled labor—thus contributing substantially to poverty alleviation among the low-income target group (Majeres 1993). Yet labor-based methods are often resisted. Target groups are generally unorganized and politically weak, so they are unlikely to have much say in program design. Where public works have been implemented by private contractors, large, powerful contractors have been successful in paying extremely low wages and substituting capital for labor when low wages were resisted. In other countries private contractors actually preferred to use labor-based methods in projects funded by bilateral donors because quick payment of contract funds was assured (Stock 1996).

Five general conclusions can be drawn from the reviewed experience.

- The wage rate is critical in determining the distribution of program benefits, as well as how well the program is targeted. Maintaining the program wage equal to the ruling market wage for unskilled labor is the best way to improve the transfer of program benefits to the poor.
- The timing and duration of employment determine the nature of benefits offered by the program. In general, the more narrowly the program is restricted to agricultural slack seasons, the lower are the transfer benefits and the higher are the stabilization benefits. It is important to bear in mind the nature of poverty in a country before rendering a public works program for only consumption smoothing. Such an approach is appropriate where poverty is transient. In countries subject to yearly fluctuations (such as Ethiopia), public works activity must intensify in bad years, lasting almost year-round. Also, in countries where poverty-gap ratios are high, the need to run the program year-round (and thus raise transfer benefits to the poor) assumes greater importance.
- The program can be designed to encourage greater participation of women, more involvement of the private sector, lower transaction costs for participation, and greater involvement of NGOs and grass roots organizations to prevent abuse.
- To enhance the program's long-term benefits for the poor, it is preferable to choose assets that have high long-term employment multiplier effects.

- To maximize the economic returns to public works activity, it is desirable to estimate economic rates of return to different projects in different regions prior to project selection, integrate the program with broader national development plans, and introduce a component to maintain the assets created.

Livelihood Programs

Programs to promote access to institutional credit date back to the early 1950s.[7] Some countries, such as India, have nationalized banking services with a view to forcing commercial banks to extend their outreach to the rural poor. The major justification offered was the need to extend credit facilities in order to encourage rural growth and technology adoption. The early 1970s, however, saw the emergence of a new view. The role of credit was not merely to channel funds to the most productive uses, it was also to bring about social justice by lending at lower (subsidized) interest rates to disadvantaged groups.[8] But channeling massive amounts of subsidized credit through state-run banks left much to be desired (see Besley 1995). The consensus in the 1980s was that private lending rates accurately reflected the costs and risks of lending, and that state-subsidized credit rarely reached the rural poor. There were simply too many rent-seeking intermediaries.

The populism of massive, subsidized, state-directed credit has abated in the 1990s. There has been a recognition that: the poor's problem is not high interest rates, but the inability to borrow because they lack collateral; although formal lending institutions can reduce the covariance of default risks, they do not have the local knowledge needed to lend to the collateralless poor and, as such, cannot avoid adverse selection (loans are sought only to be abused) and moral hazard (lenders may take excessive risks because they know that risks can be shared with borrowers); formal lending institutions lack sufficient knowledge about borrowers and, therefore, face great problems in enforcing repayment, even where legal provisions and collateral exist; and while lending to the poor is expensive, the poor are not necessarily bad credit risks (Lipton 1995).[9] Several new financial institutions, largely initiated by NGOs, have sought to overcome these problems (including market failure) with lending to the poor.

Objectives and Regional Patterns

Four types of institutions must be distinguished:
- Public banking institutions, cooperatives, and commercial banks— all with local branches but under the control of the central bank.

- Special programs, such as the Integrated Rural Development Program (IRDP) in India, administered by a central ministry, that are directly targeting the poor and are extending (subsidized) credit, usually for the purchase of income-earning assets.
- NGO-administered, formal credit institutions.
- Self-help groups, also assisted by the NGOs that operate informally and on a small scale, each with an outreach often restricted to a few villages.

The central objective of all these institutions is to advance credit, but some—particularly NGO-mediated institutions and self-help groups—strongly encourage savings as well. Specialized programs usually advance credit contingent on the purchase of an income-earning asset. While public credit institutions usually insist on collateral, special programs target credit directly to those identified as poor, and collateral is not necessary in most NGO-run programs. The institutions also differ with respect to the role played by NGOs. At least three variants can be distinguished: charismatic leadership plays an important role in the establishment, training, and administration of a credit program, such as the Grameen Bank in Bangladesh; an NGO acts as a financial intermediary between a bank or government ministry and the poor or a self-help group, as in the Philippines; or an NGO helps organize a self-help group and plays a facilitating role, for example, by linking a bank with a self-help group or advising on general performance, as with the Mysove Resettlement and Development Agency (MYRYDA) in India.

The success of credit-based programs can be assessed according to how many of the deserving poor were able to obtain credit, how many of the nonpoor managed to enter the program, whether or not the poor were able to earn a high enough rate of return on the amount borrowed to repay the loan and escape from poverty, whether or not the income generated is sustained over time, and whether or not the loans are repaid and the program is financially viable in the long term. Though several evaluations of programs are available, information is rarely found on these four criteria (Lipton 1995). There are methodological problems as well. It is often empirically difficult to disaggregate income earned from various sources. It is also difficult to track the end-use of a loan—even if the end-use is tracked, it is not clear whether the loan only encouraged the consumption of other adult goods, since all money is fungible.[10]

Targeting

Program and country experience suggests that (by far) the least effective way to reach the poor is to directly target subsidized credit to individuals and households identified as poor by bureaucrats or project managers. Where targets for poverty reduction were set, bureaucrats had a direct incentive to select people living just below the poverty line. And the nonpoor entered the scheme when powerful local interests collided with bureaucrats.[11] In practice, therefore, subsidies have attracted the nonpoor in practically every country that has experimented with such programs.[12] The principal problem with the IRDP in India is that the central ministry rates its success by the number of beneficiaries who "crossed the poverty line." Bureaucrats at the local level thus have an incentive to select people who are not poor or are close to the poverty line.[13] The scope for deliberate mistargeting is thus inherent in program design. Most credit managers at the local level lack the time to verify whether or not a household is poor. Also, many programs (including India's IRDP) measure poverty in terms of household poverty, disregarding household size. Thus substantial leakage was observed in many large-scale credit programs run by the government's usual administrative machinery.

Programs that used communities, local groups, and NGOs to identify the poor have had much better targeting records. Even in India's IRDP, the states that used village councils to select beneficiaries have had a much smaller proportion of ineligible households participate (Copestake 1992). Programs administered by NGOs or self-help groups have used various methods other than income for targeting, including geography and land ownership. Some have enforced rules that make loans more attractive to the poor than to the nonpoor (amounting to self-targeting). In Bangladesh the Grameen Bank targets credit to families owning less than 0.5 acres of land. This criterion probably ensures that most borrowers are poor (keeping inclusion errors low), though it certainly excludes many households with large families owning more than 0.5 acres, or owning poor quality land. In Indonesia the requirement for one credit program was the ownership of a house or a plot of land, which excluded the poorest from the program.

The Grameen Bank, the Bangladesh Rural Advancement Committee (BRAC), and MYRADA have generally succeeded in reaching the poor because the programs eliminated the requirement for collateral, advanced small loans, and avoided delays. In addition, the Grameen Bank relied on group lending and peer monitoring to ensure that credit was used for developmental purposes (income generation) and that loans were repaid. In many countries even commercial banks are searching for alternatives to physical collateral. Local intermediation by NGOs was used by commercial banks in some provinces in Nigeria and India; local agents (typically the influential people in villages) were used by Badan Kredet Kecamatan (BKK) in Indonesia to speak on behalf of the borrowers. MYRYDA has been more successful in reaching the poor (without resorting to group lending) than BKK, whose clients are moderately poor or not poor.

Special programs that used innovative methods to identify beneficiaries and some programs initiated by NGOs (such as MYRYDA) have reached poor women in large numbers, unlike the state-run programs. An interesting contrast is found in India: the large, state-run IRDP has less than 25 percent women beneficiaries, compared with more than 60 percent in MYRADA (and more than 90 percent in Grameen Bank).

Repayments, Sustainability, and Cost-Effectiveness

Programs administered by public banks or special programs administered by line ministries generally have very poor repayment records. Political economy factors have encouraged delinquency; it is not uncommon in some countries to promise loan write-offs prior to elections. Default risks usually increase with loan size and with a borrower's wealth (Lipton 1995). Women borrowers have had better repayment records, presumably because it is far more important for them to maintain a line of credit than for men. Subsidy-driven special programs, such as the IRDP in India, have an especially poor repayment record. Also, many rural financial institutions have incurred heavy losses, even with better repayment records, because of inadequate indexation to inflation, as in Brazil and Mexico.

It is not, however, imperative that a large government-initiated program have a poor repayment record. The two Indonesian institutions—BRI and BKK—have offered innovative monthly interest rate rebates for prompt repayment. In addition, BKK's average loan size was small, and the institution has collected repayments weekly. BKK even permitted daily repayments when justified (Yaron 1994). "A BKK staff member, for example, visited a different village each week, often on a market day, collecting savings deposits and weekly loan repayments" (Yaron 1994). Such practices have greatly reduced clients' transaction costs, standing in sharp contrast to the heavy red tape and high transaction costs clients experienced in large loan programs in India. The delivery mechanism, loan size, and innovative policies that reduced transaction costs have been critical to ensuring a high recovery rate. Government-led programs that lacked these components suffered accordingly.

Repayment records have not necessarily been high in programs mediated by NGOs. For example, many programs in the Philippines in which NGOs have acted as financial intermediaries have had exceptionally poor repayment records (Subbarao, Ahmed, and Teklu 1995).

The high repayment record of the Grameen Bank is due to group lending and peer monitoring, which ensure discipline (in repayments)—
one member's failure to repay renders the entire group liable, and the
group cannot borrow again until debts by all members are cleared. The
program's design virtually eliminated the possibility of free riding.[14]
The self-help groups also have better repayment records than the state-
run financial institutions. These operate on a small scale, saving is
strongly encouraged, and there is some oversight and advice given by
NGOs. Presumably the social stigma from defaulting is high.

Three issues are relevant to sustainability. First, clients must earn
livelihoods through activities that are sustainable over time. Second,
clients (on prompt repayment of debts) must have continuing access to
credit. Third, the program itself must be sustainable over time, which
is possible only if any subsidy elements of the loan program are minimal and repayments are prompt. (Some government-run programs
involving heavy subsidies—programs where political expediency
takes precedence over economic viability—may be sustained over time
even in the face of high default rates.)

Evidence for sustainable income generation is strong only for
Grameen Bank (Khandker, Khalily, and Khan 1995). Grameen Bank
demonstrates that it is possible for targeted credit interventions to generate sustainable livelihoods for the poor. Evidence from other programs is not as strong, yet it is reasonable to hypothesize that poor
households who have invested in self-employment ventures would
make every effort to retain their assets, even in the face of severe economic hardship. Several microeconomic studies of India's IRDP bears
out this prediction. In Uttar Pradesh, one of India's poorest states, 82
percent of the assets purchased under the IRDP were intact after two
years, and 59 percent were intact even after four years (Pulley 1989).
But evidence from India suggests significant variations in sustainability across different types of investment (Pulley 1989). Investment in
dairy (milk cows) showed the highest retention and sustainability.
Further, an analysis of the probability of retaining assets showed that
sustainability and asset retention rates were high for households that
had preprogram incomes above the poverty line, higher literacy levels,
low asset divisibility, and experienced no major weather-induced
shocks following the purchase of the asset (Pulley 1989). To the extent
that assisted households belong to a very poor population with a low
level of education, sustainable income generation requires additional
efforts (such as back-up loans, or technology or marketing support) on
the part of lending agencies.

Continuing access to credit is critical for poor households embark-
ing on self-employment ventures. Again, the BKK and the Grameen
Bank have an excellent record in this respect. By contrast, one of the

major shortcomings of India's IRDP is its failure to open up a continuing line of credit, even for those poor households that did not default on past loans (Pulley 1989). Political economy factors may be important: while the poor may want a continuing line of credit, politicians might be more interested in widening their constituency by expanding program coverage to new households (whether poor or not), rather than lending to the same poor households year after year.

The third aspect of sustainability relates to program design. In general, subsidy-driven programs impose a fiscal drain, eventually necessitating a cutback of the program itself. With limited resources largely financed by donors, programs are often discontinued when donor support is withdrawn, or scaled down to serve only more promising clients or areas. Four factors contribute to program sustainability: positive interest rates, high repayment rates, low administrative costs, and encouragement of saving (Yaron 1992a, b). Only a few programs have been successful in realizing the above goals. Barring the BKK, the BRI, and the Grameen Bank, the more successful programs are extremely small in outreach (often limited to a few provinces in a country). Thus in India MYRADA (the more successful program) manages 20 million rupees and serves about 450,000 people, compared with the nationwide IRDP (the less successful program), which manages 12 billion rupees and serves approximately 135 million people. Successful programs have endured over time, but the size of such programs is extremely small relative to the size of the country's poor population.

Finally, several programs supported by donors and implemented by NGOs have proved to be financially viable. But funds were obtained free of cost from donors. If the opportunity cost of donor funds was also taken into account, many programs (including the Grameen Bank) would not yet be economically viable (Khandker, Khalily, and Khan 1994a, b).

The Politics of Credit Programs

As Lipton (1995) remarks, most countries have "electoral credit cycles." The conflict between politicians' interests and economic viability is nowhere more real than in subsidized credit programs. With the approach of elections, default rates usually increase, and parties compete with promises of loan write-offs; program outreach is expanded, overlooking eligibility criteria; and beneficiaries' transaction costs rise as payments have to be made to local party officials (to finance elections) to gain entry into programs. The same political economy factors that tend to increase the resources available for subsidized credit programs in the budgets of provincial and central governments also tend to divert allotted resources away from the deserving poor.

Bureaucratic management has often resulted in the poor having to share some of the program's benefits with officials. Yet even if some program benefits do not leak to the nonpoor and other rent-seeking players, sustainability of the program would still be in jeopardy.

The real solution lies in the organization of beneficiaries—potential as well as actual. But organizing beneficiaries is not a costless, risk-free, or painless activity. NGOs have certainly played a role in some countries (organizing the landless labor and tribal groups in India, for example). Often, the organizing was performed by a single pioneer. One example is the social worker who organized the poor women vegetable sellers in the Indian city of Ahmedabad. The group has now blossomed into a major NGO, the Self-Employed Women's Association.

What can we learn from the reviewed experience? If credit programs are to succeed in reaching the poor, it is important to:

- Reduce transaction costs (such as many trips to the credit office, payments to officials, complex procedures for repayment).
- Subsidize transaction costs where necessary, but not interest rates.
- Avoid direct targeting of credit programs based on means tests, but use local groups.
- Alter program design (small and repeated loans, peer pressure, and group monitoring) to promote self-selection.
- Organize beneficiaries into groups and incorporate incentives for both borrowers and lenders to enforce repayment discipline.
- Incorporate savings as a necessary component.

Notes

1. This section draws from Lipton (1995), Subbarao (1997), Subbarao and Rudra (1996), Ravallion (1991), and Teklu (1994a, b).

2. The "guarantee" may have been substantially eroded following large increases in the wage rate in 1988 (Subbarao 1993; Datt and Ravallion 1994).

3. The general presumption that public works necessarily encourage more governmental involvement is clearly wrong. In fact, in some countries, such as Tanzania, public works greatly encouraged private sector initiatives. The works financed by social funds in several countries (such as Bolivia) have employed private contractors during implementation.

4. In other areas, such as education and health, most francophone countries have recorded much higher unit costs than countries in Asia.

5. Evidence also shows that socially deprived communities were overrepresented in the MEGS, and children of women who participated in the MEGS had improved nutrition.

6. The implications of using private contractors for program wages are not entirely clear. There are two possibilities. Private contractors might offer competitive market wages to laborers. In this case the wage rate may not act as a screening device for self-targeting. Private contractors have also offered wages substantially less than the market or program wage to laborers, but they actually claim the market wage rate in their costs of operation and (illegally) retain for themselves the difference between the actual wage

paid and the program wage. In this case there is a transfer of income from the government to private contractors—and the income transfer meant for the poor is reduced.

7. This section draws from Gaiha (1993); Lipton (1995); Subbarao, Ahmed, and Teklu (1995); Subbarao, Braithwaite, and Jalan (1995); Khandker, Khalily, and Khan (1995); Yaron (1992a, b; 1994); and Pulley (1989).

8. India subscribed to this philosophy in 1971 with the introduction of the Differential Rates of Interest scheme, whereby public sector banks were instructed to channel credit at less than market interest rates to families with landholdings below a certain threshold.

9. For an overview of literature on risk and consumption of the poor, see Alderman and Paxson (1992).

10. Valiant efforts have been made to collect carefully disaggregated data to isolate these effects. A recent contribution is that of Pitt and Khandker (1996).

11. Better results would have been realized had the officials been instructed to target groups (single woman without assets) or areas with highest severity and incidence of poverty.

12. See Pulley (1989); Subbarao, Braithwaite, and Jalan (1995); and Subbarao (1985).

13. On the problems associated with a criterion such as the "proportion of beneficiaries crossing the poverty line" as a measure of success of IRDP, see Subbarao (1985).

14. Although self-selection makes the program self-targeted, it has a downside. The very poor who were either extremely risk-averse or evaluated themselves as not particularly suited for self-employment could not bring themselves to agree to the rigorous discipline imposed by the Grameen Bank with respect to saving and repayment. Consequently, these poor stayed out of the program. In Grameen Bank villages only 40 percent of the poor participated in the program (Khandker, Khalily, and Khan 1995).

6

Innovations in the Delivery
and Organization of Social Assistance
and Poverty-Targeted Programs

The effectiveness of social assistance and poverty-targeted programs is influenced by the way these programs are delivered.[1] An inappropriate delivery mechanism can result in services that are unavailable to some of the poor, neither needed nor desired by the poor, captured by the nonpoor, of low quality, unsustainable, cost-ineffective, or delivered more slowly than necessary to respond to urgent needs.[2] Social assistance and poverty-targeted programs may be vulnerable to these problems for two reasons. First, the institutions that have responsibility for these programs—social sector ministries, local governments, and NGOs in remote areas—are often weak. Second, the poor are likely to lack a "voice," and attempts to transfer income to them may meet opposition.

The aim of this chapter is modest: to examine the characteristics of different delivery models and to highlight some general principles for effective service delivery based on program experiences. The aim is not to establish a unique ranking of delivery models; such an effort is infeasible because such a ranking would depend on the type of service to be delivered, the nature of poverty, and the institutional setting of the country concerned. The chapter addresses two main issues. First, it discusses the main mechanisms for delivering social assistance and poverty-targeted programs, including such recent innovations as social funds. Second, it synthesizes lessons from experience and presents some general principles for effective delivery.

Alternative Delivery Models

Service delivery includes two key activities:
- Provision—the designing and organizing of a service, often including its financing or purchasing.

- Production—the creation of a service (for example, the construction of a road or the administering of a nutrition information campaign).

Depending on who undertakes service provision and production, the different ways of delivering social assistance and poverty-targeted programs can be classified according to two main models: the traditional public delivery model—the government takes on both provision and production—and the new private delivery model—one or more private entities take on provision and production, sometimes in addition to the government (figure 6.1).

Social assistance and poverty-targeted programs are characterized by the fact that full program costs are not recoverable from beneficiaries. Hence, these programs are typically financed by governments or NGOs—either external, local, or both. While one or more of these enti-

Figure 6.1. Service Delivery Methods

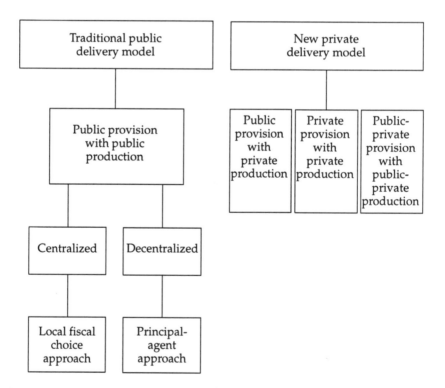

Note: The local fiscal choice approach refers to the case in which the central government gives significant decisionmaking powers to local governments. The principal-agent approach (not to be confused with principal-agent problem in welfare economics) refers to the case in which the central government retains control over decisions implemented by local governments as agents of the central government. Public includes central and local governments. Private includes private contractors, NGOs, and community groups.

ties is also involved in the provision or production of social assistance and poverty-targeted programs, in some cases the entity that finances or purchases the service may be distinct from the entity that undertakes service provision or production.

The Traditional Public Delivery Model

In the traditional public delivery model the main (and often the only) player is the government—the central government and any of the lower levels of government. The government undertakes both service provision and production. An example of this delivery model is India's nationwide public works program, the JRY. It is designed, organized, fully funded, and implemented by the government.

Public delivery may be centralized (for example, when the central government takes charge of both provision and production activities) or decentralized (for example, when the central government retains responsibility for some provision or production activities but hands the rest to local governments). In the case of decentralized public delivery two analytical approaches are relevant:[3] the local fiscal choice approach, in which the central government gives local governments (and sometimes even citizens) significant decisionmaking powers, including powers to determine the pattern of spending, and the principal-agent approach, in which the central government retains a large measure of control over program and project decisions that are implemented by local governments acting as agents of the central government (Campbell, Petersen, and Bazark 1991).[4] The local fiscal choice approach allows for power sharing among different levels of government. The principal-agent approach allows the central government to promote policy design. But the principal-agent approach may limit the ability of agents to adapt programs to local conditions. Elements of both approaches are found in some programs.

An example of the principal-agent approach is India's Integrated Child Development Services (ICDS) program. The central government controls program design, supplying a common package of services throughout the country. State governments implement the program, acting as agents of the center. By contrast, Mexico's Urban Action Program (PAU), a civil works initiative designed to rehabilitate the city of Tijuana, is an example of the local fiscal choice approach. In PAU works are developed and proposed by the municipality, do not involve the central government, and depend critically on approval (even the vote) of the citizens (Campbell and Katz 1996).

The principal-agent and local fiscal choice approaches have been combined in some programs. For example, Mexico's National Solidarity Program (PRONASOL) combines the two approaches in its matching grant system. However, the principal-agent approach is more dominant—although Mexico has a federal system of government with some powers vested in municipalities to determine local investments, municipalities are steered by strong central government control (Campbell 1995a).

While there are some successful examples of public delivery, it has often been susceptible to political interference, driven by supply pressures, and poor in quality (OED 1995), although other forms of delivery are not necessarily immune to these problems.[5] In most cases it is the lack of incentives—to public employees, financiers, and consumers—and inappropriate organizational forms and rules that have reduced the effectiveness of public delivery. Even when decentralized, public delivery has not always succeeded in adapting programs to differing regional circumstances; the incentive problem has persisted. The tightening budgets associated with structural adjustment programs may have led some governments to delegate specific service delivery responsibilities to private entities, thus speeding up the emergence of the private delivery model.

The New Private Delivery Model

The private delivery model involves a range of service deliverers, notably, private contractors, NGOs, and community groups sometimes in addition to public agencies. The different private sector providers are by no means similar—each operates under different sets of incentives.[6]

The inability to recover the full program cost from beneficiaries rules out privately financing social assistance and poverty-targeted programs. But it does not rule out the involvement of the private commercial sector in service delivery. The government can buy the services of the private deliverer if the private deliverer enjoys a comparative advantage in either managing or producing the service.

The private delivery model may incorporate any one of the following three institutional arrangements:

- The government is the provider, but a private entity produces the service (for example, the government designs and organizes a public works program, but a private contractor builds the infrastructure).[7] Senegal's Agence d'Execution des Travaux d'Interet Public (AGETIP) is an example of this delivery arrangement. Central ministries and municipalities determine the infrastructure to be built, its design, and its location, but private contractors build it.
- A private entity provides and produces the service (for example, a community-based organization designs, organizes, and administers a nutrition program). The Zambia Social Recovery Project typifies

this arrangement, with its stress on community groups as the providers and producers of social assistance and poverty-targeted programs.

- The government and private entities collaborate on service provision and/or production activities. Indonesia's Village Infrastructure project and Mongolia's Poverty Alleviation for Vulnerable Groups project are examples of this arrangement. The government and community groups are involved in designing and organizing the services, and the services are often produced collaboratively.

Both the public and private delivery models may be supported by the government or by a donor. Alternatively, one or both of the models may be supported through an autonomous intermediary agency, such as a social fund.[8] A social fund is generally managed by representatives of government and private agencies, projects are selected in response to local demands, and eligibility criteria are generally laid-out up front.[9] To this extent, a social fund is neither a service provider nor a service producer—it merely facilitates service provision and production. While social funds do not necessarily exclude the public delivery model, they are most commonly associated with the private delivery model. Social funds may include any one or more of the three institutional arrangements for private delivery.

Program Experiences under Public and Private Delivery

This section examines the experience and outcomes of some social assistance and poverty-targeted programs implemented under alternative delivery models. Four aspects of program experience are analyzed: targeting, cost-effectiveness, sustainability, and speed of service delivery. The purpose is not to rank delivery models, but to delineate patterns based on qualitative information.

Targeting

Some delivery models are more conducive to supporting particular types of self-targeting, individual targeting, and household targeting than others. Some programs are directed at individuals within a household to address, for example, the problem of intrahousehold discrimination. Leakages can occur if the intended beneficiary fails to receive the transfer, even if the household receives it. Thus where individuals are targeted, the choice of delivery model is more complex.

In general, the public delivery model is more conducive to self-targeting, through low wages, than the private delivery model. The degree of self-targeting through wages depends on the prevailing relationship between the minimum wage, market wage, and program wage, as well as how well minimum wage laws are observed. These conditions vary from country to country. In countries where market wages are higher than minimum wages, a government-run program would attract only those in need by offering the minimum wage. Enforcing wage (or quantity) restrictions can be difficult when working through private contractors or other private entities, especially if the private entities expect low wages to attract inferior workers—thus generating few overall cost savings.

India's MEGS is an example of a public delivery scheme in which the government designs and organizes infrastructure works, and carries out the construction, using government engineers and government-owned equipment. This program self-targets through wages. Until 1988 the program wage was less than the minimum wage, but equal to the farm market wage. (In Maharashtra, farmers generally do not observe minimum wage laws). As a result, the program attracted the poor—about 90 percent of MEGS workers lived below the poverty line—and employed every willing, able worker (male and female) within 5 kilometers of the worker's residence. There was no rationing of jobs (Ravallion 1991; Dev 1995a). Overall, the MEGS has helped millions of ultrapoor people. More than half are women, and many are from socially deprived communities (Lipton 1995). Given that the government was the service provider and the producer, it was possible for the government to control the wage rate. Since 1988, however, the wage offered has increased to the level of the minimum wage. The poor still participate in the program, but jobs are now rationed (Datt and Ravallion 1994).

Chile's Special Employment Programs—Minimum Employment Program (PEM) and Occupational Program for Household Heads (POJH)—are examples of public sector employment programs that pay lower-than-minimum wages. The targeting in both programs is good. On average, following participation in the program, PEM workers ended up in the second decile of the income distribution and POJH workers in the third decile. Without the PEM and POJH income (and making no allowance for alternative activities), all participant families would have been in the poorest decile (Grosh 1994). As in the MEGS wages could be used as a targeting instrument because the Chilean programs incorporated the public delivery model, with the government acting as service provider and producer.

Bolivia's Emergency Social Fund (ESF) is an example of a private delivery model in which public agencies provide the infrastructure and private contractors handle production. Bolivia's ESF offers market wages because the introduction of market signals was basic to the adjustment program, which ESF was complementing. Moreover, it was thought that any wage less than the prevailing market wage might lead to low motivation and low quality work—apart from transferring insufficient income to workers (Jorgensen, Grosh, and Schacter 1992). Outcome information shows that about 25 percent of ESF workers would have belonged to the poorest decile of the urban population had they not participated. With the ESF job, none belonged to the poorest group. Seventy-six percent of ESF workers would have belonged to the poorest 40 percent of the urban population without the ESF jobs. With the jobs, only 15 percent fell in this range (Grosh 1994).[10] Furthermore, on average, participants in the program earned 51 percent more than they would have earned without ESF. It is, however, important to consider foregone earnings. About two-thirds of the transfer was required to replace foregone incomes, and not all of the net transfer accrued to lower-income groups (Squire 1991). Thus, although it reached many poor people, the ESF was not cost-effective in transferring income to the poor. The wages paid failed to act as a screening device—those workers who participated were not necessarily the poorest. The targeting outcome of Bolivia's privately delivered ESF thus seems less favorable than the outcome achieved on the two publicly delivered programs, which used low wages as their targeting instrument.

As with public works and infrastructure programs, credit programs also exhibit a link between the price at which the service (credit in this case) is offered and the type of delivery model supported. Subsidized interest rates tend to be associated with government credit programs, while privately delivered credit programs tend to offer credit at market interest rates. The price at which the credit is offered also influences the targeting outcome. But unlike public works, in which a low wage improves targeting, a below-market interest rate encourages corruption, rent seeking, and leakage.

Bangladesh's Grameen Bank incorporates the private delivery model with an NGO as the service provider and producer. The program offers credit at market interest rates. The targeting outcome is good—a 1985 field survey of 975 Grameen borrowers showed that only 4.2 percent belonged to nontarget households (Hossain 1988). By contrast, India's IRDP incorporates the public delivery model. Unlike the Grameen Bank, IRDP provides subsidized credit. Its targeting outcome leaves much to be desired. Bribery and corruption are rampant (Dreze 1989), and affluent and influential households are well-represented among IRDP beneficiaries (Dreze, Lanjouw, and Sharma forthcoming). While NGO delivery proved better than government delivery in some credit schemes, NGO success is often due to charismatic leadership or dedicated workers who are sometimes willing to work at less-than-market wages.

The poor's access to credit is limited less by high interest rates than by high transaction costs (for example, the procedures for obtaining credit may be excessively elaborate or long distances may have to be traveled). High transaction costs may explain why poor people do not use subsidized credit even if they have access to it. The private delivery model adopted in Grameen Bank focused on reducing transaction costs and inducing behavioral changes through peer group pressure. By contrast, IRDP's public delivery model concentrated on subsidizing interest rates. The experience of these two programs indicates that delivery models that keep transaction costs low for the lender and borrower are more appropriate for reaching the poor than those that subsidize interest rates. There are few examples of a public delivery model successfully reducing transaction costs, supporting group lending, or encouraging savings among the poor. Overall, the private delivery model has been more successful. Considerable investments in social mobilization and awareness building may be required before credit can be effectively lent to the poor. Experience suggests that the private delivery model, working through NGOs, has a comparative advantage over governments in such time-intensive activities.

Geographic targeting. Social funds have typically used the private delivery model. It was thought that the demand-driven nature of social funds and their reliance on nonstate actors for service provision and production would ensure that services were delivered where they were demanded.[11] But were the areas demanding services the areas in greatest need?

For most infrastructure projects in Bolivia's ESF, public agencies were the service providers and private contractors were the producers. For most ESF social service projects NGOs or community groups were the service providers and the producers. In both cases the projects were demand-driven. Per capita ESF commitments were not well-targeted (table 6.1). The wealthiest area obtained $23.97 per capita, and

Table 6.1. Distribution of Bolivia's ESF Commitments, as of March 1989

| | | | *ESF commitments* | |
| | | *Percentage* | *Total* | |
Poverty area	*1985 population (millions)*	*of total population*	*(millions of US dollars)*	*Per capita (US dollars)*
1 (least poor)	2.3	36	56.1	23.97
2	0.7	12	20.3	27.77
3	1.3	20	17.3	13.51
4	1.4	22	16.3	11.67
5 (poorest)	0.6	10	6.2	9.45
National	6.4	100	116.1	18.20

Source: Jorgensen, Grosh, and Schacter (1992).

Table 6.2. Distribution of Bolivia's ESF Projects, as of March 1989
(percentage of amount solicited)

	Poverty area 1 (richest)	Poverty area 2	Poverty area 3	Poverty area 4	Poverty area 5 (poorest)
Percentage of total population	36	12	20	22	10
Organization					
NGO	28	12	22	31	7
Religious	48	30	9	10	4
Grass roots	28	28	27	12	5
Regional development corporation	26	33	17	17	8
National Road Service[a]	9	21	27	34	9
CONES[b]	78	13	4	5	0
Ministry of Health	55	15	18	8	5
Prefectures	27	25	24	18	5

a. The strong demand from the National Road Service in the poorest areas is explained by its focus on road construction and upgrading outside of urban areas.
b. National Council for School Construction
Source: Jorgensen, Grosh, and Schacter (1992).

the poorest received only $9.45 per capita (Jorgensen, Grosh, and Schacter 1992). Performance of the different service providers was also disappointing (table 6.2). While NGOs and religious and grass roots organizations have stronger demand coming from poorer areas than do centralized public agencies, none of these groups directed the majority of their resources to the poorest, most remote regions (van Domelen 1992).

Zambia's Social Recovery Project relies mainly on community groups for the provision and production of services.[12] This project also incorporates the demand-driven private delivery model (table 6.3).

Table 6.3. Expenditures of the Microprojects Unit of Zambia's Social Recovery Project, up to December 1993
(US dollars)

Province	Total expenditures	1991 population	Per capita expenditures	Poverty index [a] highest poverty = 1 P^0	P^1	P^2
Central	3,056,452	751,677	4.1	7	7	8
Copper Belt	3,876,754	1,618,279	2.4	8	8	7
Eastern	2,398,557	1,013,954	2.4	5	6	6
Luapula	2,823,908	538,868	5.2	2	2	4
Lusaka	5,339,134	1,277,965	4.2	9	9	9
Northern	2,293,958	890,063	2.6	3	5	5
Northwestern	3,445,991	392,782	8.8	6	2	2
Southern	1,852,478	979,869	1.9	4	2	2
Western	2,290,542	621,831	3.7	1	1	1

a. P^0= Poverty headcount index, P^1= Poverty depth index, P^2= Poverty severity index.
Source: World Bank data.

Actual per capita expenditures of the Microprojects Unit (MPU) as of December 1993 were not well-targeted across Zambia's nine provinces: the higher was a province's poverty headcount index, the lower was the actual per capita expenditures it received from the Microprojects Unit (the estimated Spearman rank correlation coefficient was negative).[13] As in Bolivia, reliance on community groups did not ensure that the poorer regions received higher per capita resources.

Egypt's Community Development Program (CDP) uses a demand-driven private delivery model (table 6.4). The three governorates with the highest poverty index (Minya, Beheira, and Sharqiya) had received

Table 6.4. Disbursement in Egypt's Community Development Program, as of March 31, 1995

Governorate	Poverty index[a] (percent)	Expected project funding (dollars)	Disbursement (dollars)	Expenditures as a percentage of expected project funding
Alexandria	2.87	9,315.96	3,532.67	37.9
Assuit	7.08	22,961.87	9,867.57	43.0
Aswan	1.78	5,773.27	9,151.96	158.5
Beheira	8.14	26,373.35	5,772.00	21.9
Beni Suef	4.88	15,810.84	4,066.97	25.7
Cairo	6.05	19,616.00	4,425.13	22.6
Damietta	0.97	3,149.06	1,026.59	32.6
Daqahliya	6.76	21,912.18	6,299.48	28.7
Fayoum	5.38	17,451.02	2,086.65	12.0
Gharbiya	5.71	18,500.71	2,632.34	14.2
Giza	6.92	22,437.03	4,098.32	18.3
Ismailia	0.87	2,821.03	3,295.10	116.8
Kafr El Sheikh	4.78	15,482.86	4,143.66	26.8
Matruh	0.43	1,377.71	1,883.26	136.7
Menufiya	5.30	17,188.60	4,345.48	25.3
Minya	9.13	29,558.01	9,875.51	33.4
New Valley	0.16	524.84	1,020.00	194.3
North Sinai	0.22	721.66	160.00	22.2
Port Said	0.36	1,180.90	1,931.54	163.6
Qalubiya	4.72	15,286.04	3,919.84	25.6
Qena	6.84	22,174.61	4,453.22	20.1
Red Sea	0.12	393.63	334.08	84.9
Sharqiya	8.06	26,110.93	8,859.00	33.9
Sohag	1.88	6,101.30	6,894.63	113.0
South Sinai	0.20	656.05	80.00	12.2
Suez	0.38	1,246.50	5,720.47	458.9
Total	100.00	324,156.00	109,875.45	33.9

a. The poverty index is the maximum-normalized, first principal component of six variables. They are the female illiteracy rate, proportion of individuals in households without drinking water from a public network in the housing unit, proportion of individuals in households without a kitchen, ratio of expenditures on food to total household expenditures, relative drop in the average annual expenditure per person in households, and proportion of households using kerosene as the sole source of energy.
Source: Ferghany (1992).

33 percent, 22 percent, and 34 percent, respectively, of their individual CDP resource allocations in 1995. Seven governorates with low poverty indices (Suez, New Valley, Port Said, Aswan, Matruh, Ismailia, and Sohag) received more resources than were allocated to them. Broadly, the geographic distribution of resources is not well-targeted. But a beneficiary profile survey carried out in five governorates where the social fund was operational showed that social fund beneficiaries were poorer than the population at large.

In Sri Lanka's Poverty Alleviation Program—another demand-driven program—infrastructure was mainly provided and produced by local governments (table 6.5). Was its outcome any different from that of Egypt's privately delivered programs? The analysis here shows that the resources in Sri Lanka's rural works program were also not well-targeted: the higher was the poverty incidence of a province, the lower was its per capita disbursement (the estimated Spearman rank correlation coefficient was negative).

Thus the geographic distribution of resources is poor in the demand-driven programs examined here.[14] The higher absorptive capacity of the wealthier regions probably accounts for this outcome (Subbarao 1985).[15] But this outcome can be improved through effective promotion and outreach. For example, special promotion efforts improved the geographic targeting of social funds in Honduras and Bolivia (World Bank 1994e; Jorgensen, Grosh, and Schacter 1992).

Programs that are not demand-driven. It is instructive to compare the above outcomes with that of programs incorporating private delivery without the demand-driven component. The Grameen Bank is an example, in which an NGO is responsible for designing and organizing the credit operations. The NGO also undertakes the lending operations. While Grameen Bank responds to the needs of the poor, it does

Table 6.5. Sri Lanka's Poverty Alleviation Project Rural Works Fund, Disbursements as of December 31, 1994

Province	Number of projects	Actual disbursements (million rupees)	Per capita disbursements (rupees)	Poverty incidence 1981 (percent)
Central	336	64.5	29.06	26.8
North Central	242	39.6	38.22	24.5
Northwest	492	88.2	43.56	29.0
Sabaragamuwa	227	31.0	18.31	40.0
Southern	262	42.5	18.99	30.7
Uva	228	30.3	28.30	29.7
Western	289	44.1	9.93	17.8
Total	738	353.6	n.a.	n.a.

n.a. Not applicable
Source: World Bank data. The 1981 provincial poverty incidence figures are from Ranji and Salgado (1989).

not respond to formal project proposals from community groups or other agencies.

What determines the geographic distribution of Grameen Bank branches? In theory, the chances of a branch remaining profitable would be higher in areas with more favorable characteristics (such as areas less prone to flooding and areas with good roads), but the poverty objective would be better addressed by locating branches in less favorable areas. A study of Grameen Bank branch placement showed that placement does not respond to better agroclimatic and locational factors (Khandker, Khalily, and Khan 1995). In contrast, both government and commercial banks respond positively to better agroclimatic and locational conditions. For example, both locate their branches in subdistricts that are closer to district headquarters, thus reducing their transaction costs. On the other hand, Grameen Bank's decision to open branches in a certain area is not conditioned by its proximity to administrative centers. To serve the poor, Grameen Bank may locate its branches in some areas that other banks would deem too risky. Thus Grameen Bank is more concerned with the behavioral risk of lending due to adverse selection than with the risk of low or saturated demand in poorly endowed regions. Its non-demand-driven delivery mechanism may be better targeted geographically than demand-driven social funds.[16]

Cost-effectiveness. It is difficult to compare costs across projects. First, weaknesses in reporting cost data often make it difficult to determine which costs are excluded and which included in average cost figures. Second, it is almost impossible to obtain cost information for different programs that control the speed of service delivery, quality of services, and the location of services.

Reviews suggest that classrooms built under Honduras's Social Fund, through the private delivery model, cost many times less to build than ministry-supported classrooms (World Bank 1994h). Projects financed by PRONASOL in Mexico through the Municipal Fund have a much lower cost than similar projects implemented by line ministries. In the case of primary school construction the savings amount to 30–40 percent (Silverman 1993). Also, in Mexico's Mendoza Provincial Program for Basic Social Infrastructure (MENPROSIF) private contractors' bidding for projects has resulted in savings of up to 35 percent compared with works carried out by the public works ministry. In addition, contractors are offering warranties for their works, sometimes up to five years (Campbell 1995a). In Senegal privately delivered AGETIP-supported projects are able to achieve unit prices 5 to 40 percent lower than government programs (World Bank 1992e).

Grameen Bank's experience with credit programs is interesting. Its investment in organizing groups, mobilizing resources, and supervising loan repayments raises its administrative costs above those of programs not offering such services—such as the Small Farmers Development Program in Nepal (SFDP) and the Small Farmer Credit Institutions (SFCIs) throughout the world (Holt 1991). Grameen Bank's administrative costs as a percentage of total disbursements in 1984 was 12.3 percent compared with 7.6 percent for SFDP and 4.68 percent for SFCIs. But for Grameen Bank higher administrative costs translated into reduced loan arrears: in 1983–84 its arrears rate was 1.6 percent compared with 11.7 percent for SFDP and 39 percent for SFCIs. And the high repayment rates contributed to Grameen Bank's ability to cover costs and sometimes even make a profit.

Chile's publicly delivered Special Employment Programs (PEM and POJH), though successful in targeting the poor, were not cost-effective. Their design contributed to high costs. The requirement that labor costs be at least 80 percent of total project costs was difficult to enforce without inflating the cost of the work. Generally, work days were shorter than stipulated, and even while workers were ostensibly working, they were not required to work hard. A survey of project workers reported that they could accomplish their work in about twenty-seven hours as opposed to the statutory thirty-five hours. Thus the actual work done was 22 percent less than the programmed work. Absentee rates ran at about 12 percent. Consequently, the effective work done was about a third less than the programmed work (Grosh 1994).

Within public delivery, it is instructive to compare two large nutrition programs in India with similar objectives: Tamil Nadu Integrated Nutrition Project (TINP) and the nationwide ICDS. Though both programs were publicly delivered, there were considerable differences in the cost of delivery. The annual per capita cost for TINP is 10 rupees, compared with roughly 18 rupees for comparable services in the same state under ICDS. The cost of expanding TINP to cover the full state would account for less than 0.5 percent of state GDP, compared with more than 1.0 percent for ICDS. ICDS in Tamil Nadu has reduced cases of advanced malnutrition by 20 to 25 percent—an impressive achievement. If the reduction in malnutrition achieved by TINP is assumed to be 50 percent (the approximate midpoint between the monitoring and evaluation data), TINP delivers about twice the benefits for slightly more than half the cost. This finding is fairly robust for different definitions of costs (Subbarao 1989; Heaver 1989; Shekar 1994).

What factors account for the observed variations in cost-effectiveness? The most important factors contributing to lower costs include the use of private contractors who had to compete for projects; the involvement of beneficiary communities in project execution through contributions of management time, labor, and cash; and the highly motivated and qualified staff of social funds compared with their often inefficient counterparts in government public works departments. In the case of Grameen Bank up-front investments in social mobilization appear to have paid off in terms of better repayment rates. In Chile the reduced cost-effectiveness of the Special Employment Programs was due to weak program design—particularly the programs' excessive focus on labor use.[17] In India's TINP cost-effectiveness came as a result of a tightly targeted approach to nutrition that concentrated on targeting children during the most important two and a half years of their lives nutritionally; maintaining high worker quality by training workers to perform only a few critical tasks; ensuring high motivation among nutrition workers by encouraging supportive supervision that emphasized problem solving rather than fault finding; ensuring adequate supplies for workers, enabling them to perform their tasks efficiently; requiring nutrition workers to reinforce health and family planning messages (thus maximizing beneficial externalities); and selecting nutrition workers from the community itself (Berg 1987a; Subbarao 1989; Shekar 1994).

Sustainability of Services

Four issues are relevant to sustainability: consistency with sectoral priorities, recurrent costs, beneficiary participation, and flexibility in service delivery.[18]

Consistency with sectoral priorities. Coordinating interventions with sectoral plans is critical to the success of social assistance and poverty-targeted programs. Programs' services will be difficult to sustain if they are uncoordinated or conflict with other interventions in the sector. Services provided through social funds (which are typically independent of government structures) are particularly susceptible to this problem. Their activities often have little input from sectoral ministries about how well they fit with other planned or ongoing activities. Unless special measures are taken, social fund activities may be uncoordinated with government interventions (Carvalho 1994b). In Bolivia's ESF the services that were funded were not necessarily the ones that best met sectoral priorities. ESF's emphasis on speed and its autonomy from the line ministries worked against fitting each project into a predetermined sectoral plan. But adopting the public delivery model does not necessarily guarantee that consistency with sectoral priorities will be achieved. A mission studying India's publicly delivered MEGS reported this finding: the annual plan for the implementation of MEGS was a mere collection of ad hoc works suggested by various government departments. Also, the plan lacked sectoral coordination.

Governmental agencies, such as sectoral ministries, have information about sectoral needs and the actions proposed by various public bodies. These agencies might, therefore, be better able to design interventions consistent with sectoral plans. Hence, some recent social funds have tried to involve sectoral ministries in defining technical standards for the planned activities and in clearing projects for social-fund financing. For example, in Cambodia's social fund the line ministries will define the fund's sectoral policy guidelines and standards for infrastructure construction. The line ministries will also provide a "no objection" clearance to projects before they are funded. In Zambia's Social Recovery Project (SRP) local government officials accompany SRP staff on appraisal visits and participate in desk reviews of project proposals.

Recurrent costs. Sustainability also depends on adequate financing of recurrent costs. The experience of Bolivia's ESF indicates that public agencies are better equipped to meet recurrent costs through the national budget process than are NGOs and community groups. The latter's biggest challenge is the continued financing of recurrent costs over the long term (Jorgensen, Grosh, and Schacter 1992). A 1990 survey for ESF in Bolivia found that projects sponsored by central government agencies were most likely to survive, while projects sponsored by grass roots organizations were least likely to survive (World Bank 1992a).

But governments do not necessarily meet recurrent costs effectively. Consider India's publicly delivered MEGS. One of the weakest aspects of the program was the virtual absence of operation and maintenance of completed works according to the 1992 fact finding mission study in the MEGS. Similarly, in Egypt's social fund the public works program (with the government as provider) had difficulty maintaining works after completion. Regional and local authorities had given assurances to provide maintenance funds, but these intentions were not always honored in an era of shrinking resources (World Bank 1995h). Maintenance of completed works has become a problem in most government-implemented public works programs (Teklu 1994a, b; 1995a, b).

The recurrent cost problem can be particularly severe in social funds because individual projects are not determined up front (only the eligibility criteria are). Thus the precise recurrent costs may be difficult to pin down when the government sets its annual budget. To address the recurrent cost problem, the eligibility criteria recently adopted in social funds (and some other privately delivered programs) require that the service provider has established links with public agencies and has presented evidence that some public agency will pick up at least part of the recurrent cost. Contributions in cash or labor from the beneficiaries for the operation and maintenance of the works are also being encouraged.

Beneficiary participation. A recent empirical study of 121 water supply projects showed that participation by beneficiaries in decision-making made a major contribution to project effectiveness (Narayan 1995).[19] Proximity of the service deliverer to beneficiaries, the capacity to respond creatively to unforeseen problems, and a project cycle that is not time-bound all promote beneficiary participation. The private delivery model operating through NGOs and community-based organizations will likely display these characteristics more frequently than the public delivery model.[20]

In general, few central government agencies have the necessary skills and orientation to foster continued interaction with a wide range of small, and perhaps scattered, beneficiary groups. For example, a fact-finding mission for the MEGS found that works under this program were designed and implemented by government departments with minimal participation from beneficiaries or NGOs. Consequently, designs did not take into consideration the socioeconomic situation at the grass roots level according to the 1992 fact finding mission study in the MEGS. However, the MEGS did enhance the economic power of the poor by generating workers' pressure groups, especially women's groups (Dev 1995a).

Making governmental structures participatory is important. Small NGOs have an impact only in a few villages. The problem remains of how to assist all other villages (Korten and Siy 1988). Governments are major investors in development, so finding ways for government agencies to implement participatory strategies may be one solution. Significant to this point is the experience of the Philippines Communal Irrigation Program. The initiative for developing a participatory approach in this program came from a government agency that had been developing and testing the approach for five years (Nagle and Ghose 1990).

Beneficiary participation can be costly and difficult. Most importantly, poor peoples' time has opportunity costs (especially if they are working poor), and they will get involved only if they anticipate sufficient returns. Zambia's Beneficiary Assessment for the Social Recovery Project (SRP) reports that some women declined to be on project committees; they argued that they were simply too busy (Milimo and Njobvu 1993). Moreover, the rationale for community participation is often that local entities know best what their clients need and the appropriate way to meet those needs. But local entities may lack the broader sectoral perspective of public agencies, and they may not necessarily be propoor. For example, in Pakistan's Zakat and Ushr program beneficiaries are selected by local committees mainly according to personal preferences rather than poverty criteria. Consequently, only 2–10 percent of beneficiaries are from low-income households, and although lists and committees are supposed to change every six months, neither does (OED 1995). Communities are rarely harmonious units, and traditional structures often reflect the interests of the elite (Holt 1991). Beneficiary participation through NGOs may run into other problems. For example, many NGOs are located in cities or towns and tend to work in these areas rather than in the poorest regions.

The experience of Zambia's SRP with beneficiary participation shows interesting trade-offs. Parent-teacher associations implemented about 48 percent of projects, NGOs and churches about 18 percent, district councils about 7 percent, project committees about 18 percent, and political functionaries about 8 percent. Where there was maximum beneficiary participation (parent-teacher association projects, for example), workmanship tended to suffer (table 6.6). The Zambian example also shows that community groups such as parent-teacher associations can be highly participatory, yet not necessarily accountable to beneficiaries.

Flexibility in service delivery. Social assistance and poverty-targeted programs aim to address the needs of target groups whose response is not always easy to predict in advance. The more uncertain is a program's operating environment, the more flexible must the delivery mechanism be. The mechanism must allow considerable learning to take place before the program can be successfully implemented (Holt 1991). Flexible and learning-oriented organizational setups are more likely to be found among NGOs and community-based organizations than in government bureaucracies. NGOs and community-based organizations may have greater field presence and orientation. They thus enjoy an advantage in initiating new approaches at the grass roots level and responding flexibly to emerging problems. The limited flexibility of bureaucracies may restrict their ability to respond to the poor, who often need customized assistance.

Pakistan's NGO-run, privately delivered Aga Khan Rural Support Project (AKRSP) features an open management style, free communication along the management chain, and meticulous record keeping. All of these characteristics contribute to a dynamic and responsive problem-solving environment. The closeness of AKRSP's general manager and senior management staff to events in the field is critical to the project's successful implementation. The time that they spend in the field is well-structured (the length of time is not as important as its quality) and fully recorded. The management and villages are close and are in frequent contact with each other. The net effect of the field visits and extensive reporting is a system of written and oral communication that enhances decisionmaking by managers, field staff, and beneficiaries. It also enables midcourse corrections. AKRSP establishes its objectives,

Table 6.6. Characteristics of Implementing Agencies in Zambia's Social Recovery Project

Implementing agency	Community participation	Transparency	Accountability	Workmanship
Churches	Minimal	Low/zero	High	Excellent
Parent-teacher associations	High	High	Low	Poor
NGOs	Low	Low	High	Mixed
District councils	Fairly good[a]	Low	Low	Poor
Political leaders	Fairly good[a]	Low/zero	Low	Poor
Strong personalities	Fairly good[a]	Low/zero	Low	Good

a. Usually, communities will have started contributing materials, labor, and resources to a project; after the start-up politicians and council officials assume overall control of the projects. It is then that issues of transparency and accountability arise.
Source: Milimo and Njobvu (1993).

principles, and functions through an iterative implementation process. The result is a project that is characterized by open communication at all levels, is prepared to learn from its mistakes, and is driven by results (OED 1986).

Another program incorporating the private delivery model is Bangladesh's Grameen Bank. Effective leadership (and generous donor support, including a subsidy from the International Fund for Agricultural Development) have played a significant role in Grameen Bank's success. In addition, the program's decentralized management style (emphasizing adaptability in decisionmaking) has been a key to success. Grameen's management structure features built-in flexibility that has been refined through field experience. This style combines learning, innovation, and adaptability at all levels. With the expansion of bank branches, the management gradually delegated more decisionmaking authority to intermediate administrative units; the head office could no longer effectively handle the volume and variety of issues involved. Unlike most hierarchical bureaucracies, the Grameen Bank evolved into a decentralized organization as it grew. With selective supervision from the head office, field office managers are expected to plan, organize, and implement Grameen Bank services and activities at various levels. Grameen Bank has a strong staff training program. It features a structured learning process that is continually fine-tuned by trial and error.

There are few data on the time that different delivery models take for service delivery. The private delivery model appears to be faster in delivering services in the few cases examined here. Simple and clear operating procedures, well-defined division of responsibilities between individuals and organizational units, adequate equipment, good information systems, and qualified and motivated staff all seem to be associated with quick service delivery. While these characteristics can be found in public agencies, they are more common in private agencies. In fact, one reason to create social funds as autonomous bodies outside the normal bureaucratic structure is to avoid the red tape and delays associated with public delivery.

Faster turnaround time in managing such processes as bidding and procurement should mean speedier service delivery. It takes Senegal's AGETIP two months to complete the whole bidding process, while it takes the government administration six months to do the same (World Bank 1992c). In the Honduras social fund, while line ministries sometimes take up to a year to complete the bidding process, social fund management turns in a bid for the same type of project within a month (World Bank 1994f). In India's publicly delivered ICDS program there is often a considerable lag between the program's sanctioning by the central government and the program's becoming operational. Sometimes the lag time runs up to seven years (Subbarao 1989). Anecdotal evidence indicates that private contractors and NGOs try to minimize delays to keep costs down; hence they are typically quicker service deliverers than are public agencies.

Lessons of Experience

Based on program experiences, it is possible to identify some key principles for the effective delivery of social assistance and poverty-targeted programs. These principles include tapping institutional complementarity, balancing demand-driven systems and demand management, and fostering beneficiary participation.[21]

Tapping Institutional Complementarity

Many countries have a weak institutional capacity for reaching the poor. Hence, it is critical to tap the strengths and resources of all development agencies—whether private or public, central or local—according to their comparative advantages. Generally, some blend will be most appropriate. The issue is to determine the optimal mix of inputs required in each case and to divide responsibilities among organizations accordingly.[22]

The case of the infrastructure component of Bolivia's ESF is a good example of tapping the complementarities between public and private agencies. Most of the infrastructure projects financed by ESF were designed and organized by public agencies, but the actual building was contracted out to private firms. This division of labor reflects the comparative advantages of public and private agencies. Because public agencies were in a better position to fit activities within sectoral priorities and ensure that the recurrent costs implied by the capital investments would be met, ESF vested service provision in public agencies. On the other hand, given their capacity to deliver services fast, private contractors were hired to produce the infrastructure.

There are also more and more cases in which an effective division of labor is established between public agencies and NGOs. This trend is growing as governments take advantage of NGO flexibility and grass roots orientation, and NGOs benefit from governments' sectoral information base and resources. For example, Professional Assistance for Development Action (PRADAN)—an Indian NGO—has been working with government IRDP officials to improve the effectiveness of poverty alleviation programs at the subdistrict level. This effort has improved targeting and loan repayment (Holt 1991).

The sanitation component of the Honduras Social Fund is a good example of the partnership between different service deliverers. The social fund works closely with the Ministry of Health's Health Education and Sanitation Division and NGOs to design the component (public-private provision). The social fund hires private contractors to build latrines (private production) and NGOs to provide simultaneous sanitation education (private production). A 1994 ex-post evaluation of the social fund showed that about 88 percent of the beneficiaries were using the services and were adopting appropriate sanitary practices (Webb, Lee, and Sant' Anna 1995).

Balancing Demand-Driven Systems and Demand Management

Though sensitive to the needs of the poor, demand-driven institutions (such as social funds) are not free from problems. First, some types of projects (such as family planning) may not be demanded at all (for cultural or other reasons), although these activities may have high social returns. Second, social funds do not necessarily have favorable geographic targeting because the poor may have a limited capacity to absorb and hence demand projects. Third, reliance on a purely demand-driven approach may lead to the financing of projects that can be prepared quickly rather than those that are most needed. For example, in Honduras's FHIS about 62 percent of the funds allocated to the basic needs component had gone to a school desk manufacturing program, an arguably low-priority item. In Zambia's SRP about 70 percent of the projects were in the education sector, mainly school construction and rehabilitation.[23] In Honduras manufacturing desks was popular because such project proposals could be easily prepared. In Zambia the fact that the parent-teacher association was active and experienced in undertaking school projects led to a profusion of viable project proposals for schools, neglecting other potentially needy projects in the process. Fourth, demand-driven programs without a funding constraint leads to demand for everything—the wish-list problem. Even if there is a funding constraint, people may prefer that resources are used to generate pure benefits (such as a road) rather than for things that provide a flow of benefits but require complementary inputs (such as an irrigation canal). Finally, demand-driven projects may be biased against the poor because the poor are often less ready than the non-poor to articulate their needs.

In response to these shortcomings the fully demand-driven approach has evolved into a demand-managed approach. Demand management, for example, in the Cambodia Social Fund has been achieved by using several instruments:

- Eligibility principles, which lay out the broad policy framework governing the social fund's activities.
- A project menu, which lists the different kinds of projects that can be financed by the social fund.
- Eligibility criteria, which outline the various activities that are eligible for social fund financing.
- Appraisal criteria, which further narrow the activities and the form of acceptable projects.
- Targeting criteria, which lay out the groups, type of projects, and provinces that will receive priority in processing applications in order to ensure that the poor benefit.[24] An additional instrument of demand management used in social funds, especially to stimulate demand for projects among poorer communities, is outreach and promotion. Outreach and promotion may include one (or more) of three activities, each representing progressively higher levels of assistance.

  - Information dissemination, which aims at making a social fund popular by passing out general information about its objectives and project selection criteria.
  - Facilitation, which aims at explaining the project selection criteria, helping to determine if specific projects meet those criteria, and clarifying procedures for proposing projects.
  - And, lastly, training and technical assistance, which focuses on helping communities acquire skills to effectively prepare, manage, and implement projects (Carvalho 1994b).

Demand management is not without limitations. It may increase the time it takes to appraise projects, thereby, reducing the social fund's agility in responding to demand and increasing its administrative costs. It may also result in less ownership of projects. Whatever the delivery model, the key is to strike an appropriate balance between demand-driven systems and demand management.

Fostering Beneficiary Participation

Where programs have succeeded, they have been tailored to the local environment, and beneficiaries have felt involved and "owned" the programs. The highly successful Philippines Communal Irrigation project (NIA) showed that securing beneficiaries' full-scale participation takes a tremendous effort—but such an effort pays off handsomely with a sustainable project in which farmers truly assume ownership and are motivated to maintain it. In general, the short-term costs of participation are likely to be outweighed by the longer-term benefits emanating from more effective and sustainable projects. Important policy and design features needed for effective beneficiary participation include: creation of social infrastructure (identification of key actors, their social organization and leadership, and their interest and capacity to manage the physical infrastructure) to sustain the physical infrastructure, and flexibility in allowing different forms and intensity of participation (Narayan 1995).

Beneficiary participation will be more desirable in some projects than in others. For example, in projects that depend on participation by a large number of beneficiaries and require regular maintenance and supervision, local involvement and grass roots participation at almost all stages of project design and implementation may add significantly to project effectiveness and sustainability. By contrast, in projects that require lumpy capital investments, such as infrastructure construction, ensuring that the needs of beneficiaries (for example, project location or resettlement) are taken into account may be enough. Participation in such projects tends to be more consultative than participatory. In these circumstances services can be provided through existing central organizations or private contractors.

Notes

1. The term "delivery" includes both institutional and organizational issues. Institutions refer to the "rules of the game" and organizations to "how the game is played" (North 1990).

2. Being unsustainable is not bad under all circumstances. A poverty-targeted program need not be sustained forever. It must be sustained only until the problem it tackles has gone away or can be better handled by other means.

3. The two approaches are based on a distribution of responsibilities among different levels of government—the distribution of resources is a separate issue. Block grants either earmarked (for specific activities that are to be encouraged) or unearmarked are instruments for distributing resources. Block grants may include matching grants, especially if domestic resource generation is desired.

4. Under the fiscal choice model local authorities can also raise revenue for the program.

5. Moreover, it is worth stressing that some disincentive effects—such as crowding out family and community thrift—are not delivery system issues. Disincentives raise costs and harm program objectives whatever the delivery model is.

7

Modes of Financing
Social Assistance Programs

The mode of financing influences the choice of social assistance program, its sustainability, and its ultimate impact on the poor. Alternative sources of financing are discussed, and some of the trade-offs and implications for program sustainability are described. That discussion is followed by an empirical analysis of the limited information on how countries have chosen to finance social assistance programs. Because such programs make competing claims on real resources, it is important to assess whether they crowd out other long-term investments for growth. This issue is reviewed using a small sample of countries for which data are available. Further, we explore the growing tendency to decentralize fiscal responsibility for social assistance programs. Finally, financing issues are addressed. Financing social assistance programs is particularly challenging in the economies in transition because of their output and fiscal contractions.

Because funds have alternative uses, it is important to be aware of the extent to which a particular financing mechanism displaces others. But the lack of adequate data precludes sorting out the effects of fungibility. For the purposes of this chapter zero fungibility (perfect earmarking) is assumed, and the different sources of financing are treated as mutually independent and exclusive. Obviously, this view is an oversimplification.

Sources of Financing and Trade-Offs

There is considerable heterogeneity among countries when it comes to financing social assistance programs. Broadly, social assistance programs may be financed from external or internal (domestic) sources (figure 7.1). Internally, a program may be funded from general tax revenues, payroll taxes, or specific taxes, or "covered" by arrears.[1] If financing is intended to come from general revenues, but there is a deficit, the deficit can be covered domestically by money financing, debt financing (bond sales), or arrears.

Figure 7.1. Sources of Financing

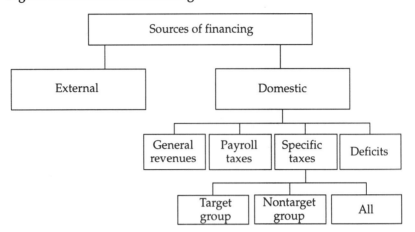

Because social assistance programs are for the poor, they are best financed with general progressive tax revenues. The growth of such revenues in both developing and transition economies, however, is constrained by the ability of the tax administration to implement redistributive taxation with few distortions. Political economy factors are also a constraint. Further, if social assistance programs are funded from general tax revenues, tight fiscal and budgetary constraints make it possible that programs could end up being financed from fiscal deficits. In such a case the poor may lose because of inflation. In addition, levying taxes may have important effects on labor supply and investment decisions.

Earmarked payroll taxes are also an important source of financing. But payroll taxes are a tax on labor, and they tend to raise the unit cost of production, reducing competitiveness. This effect may have adverse consequences for the poor, especially because the poor lack assets other than their own labor. In the long run such taxes may encourage factor substitution away from labor and may induce employers to curtail output. A vicious circle may arise: taxes on employment reduce the demand for labor, thereby raising unemployment. In turn, the greater need for social assistance may exert pressure for higher taxes.

If social assistance programs are funded from specific taxes, governments have a choice: tax nontarget groups (only the nonpoor) or tax the whole population (including the poor). For instance, an urban employment tax in Maharashtra, India, was used to partially finance an employment guarantee program; a tax on horse race betting was used to garner resources for social assistance programs in Morocco; and a gambling tax was used to finance poverty alleviation programs in Paraguay. Such funding may seem equitable in the sense that resources are being redistributed. But if every program is funded this way, the administrative burden will become heavy as the tax machinery grows increasingly complex. Furthermore, in some countries the poor are disproportionately represented among those participating in lotteries and gambling. And depending on the political clout of the groups being taxed, the fiscal sustainability of these sources of financing is questionable.

Programs may also be partially funded from resources obtained from target groups in the form of "self-help" contributions. One example would be the public works programs in some Asian and African countries (for example, some public works programs in Africa have used free labor and user-contributed land).[2] To the extent that the contributors of land are from the poorer strata of society, this form of financing may be less equitable, because there is no guarantee that the contributions will be offset by program gains.

User charges are a potentially important source of finance for continuing programs or meeting recurrent costs. They may benefit the poor if the revenue generated is used to extend the supply of essential services or improve quality. But if instituted at equal levels for all program participants, they are likely to be regressive. The impact of user charges on revenue collected is determined by the elasticity of demand for the services rendered. If demand is elastic, the imposition of user fees may reduce service use and hence revenue. Conversely, if demand is inelastic, households may not greatly reduce their use, but they may have to reduce their consumption of some other commodity (in the absence of savings)—and suffer a welfare loss. Further, while there is often untapped potential to collect user fees and partial cost recovery, there are likely to be poor groups in every society that must be exempt from such fees.

If properly structured, user charges incorporate signals and incentives that help curtail leakage and lead to a more efficient use of resources. In addition, the patterns of demand observed when there are user fees may convey information to planners about how different consumer groups value different services. These considerations suggest that, while being an important source of cost recovery, user fees by themselves may not automatically improve the efficiency or the quality of social assistance programs. The structure adopted is crucial. Who is responsible for collecting fees? What happens to the revenue generated from such fees? What incentives are created? These questions must be addressed when designing the program.

Asset sales are yet another option for raising revenue. This option is possible in countries with large publicly held natural resource reserves or in countries emerging from state planning and state ownership of enterprises (such as Chile, Mexico, Russia, and Venezuela). For instance, in Russia the Fund for the Social Support of the Population has received 10 percent of privatization proceeds and some assets of the communist party. But the real value of these assets eroded because of rapid inflation.[3] An important problem is that asset sales offer only a one-shot source of financing, not a continuing source. They are therefore unlikely to sustain programs if they are the sole source of financing.

Finally, programs can be funded externally. The sustainability of a program that is fully funded externally is always in doubt. Moreover, the availability of donor financing may slacken efforts to mobilize domestic resources in the recipient country. External funds may be regarded as a substitute for domestic funds and may discourage redistributive taxation. These problems notwithstanding, donor funds have played a major role in financing social assistance programs in Africa, Asia, and Latin America.

A few countries have adopted other financing strategies. These include reducing current government expenditures; converting external debt into social assistance programs (as in Chile, the Dominican Republic, and Ecuador); and increasing contributions from participants.

Like every other spending activity, the financing of social assistance programs claims scarce resources. Therefore, it is necessary to assess the opportunity cost of forgone alternatives. Trade-offs arise between long-term investments in growth and human resources, and short-term investments in social assistance programs. Whether a particular program has crowded out other long-term investments, is, however, an empirical issue. Not every social assistance program competes for scarce resources. In fact, social assistance programs could complement developmental expenditures in some countries. For example, a well-designed public works program could create socially useful rural infrastructure, enhancing economic growth. Similarly, cash transfers to the poor may be both desirable and necessary to the extent that they complement the reform or adjustment process by preventing the erosion of living standards in the interim and harnessing political support for reform. Some consumption-smoothing programs can encourage the poor to accept high-risk portfolios with greater expected returns or income, thereby raising GNP.

The mode of financing affects the ultimate impact on the poor. The cost of poorly targeted social action programs may be prohibitive and require deficit financing. If the deficit is monetized, ensuing inflationary pressures may hurt the poor disproportionately.[4] The Latin American experience of the 1980s highlights the narrow limits of inflationary finance—and its dramatic costs. Insofar as inflation is a tax on real resources and the poor have less access to other forms of wealth, benefits can be more than offset by inflation, which erodes the real value of the poor's limited cash balances. In addition, social assistance programs requiring a larger slice of the budget (the case in some transition economies) are difficult to sustain in an era of structural adjustment or austerity, as governments take corrective measures to reduce deficits.

A Cross-Country Analysis of Funding

Four findings emerge from the regional patterns of financing social assistance programs. First, food and nonfood external aid were the dominant funding sources in Africa and Asia for most programs. Many Asian countries (India and Bangladesh in particular) supplemented external aid with several programs funded out of general tax revenues. Second, few countries have used special taxes (India's employment tax is a notable exception). Third, in countries in transition social assistance programs are funded from general taxes, particularly from state and local budgets. So far, external aid has played little or no role. Fourth, all public works programs (regardless of geographic location) for which there are data have relied on some form of external food aid (except for the program in India).[5] Many African countries received both food and nonfood external aid for their public works projects (for example, Burkina Faso, Kenya, and Niger). Some major credit-based programs (for instance, the Grameen Bank in Bangladesh, the Banco Solidavio in Bolivia, the Credit Solidaire program in Burkina Faso, and the Bumkin Raya Karkara program in Niger) relied partially or wholly on nonfood external aid. The value of aid is partly dependent on whether it is given in-kind (food aid) or in cash.

Nearly 80 to 90 percent of total social assistance spending in Africa is supported by external finances. In Latin America external financing is also an important source. But within Latin America external financing did not necessarily focus on the poorer countries; some middle-income countries like Venezuela also obtained a high proportion of external funding. Mexico is the only country where the entire program was domestically funded.

Data on annual average spending on social assistance and the proportion of the total population below the poverty line suggest that average spending is usually higher in countries that have more people living below the poverty line (figure 7.2). For example, countries like Madagascar, Mexico, Uganda, Venezuela, and Zambia had higher average annual levels of spending on social assistance programs. These were also the countries that had more of their population living below the poverty line. El Salvador and Somalia rank low in both areas.

**Figure 7.2. Selected Countries Ranked According to Average
Annual Financing of Social Assistance Programs and Population
Below the Poverty Line, Late 1970s–Early 1990s**

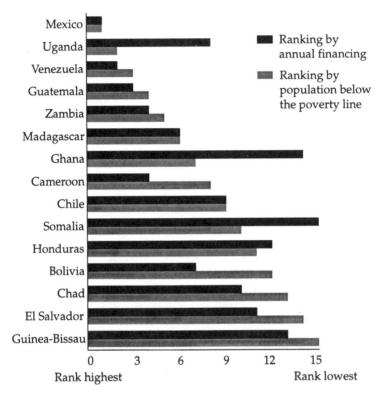

Source: World Bank estimates and Mesa-Lago (1993).

Did donor support increase social assistance spending in countries
with the largest poor populations?[6] To determine whether the ranks
(based on average annual spending) would have been different in the
absence of donor funding, scores were derived when external funding
was removed from total spending. Whether external financing has any
impact on a country's rank presumably depends on its initial conditions. External financing may be expected to be important in countries
that have a larger absolute number of people living below the poverty
line (figure 7.3). This seems to be the case.

An excessive dependence on external financing (averaging about 88
percent of total financing in Africa and 72 percent in Latin America)
exposes social assistance programs to fluctuations in available finances
and therefore jeopardizes their sustainability. Domestic financing has
its own problems and advantages. Many of the Asian countries

Figure 7.3. Selected Countries Ranked According to Annual Foreign Financing and Population Living Below the Poverty Line, Late 1970s–Early 1990s

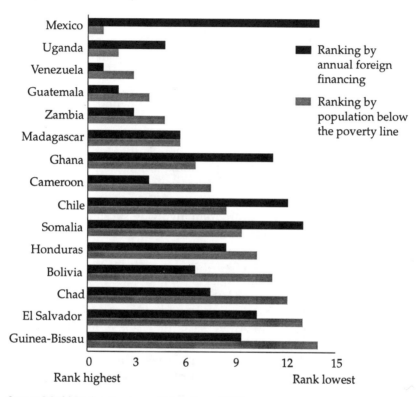

Source: World Bank estimates and Mesa-Lago (1993).

financed social assistance programs out of domestic sources. Such practices contribute to ownership and sustainability, though force a tough choice between allocating scarce resources for long-term investment and growth or for short-term poverty alleviation.

The number of donors involved in funding a particular program influences its outcome. A large number of donors with smaller contributing shares may create an environment in which negotiations, approvals, and disbursement of funds are difficult. Conversely, a smaller number of donors with a higher concentration of shares would probably make these tasks easier. The Bolivia ESF is an example of the latter, having only nine donors (with two financing more than half of the requirement). Hence negotiations, approvals, and disbursement were accomplished rapidly—in about one-sixth the average time (Mesa-Lago 1993). Honduras has almost twice as many donors (sixteen), but two of the donors provided most of the funds, so start-up was rapid. Ghana received less than half the funds allocated to Bolivia's ESF, but it had twice the number of donors, each with very small shares. Disagreements between the government and the donors (compounded by the donors' unwillingness to simplify and shorten their procedures) contributed to massive delays in start-up (Mesa-Lago 1993).

To the extent that social assistance programs can target the poor, the best form of financing is clearly redistributive taxation. But all taxes are distortionary to some extent. If resources needed for financing transfers from general tax revenues are not kept within limits, the distortions imposed by increased levels of taxation might more than outweigh the benefits accruing to the poor from transfer programs. For example, indirect taxation, with all its attendant distortions, is exceptionally high in some countries (like India). Moreover, while the coverage of any given direct tax is low, the levels of taxation are high, thus inducing evasion and other inefficiencies. These considerations suggest that a desirable transfer program involving substantive domestic financing depends very much on how efficient countries are in raising tax revenues.

Another aspect of domestic financing is participant financing. The data suggest that participant financing (as measured by the contribution of managing agencies and beneficiaries) is not a significant source of finance for social assistance programs (about 8 percent in Latin America and 1 percent in Africa). The Bolivia ESF has the highest counterpart share (23 percent), and it allows labor contributions, thereby reducing the charity stigma from the program. But this practice raises the issue of how to measure contributions and monitor financial flows. Shares in rural projects are usually higher than shares in urban areas (Jorgensen, Grosh, and Schacter 1992). Honduras generally sets a share of 10 percent, and participants are expected to contribute at least 15 percent in cost recovery for sanitation projects. In Mexico, as in Bangladesh and other Asian countries, beneficiaries' contributions (particularly in primary health care projects) are made in communal work and occasionally in land or local materials.

A few countries have imposed specific taxes designed to fund social assistance programs. For instance, Paraguay, though providing no formal safety net, allows the autonomous agency DIBEN (which was designed to help the poor satisfy their basic needs) to impose a levy on gambling. The Entraide National, a public establishment mandated to promote social welfare in Morocco, is financed by taxes on horse betting, festivals, and plays, and a surtax on animal slaughtering. Yet another example is the MEGS in India. It is partially funded from an urban tax that was initially envisaged to dampen rural-urban migration.

In transition countries social assistance programs are quite limited and financed primarily or exclusively by payroll taxes. Payroll taxes finance predominately social insurance programs, which are not targeted to the poor. But such taxes increase the costs of production, introduce tax compliance problems, reduce competitiveness, and are distortionary. Payroll taxes are very high—ranging from 35 percent to 52 percent (Ukraine).

Finally, some countries (the poorest in Africa, or those caught up in the tumult of transition) may lack resources to finance any social assistance programs, and thus may have to incur a budget deficit. In this situation financing recommendations for social assistance programs do not differ from general recommendations about financing the overall deficit, although, typically, the share of the deficit devoted to social assistance (though difficult to pin down) is usually not large. This is because absolute spending on social assistance programs is small.

Transfer Spending, Social Services, and Budget Deficits

Does spending on social assistance programs crowd out other critical expenditures on health and education, and increase the budget deficit? It is difficult to test this proposition empirically. First, data on welfare spending are available only for a few countries, and only for central government sources. Second, available data are aggregated for social security and welfare, which includes social insurance and social assistance. Public spending on social security is generally for the nonpoor, while welfare is generally for the poor. Third, the budget deficit, as well as social sector spending, might rise or fall for other reasons. In Jordan, Nepal, and Nicaragua social welfare expenditures increased substantially in 1980–93. In Nepal this increase was financed through a budget deficit. In Nicaragua, while the deficit decreased slightly, the relative spending on health declined. Moreover, Nicaragua was faced with massive macroeconomic instability—its inflation rate hovered over 600 percent. In such a situation it is questionable if raising welfare spending will bring any relief to the poor.

In some countries social welfare spending has increased modestly, and in most the budget deficit position has improved. Thus, there is no evidence of a worsening deficit, even in countries where spending on social assistance programs has increased. In a few countries the relative share of health and education expenditures have also increased. But in others spending on one of the two sectors has increased only slightly or decreased. Thus the evidence is not robust. However, countries that managed to sustain welfare spending without hurting education or health spending were typically successful in raising tax revenues (such as Ghana) or curtailing expenditures (such as Sri Lanka). Generally, countries unable to raise revenues were unable to sustain spending on social welfare without hurting either health or education.

In many countries the responsibility for financing social assistance programs is devolving to local governments. Where such fiscal decentralization is taking place, the sustainability and viability of programs, as well as interprovincial equity, are real concerns.

Fiscal Federalism, Decentralization, and Public Expenditure Management

Spending and revenue decisions must be decentralized to ensure that poverty alleviation programs and policies reflect the preferences, needs, and fiscal abilities of different regions of the country. The nature of decentralization and the driving force behind it depend on a country's specific circumstances. The momentum to decentralize public administration and public finances has partly reflected the decentralizing objectives of each government and, in transition countries, the disintegration of the centrally planned economies.

Decentralization is a paradox. It demands more sophisticated political skills at the national level to guide the process, but at the same time it requires that the dependence on the center be broken. This is the case in Latin America and some Asian countries, such as China, where decentralization represents a clear break after many decades of centralism. A complicated dynamic emerges as national governments and political elites transfer power to local authorities. Governance becomes more difficult just when it is most important for providing a common, coherent set of goals for social programs.

Not surprisingly, decentralization has had limited success. For instance, the propoor services throughout Vietnam are underfunded (Bird, Litvack, and Rao 1995). This problem is particularly acute in poorer areas compared with larger cities. Improvements in the system of intergovernmental finances could help ensure that each level of government, even in the poorer provinces, is adequately funded—and given sufficient expenditure and revenue-raising autonomy—so as to support, operate, and maintain local investments. Because poor provinces are often less able to mobilize local revenues to support social services, well-designed intergovernmental transfers are particularly important.

Provinces must play a greater role in raising revenues and in allocating expenditures. Incentives should be built in to ensure that provinces perform these roles responsibly and efficiently. Now, most local governments raise very little revenue, the extent of which varies from year to year, depending on central transfers. Such uncertainties affect most local expenditures, including transfer expenditures. Local governments must—to be accountable—have some responsibility for determining local tax rates. This power would give them the flexibility to collect more revenue to finance more social programs if they so choose. At the same time it would allow the central authorities to design its transfers to ensure that they do not discourage local fiscal efforts. This concern is real because local authorities may simply regard central transfers as an easy alternative to their own revenue-raising efforts.

Countries that have decentralized revenue sharing, such as Brazil and India, have assigned some major tax bases to subnational governments. Such assignments aim to ease the revenue situation at the provincial level. For example, in Brazil the general value added tax (ICM) has been assigned to the states. In India the sales tax has been assigned to the states. In the former Soviet Union the individual income tax and many excise taxes have been assigned to subnational governments (Bahl 1994), though this strategy has raised insignificant amounts of revenue.

Richer provinces will undoubtedly collect more revenue. A particularly striking feature in almost every country, developed or developing, is the difference between big city governments and other local governments. In Colombia, for example, per capita tax revenues were almost ten times higher (in the 1970s) in Bogota than in the other, smaller rural municipalities. Some redistribution is therefore necessary if national social action programs are to succeed across heterogeneous locales. This is an important consideration because decentralization is often viewed as a means used by richer communities to opt out of social assistance programs run by higher levels of government.

For decentralization to be successful both expenditures and revenues must be decentralized. But the search for "good taxes" that could be exploited by local jurisdictions has not produced very good results (Bahl and Linn 1994; Bird 1986). The verdict on this issue is that the taxes local governments often raise, especially in developing countries, tend to be poor in quality. And their poor quality generates many economic distortions. Thus a question arises: if decentralization is defended on the grounds that it improves the allocation of resources on the expenditure side, how much efficiency is lost when resources are raised using distortionary methods?

These issues underscore the difficulty of financing social assistance programs under fiscal decentralization (box 7.1). The process is typical of economies undergoing structural changes and market reforms. Fiscal pressures at the local level increase as national governments transfer many of the expenditure responsibilities of social assistance programs to local authorities. At the same time the revenue crisis is

Box 7.1. Budgetary Problems and Decentralization in Kyrgyz Republic, Latvia, and Hungary

In the Kyrgyz Republic expenditures on state pensions are taken from an extrabudgetary fund called the social fund. The social fund collects revenue from employers and employees, and passes the money to the Ministry of Labor and Social Protection to pay pensions. The money never passes through the Ministry of Finance and therefore never shows up as an entry on the general budget. Social assistance spending comes from the general budget and does show up as a line item. (The aim for 1996 is to keep social assistance to 4.7 percent of GDP). A problem arises because the budget line item for social assistance must cover all social expenditures, including currency shortfall in the social fund budget. Although it appears that social insurance is self-contained and is almost 5 percent of GDP, in fact the first claim is to cover the deficit in social insurance revenue collection. Social assistance receives only the remaining balance. The effect is a budget line entry that appears to show 4.7 percent of GDP going to the poor. In fact, most covers revenue collections from defaulting enterprises and is thus an indirect subsidy to enterprises.

Latvia has a different problem. Latvian social assistance legislation provides for a uniform income-tested benefit across the country. But in attempt to give local authorities more control, budgets have been devolved to local authorities. Each local authority is allocated money from the general budget to meet its estimated needs. This devolved budget includes an amount to cover social assistance. But the money allocated for the estimated social assistance needs can be used however the local authority decides. The result is provision in some areas above the envisaged level, because the local authorities supplement the general budget allocation, and provision in other areas below the envisaged level. Therefore, there is considerable variation in actual spending across regions.

In Hungary the financing of local government spending does not allow for earmarking resources for social assistance. Fiscal pressures on local governments, especially on poorer ones, are likely to divert increasing parts of social assistance allocations to other purposes. Given that local governments rarely levy local taxes, there is a danger that the safety net system might break down and add to the increasing differentiation of social services across localities. Local pressures for equal treatment may easily lead to benefits that are too low and doled out to too many clients (inclusion errors). Or, such pressure may lead to exclusion errors.

forcing central governments in transition to withdraw revenue-sharing instruments from local governments without providing substitutes. Uncertainties of the transition, including lack of clarity in tax assignments, give rise to ambiguities in intergovernmental relations and obligations. The danger that financing programs for the poor will "fall between the cracks" of vague responsibilities is very real.

The Specific Challenges of Financing in the Economies in Transition

Financing social assistance programs poses a special challenge for the economies in transition because of their past economic structure and the nature of their transition to market economies. First, the transition has been accompanied by a severe contraction of GDP. Though some countries in Africa, Asia, and Latin America have also experienced reductions in GDP, the severity of the contraction experienced in transition economies is unprecedented (figure 7.4).[7] Second, the extent and level of consumer subsidization before the transition has contributed to high expectations concerning the role of the state in social protection during and after the transition. Third, the disruption of the interstate trade and payments system, and the vertically integrated system of the former Soviet Union further aggravated pressures on the external sector. Added to these trends, the proliferation of armed conflicts in the region increased the number of poor demanding social assistance—while further reducing GDP.

The situation described above heightened fiscal constraints, which were a major difficulty during 1992–94 for most countries of the former Soviet Union. As a part of stabilization programs conducted with the International Monetary Fund (IMF), most countries sharply reduced the volume of consumer subsidies (table 7.1). These subsidies had

Figure 7.4. Growth Rates in Some Countries of the Former Soviet Union, 1993 and 1994

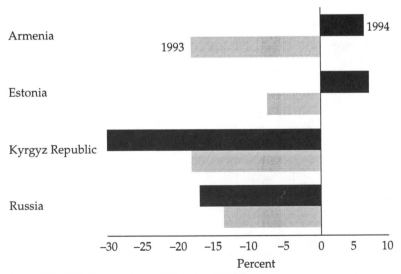

Percent

Source: World Bank estimates and Mesa-Lago (1993).

reached massive proportions by the 1980s (especially in the food sector).[8] The contraction of GDP during 1992–94 was accompanied by lower revenue collection and, consequently, large fiscal deficits (figure 7.5). Lacking domestic financial markets for bonds and faced with severely limited external financing, most countries of the former Soviet Union were forced to monetize these deficits. As a result, most experienced hyperinflation (figure 7.6).

High expectations for the transition and the historical role of safety nets also reinforced the problem of fiscal constraint. Also bolstering high expectations was the extension of Eastern European-style child allowances to countries of the former Soviet Union. Implemented in 1992 in most countries of the former Soviet Union, these child allowances were intended to compensate the entire population for price increases. But sustaining these high levels of assistance is proving difficult.

High expectations may also constrain the state's capacity to finance domestic social action programs. These expectations limit how fast and how far the tax system can change from a posttransition structure to a progressive structure. In addition, limited revenues hurt fiscal decentralization, slowing efforts to improve the tax administration at the local level.

Creating a new and effective safety net means correcting errors of exclusion and leakage. Universal systems have high leakage. For example, all individuals can take advantage of generalized consumer

Table 7.1. Social Safety Net Spending in Some Countries of the Former Soviet Union, 1993–94
(percentage of GDP at current prices)

Country	Item	1993	1994
Armenia	Total	7.1	5.0
	Transfers	6.1	2.9
	Explicit subsidies	1.0	2.1
Estonia[a]	Total	8.7	9.1
	Pensions	5.1	5.4
	Family allowances	1.8	1.6
	Social assistance	1.6	1.6
	Unemployment and labor market	0.2	0.5
Kyrgyz Republic[b]	Transfers	10.4	—
Russia	Total	20.3	17.9
	Subsidies	2.8	0.0
	Social programs	17.5	17.9

— Data not available.
a. Data for 1994 are World Bank projections.
b. World Bank (1995b) reported much lower shares for social assistance of 6, 3, 3, and 3 percent of GDP, respectively, in 1991–94.
Source: World Bank data and World Bank (1994k).

subsidies. The first round of fiscal contraction in the former Soviet Union and Eastern Europe led to a necessary, sharp cut in the volume of generalized consumer subsides. Cutting back subsidies is a straightforward process. It does require, however, significant political will. Defining who is poor and devising methods to best help them are clear goals, but the tasks themselves are highly complex.

The first obstacle for many countries is the lack of reliable information about who constitutes the poor and what an appropriate poverty line might be. In some Eastern European countries, however, the poverty line and systematic information on the poor are readily available. In several countries poverty assessments based on representative household income and expenditure surveys have been prepared.[9] For adequate poverty monitoring, surveys must be routinely incorporated into the regular workings of the statistical agency (such as in Poland and Hungary, and as envisioned in Armenia through the World Bank–sponsored Social Investment Fund).

The second challenge is to devise better ways to help the poor. Three major problems remain: retirement ages are too low and pensions are given to too large a fraction of the population (pension benefits are extremely regressive), countries are prematurely introducing means testing—before considering administrative capacity or cost, and most countries do not have the fiscal resources to introduce poverty benefits.

Figure 7.5. Fiscal Balance in Some Countries of the Former Soviet Union, 1993 and 1994

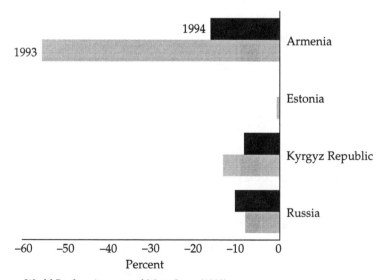

Source: World Bank estimates and Mesa-Lago (1993).

**Figure 7.6. Annual Inflation Rates in Some Countries
of the Former Soviet Union, 1993 and 1994**

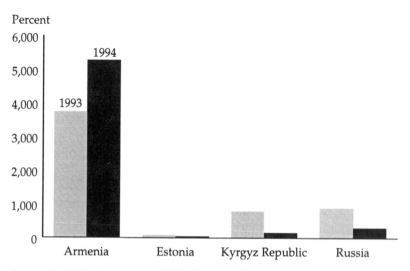

Source: World Bank estimates and Mesa-Lago (1993).

Universal child allowances have been modified in several countries
of the former Soviet Union in attempt to reduce overall spending and
improve targeting, even though child allowances overall were found
to be progressive transfers for countries in Eastern Europe and the former Soviet Union (Krumm, Milanovic, and Walton 1995).

Most countries do not have the fiscal resources to finance poverty
benefits, even if the extreme difficulties of means testing could be overcome. In Russia a means-tested poverty benefit was legislated in 1993,
but general fiscal resources were not made available until 1994. The
means-testing process has been carried out on an ad hoc basis, and
localities use different poverty lines that do not always correspond to
the national poverty line. Additionally, it is not clear that localities are
receiving their mandated resources (a certain percentage of national
value-added tax revenues). The general revenue decline has exacerbated the problem of financing this benefit.

In all of the countries of the former Soviet Union and in most of the
countries in Eastern Europe, however, significant efforts are underway
to improve fiscal performance, particularly in the areas of tax policy
and tax collection. In most countries treasuries, tax inspectorates, and
customs have been established, and improving revenue collection is a
major focus of technical assistance. Some problems of revenue collection are temporary—tax administration is improving, and when positive economic growth resumes, revenue performance will improve.

Notes

1. These sources are not mutually exclusive. A single program could be funded from any combination of these sources.

2. The Harambee schools in Kenya and the *ShramDan* (donate labor) movement in India were early harbingers of these kinds of programs.

3. Asset sales may have other macroeconomic and microeconomic effects whose impacts on the poor are difficult to assess a priori.

4. In addition, excessive inflation also has adverse effects for the poor with respect to resource allocation (capital flight) and income distribution.

5. Prior to the 1960s India also financed some of its food-for-work programs with P.L. 480 grain assistance from the United States.

6. The approach in this paragraph draws on behavioral and theoretic analyses of whether more donor spending is associated with more or less domestic spending per person. As such, the approach here is ex post and merely provides a descriptive scenario.

7. Some of the contraction in output arises from data limitations, concealment (non-recording), and informalization of output. The extent and significance of these biases are difficult to quantify.

8. These subsidies were financed through general budget revenues. In addition, significant noncash benefits were provided by state enterprises, including housing subsidies, day-care centers, clinics, cafeterias providing subsidized meals (and often kitchen gardens to stock cafeterias), and a system of subsidized stays at health and recreational facilities. Depending on the type of enterprise, workers with seniority could have preferential access to waiting lists for automobiles and other consumer durables. A strict system of residence permits (propiska) meant that larger enterprises could offer authorization to live in the more desirable cities and large towns. When food and consumer shortages increased significantly in the 1980s, many enterprises organized buying services for employees or maintained small shops where employees could purchase food and other goods (Braithwaite 1991).

9. The World Bank financed or provided technical assistance for household income and expenditure surveys in Kyrgyzstan, Romania, Russia, and Ukraine. The World Bank is able to use existing or new surveys in Armenia, Bulgaria, Estonia, Hungary, Poland, and Slovakia. World Bank–sponsored (or administered) work on various other sorts of surveys is occurring in Azerbaijan, Kazakstan, Moldova, and Uzbekistan. But most of the surveys in the former Soviet Union were one-off, and, more seriously, little significant financing to date has been provided for social assistance programs.

8

The Political Economy
of Social Assistance Programs

Social assistance programs are influenced strongly by domestic political economy concerns.[1] Targeting objectives and outcomes, and cost-effectiveness, for example, vary a great deal according to political contexts. While focusing the benefits of social assistance on poor and vulnerable groups may make sense based on fiscal and poverty concerns, many governments face competing claims for assistance from more vocal and organized, but far less needy groups. Because these groups often wield more political influence than the poor, at least some of the benefits of social assistance are often allocated to them. This motive leads to outcomes that are less cost-effective but often more feasible politically.

In addition, political objectives can often influence how social assistance programs affect beneficiaries' incentives to seek alternative employment or to save. For example, if the target group of unemployed previously earned relatively high wages and are highly organized and politically influential, they may refuse to work in a low-wage public works program that provides minimal income relief. In this case the optimal employment program from a technical standpoint may be insufficient to meet the government's political need to placate a potentially powerful opposition.

Politics often affect the sustainability of social assistance programs. In some contexts it may be necessary to divert part of the benefits of social assistance to less needy groups to ensure political support for those programs. In other contexts, where demand-based programs (such as social funds) are able to effectively incorporate the poor, the poor's organizational potential and political ability may be enhanced. Then, shifting public expenditures toward the poor is more likely to be sustainable.

Finally, choices about the speed of service provision are directly affected by politics. Although designing the optimal social assistance program takes time—to compile adequate information about who the poor are and how to reach them—many governments implement social assistance programs during economic transitions or crises, when politics demands rapid and visible assistance. Many governments, for example, face strong and immediate pressure to "do something about the social costs of adjustment." In such situations objectives such as targeting often become secondary to political expediency.

This chapter describes the effects that politics can have on social assistance programs. It also identifies approaches to social assistance that, at least in some cases, allow governments to avoid the political trade-offs in which social assistance benefits are provided to less needy groups at the expense of the poor. Using a country case-study approach, the chapter explores three central propositions: that particular political and institutional contexts affect social assistance programs and their beneficiaries, that safety nets can (but do not always) reduce poverty in the long term, and that safety nets can contribute to the political sustainability of ongoing economic transition. The findings are based on field studies of social assistance programs in several countries. While the cases under study are all of economies undergoing reform, some of the lessons that emerge are also relevant to countries not undertaking reform. Particular attention is paid to the political economy of using the demand-based approach to implementing safety nets. This approach is emphasized because of its increasing predominance and its potential to enhance the political voice, as well as the economic capacity of the poor.

On the policy front establishing a consistent macroeconomic framework that will enable poverty reduction requires economic adjustments that are often difficult to sustain politically. On the program front implementing safety nets directed at particular groups entails the allocation of scarce public resources. Therefore program choices are based on politics and on efficiency considerations. The conventional wisdom holds that the poor have a weak political voice. In addition, while the poor may bear some of the social costs of adjustment or have the least ability to absorb negative shocks or cyclical downturns, they are often not the most negatively affected. Governments usually have legitimate concerns about sustainability in the face of opposition from organized or powerful groups. These groups range from organized labor and political parties to the private sector. Thus governments have few immediate political incentives to help the poor. An additional dilemma is that the poorest and most needy groups are often the most difficult (and costly) to reach. Therefore, compensatory efforts during transition tend to focus on more vocal, organized, and privileged groups for reasons of political sustainability. Such efforts are usually made at the expense of poverty alleviation objectives.

The country experiences reviewed here suggest that this need not be the case. Safety nets can be designed to contribute to long-term poverty reduction, as well as to the sustainability of economic reform programs. Some of the cases in this chapter yield lessons about how to reduce poverty and enhance the political sustainability of adjustment. Dramatic political change or extreme economic crisis, for example, can alter or undermine the relative weights of powerful interest groups. Such change can create opportunities for governments to redirect public resources to less-privileged groups. Reaching out to previously marginal groups rather than focusing on the vocal opponents of reform may allow governments to circumvent the traditional "new poor" and "old poor" dilemma. This approach may also require encouraging the participation of the poor, both in the implementation of social assistance programs and in politics. Such efforts are needed to make resource shifts toward the poor sustainable in the future. Effective communication on the part of governments can be crucial to such a process.

Still, in some cases it may be necessary to extend safety net services to nonpoor groups that lose out in relative terms during reform. But, ultimately, if reform efforts are abandoned for a return to unsustainable fiscal distortions or "populist" economic policies, the poor will suffer most.

Recent international trends demonstrate the possibility of directing safety net services to the poor rather than to vocal groups. In some countries the focus of government spending has shifted from development efforts that relied on large-scale infrastructure projects and universal subsidies to universal provision of only basic health and education services combined with targeted interventions to help the neediest groups. In several other countries, however, such shifts have been postponed—mainly for political reasons—at a high cost in terms of fiscal sustainability and effective protection for the poor.

Largely influenced by the experience of Bolivia's ESF, social funds have become a primary means for delivering social assistance. The concept of incorporating market principles—through the demands of beneficiaries—into program design has proven a powerful tool for enhancing poverty alleviation and institutional development locally. The most evident drawback of the social fund approach is that the poorest groups, which tend to be poorly organized, are the least equipped to solicit benefits from demand-based programs. While both the nonpoor and poor can benefit from a variety of productivity-enhancing measures, such as credit schemes or increased investment in education, the poorest often face other obstacles, such as malnutrition or chronic diseases, that may prevent them from benefiting from such policies.

Three messages emerge from the reviewed country experiences. First, open political environments provide greater opportunities for building broad-based support for economic reform and, therefore, a policy environment in which effective poverty reduction can take place.[2] Effective government communication with the public is an important element, because there is a need to increase popular understanding of the reform process in order to create support for change.[3] Second, open political systems are more likely to encourage the participation of diverse groups, such as NGOs and local institutions, in their antipoverty strategies. And, third, in the absence of strategies to encourage participation of the poor, vocal and organized groups are likely to make more effective claims on government resources. In contrast, closed political regimes, which are less vulnerable to the demands of interest groups, may have less difficulty targeting resources to the poor, even without the poor's participation.[4]

Strategies that rely on participation of beneficiaries and the organizations that represent them (such as social funds) can strengthen the capacity of these institutions. Stronger capacity gives previously marginal groups a more effective political voice and makes longer-term contributions to poverty reduction through institutional and political development. Giving previously marginalized groups a new stake in the system and increased influence may result in the creation of new coalitions supporting economic reform.

Protecting the Poor during Adjustment in Latin America and the Caribbean

Latin America and the Caribbean was the first region to begin the process of policy reform and to grapple with the social dimensions of reform. As a result this regioin has had a longer time in which to examine the political consequences of policy reform. The duration of programs, along with the variety of experience, makes this region an ideal starting point for examining the effects of safety nets during reform. This section reviews the experiences of Chile, Peru, Bolivia, and Mexico, which mirror the regional variation in political economy and program outcomes.

Chile

One of the first and most effective efforts to protect the poor during adjustment was implemented in Chile (1973–89). But the authoritarian nature of Chile's regime limits the ability to replicate that experience, at least in terms of the political dynamics determining the allocation of public resources. Chile had an extensive social welfare structure prior to adjustment; the system was revamped and targeted to the poorest groups during the Pinochet years. While social spending per capita declined overall during the adjustment years, it increased for the poorest two deciles. Still, many people at the margin lost access to what had been one of the most comprehensive social systems in Latin America. This loss was not necessarily a positive result, nor was it one that a more responsive government could have prevented. But the system proved extremely effective in protecting the poorest sectors during severe economic crisis. The infant mortality rate, for example, not only continued to decline, but accelerated its rate of decline. It is now one of the lowest on the continent, below that of Argentina, Colombia, and Mexico.

In conjunction with targeting social sector spending, large-scale employment programs were implemented in 1975–87. At the height of the economic crisis in 1982, with unemployment at almost 30 percent, the programs employed up to 13 percent of the workforce. Programs paid between one-fourth and one-half of the minimum wage, providing a self-targeting mechanism, although many critics argue that the subsidy was far too low. Implementation at the beginning was a bit haphazard—labor was often used unproductively, tainting the image of the programs. With time, program design was improved, incorporating some private sector hiring and training. Workers in the private sector–linked programs were often able to find permanent jobs with the same firms: a positive effect in terms of poverty alleviation.

While the programs had several flaws—particularly their authoritarian manner—even their harshest critics agree that their existence, and their sheer scale and duration, reduced the potential for social explosion at a time of unprecedented unemployment. It is unlikely that a demand-based program could attain the systematic coverage, scale, and speed in implementation that the Chilean programs did, particularly with the resources available relative to population size. In 1987 the programs were allocated 5 billion pesos (approximately $20 million) from the government's total social spending budget of 274 billion pesos and employed approximately 165,000 people (about 13 percent of the labor force). In comparison, Bolivia's ESF had approximately $240 million for its four years of operations, and on average it employed approximately 3,000 or 0.3 percent of the economically active population.

Chile's record (compared with that of its neighbors) in protecting the basic health and welfare of the poor during a period of adjustment, and targeting and reaching the poorest is indeed remarkable. Yet according to other indicators, such as income distribution and per capita consumption, Chile fares less well. Further, a major flaw in the Pinochet government's approach was its failure to incorporate beneficiary participation. The authoritarian government's top-down manner precluded the kind of participation from below that often enhances the sustainability of programs. It also limited the program's positive political effects. Jobs were withdrawn from shantytowns that were active in political protests, for example. Because targeting of social welfare spending entails political as well as economic choices and because the Pinochet regime was free of the constraints faced by most democratic regimes, Chile's lessons on political sustainability are not clear cut.

Peru

The Peruvian case demonstrates that programs designed to protect or benefit the poor, if poorly implemented, can do more harm than good. They often alienate potential beneficiaries, as in the case of the Peruvian Temporary Income Support (PAIT) program. The PAIT program was a public works employment program modeled on Chile's programs. It was implemented in Lima's shantytowns by the 1985–90 American Popular Revolutionary Alliance (APRA) government.

The program provided sorely needed income support and some socially useful infrastructure. Yet it was implemented in an extremely top-down and partisan manner, with a great deal of clientelism in hiring and constant political manipulation of the workers. PAIT workers were often taken to political rallies, for example. The program's budget was also manipulated. It rose drastically prior to elections and then quietly faded out afterward. Consequently, applicants were in a constant state of uncertainty. And while some PAIT projects provided useful services for poor areas, such as painting schools or laying sewerage pipes, in many cases such projects were begun and left unfinished. Many projects achieved very low worker productivity and had no permanent effects, such as the cleaning of beaches for primarily upper-income residents in Lima. Finally, jobs were concentrated in Lima, which is extremely important politically, but has lower poverty rates than the rest of the country.

The perception that the program was used as a tool by the governing party ultimately undermined its public image. Most damaging, however, was the program's excessive centralism and top-down implementation. The program duplicated and undermined the efforts of local self-help groups, which are critical to the survival of the poor in Peru. It is little surprise that the program's paying of wages for the same work that had previously been volunteered by communities undermined ongoing projects. Its effects ran directly counter to the capacity building that is integral to poverty reduction. The marginal effects the PAIT program had on poverty alleviation were temporary, while the disruption of local organizations often had permanent effects.

Bolivia

Bolivia's ESF was the first social fund of its kind, and it attracted a great deal of national and international attention.[5] Enthusiasts of the ESF cite its demand-based approach, its efficiency and transparency, and its quick results. Critics question the program's ability to permanently alleviate poverty or to target the poorest sectors. They are also wary of the fact that the program is separate from the government bureaucracy. The program did not reach the people most directly affected by adjustment (for example, the tin miners). It also had a disproportionately low reach to the two poorest deciles. The poorest regions benefited least from the ESF in per capita expenditures: the wealthiest of five income areas received $23.97 per capita, while the poorest received $9.45. ESF workers represented 6.25 percent and 7.75 percent of workers in the two poorest deciles, but 13.25 percent, 21.5 percent, and 15.3 percent in the next highest deciles. By regional standards, however, the three higher deciles in Bolivia are still considered quite poor. Because the program operated separately from government ministries, it did little to further central-level institutional or social sector reform. Indeed, its large and visible scale may have even provided the government with an excuse to postpone more difficult institutional reforms. Still, the program clearly had positive effects, particularly in demonstrating that different types of public sector operations were possible.[6]

The ESF administered $240 million in its four years of operation. The projects that it created, which ranged from infrastructure (such as health posts, schools, and low-income homes) to services (such as job creation and school lunch programs), benefited more than 1 million poor people—a large number in a population of less than 7 million. Despite relatively weak targeting, the program had a substantial impact on the political sustainability of economic reform and on poverty alleviation.

The ESF had a positive political impact. It demonstrated that such a program could work in a transparent and nonpartisan manner—with local governments and NGOs of all political bents—in a country where aid programs were usually influenced by patronage politics. The ESF resulted in an unprecedented collaboration of efforts between NGOs—the groups with the closest ties to the poor—and the state. This teamwork allowed the fund to reach the poor in remote communities, which had rarely, if ever, seen the state follow through on promises. The fund also enhanced local governments' capacities by providing them with funds independent from the central government. And, because of its demand-based structure, the fund could not be monopolized by any one political actor at election time: a diversity of actors, from the governing party to local governments and NGOs, could claim credit for ESF projects. Thus there was no correlation between the allocation of ESF funds and the outcomes of the 1989 presidential election and 1987–89 municipal elections.[7]

The Fund handed the poor a way to help themselves, thereby giving them a stake in the ongoing process of economic reform. By doing so it generated support for the government at a critical time—if not for the adjustment program per se—among previously marginal groups, which enhanced the feasibility of economic reform. Even if the ESF had focused its efforts on people who were directly affected by the adjustment program—the tin miners—it is unlikely that it could have eroded their entrenched opposition to the government's economic strategy. Meanwhile, the rapid pace of adjustment, coupled with the crash in world tin prices, reduced the political power of the miners' traditionally influential confederation. This does not imply that people who are directly affected by adjustment do not merit compensation.[8] Rather, it implies that most efforts directed at those groups will have a marginal impact on the political sustainability of adjustment. Propoor programs implemented during adjustment may create opportunities for building proreform coalitions among the poorest groups by enhancing the poor's economic potential and political voice.

Mexico

A program that is gaining increasing national and international attention is Mexico's PRONASOL. The program is a Bolivia-style, demand-based social fund, but it is being implemented on a much larger scale. The ESF administered $240 million in four years; PRONASOL started with a budget of $680 million in 1989, which rose to a projected $2.3 billion for 1992.[9] If administrative and infrastructure costs were waived, the ESF would have spent approximately $50 per year on each of its 1.2 million beneficiaries.[10] With its 1992 budget, PRONASOL would spend $135 on each of the 17 million people living in extreme poverty in Mexico. PRONASOL's highly visible nature—such as its prominent appearance in President Salinas' 1992 annual address to the nation—also suggests that the program is having an impact politically. And like the ESF, the effects of PRONASOL's outreach to groups that had rarely, if ever, received state attention in the past cannot be underestimated.

PRONASOL's design was influenced by the ESF and other demand-based social funds. It was also an outgrowth of President Salinas' doctoral research,[11] as well as of previous government programs that relied on community initiatives in the form of manual labor and food for work.[12] There are 64,000 solidarity committees nationwide; they are elected locally. In response to popular demands the committees design projects in collaboration with government staff. There are four program areas: food support, which includes extensive support for ongoing targeted food subsidy programs; production; social services; and infrastructure (Dresser 1991). In addition to these activities PRONASOL has three programs aimed at increasing the earning potential of the poor. Solidarity funds for production provide credit to farmers undertaking high-risk, low-yield activities; solidarity funds for indigenous communities support ethnic groups involved in local development activities; and solidarity funds for women provide credit to workshops and small industries run by women. PRONASOL supports sectoral ministries by expanding the country's health and education facilities, and through scholarship and school feeding programs. Finally, PRONASOL supports municipal development and builds infrastructure for poor communities through its municipal and regional solidarity funds (Dresser 1991).

The wide range and large number of programs makes it difficult to form a singular judgment of PRONASOL. In addition, it is difficult to separate what may be justified criticisms of the political system—a semi-authoritarian system in the process of liberalizing (in theory)—from those of the actual design or content of the program. Ultimately, PRONASOL's success as a demand-based program hinges on how committed the government is to genuine political opening and to allowing actors and organizations of all political bents to join.

PRONASOL's record varies depending on the nature of the local party power structure and the capacity of grass roots and community organizations. In many regions the program has conflicted with authoritarian party bosses at the local level. Such clashes indicate that nontraditional actors have been able to benefit to some extent.[13] While President Salinas demonstrated a willingness to let solidarity committees undermine local authorities, he was less willing to allow the committees to operate independently in municipalities controlled by the opposition.[14] The extent to which PRONASOL is able to reach previously marginalized groups and to serve as an alternative to Mexico's dominant political party, the Institutional Revolutionary Party (PRI), by providing a channel "through which popular groups can express their demands" (Dresser 1991:26), will determine whether it can raise the economic potential and political voice of the poor as did funds like the ESF.

As with many similar programs, the origins of PRONASOL can be traced to politics. In the 1988 elections, given new mobilizing forces on the left, the PRI had the worst electoral showing in its history, and President Salinas took power amid widespread accusations of fraud. While Salinas did not fear massive social unrest as did the governments of Chile, Poland, and Senegal, for example, he was well aware of how unpopular the cutting of social services by the de la Madrid government had been. PRONASOL was a gamble that reversing that trend would change popular perceptions of government legitimacy. The government increased PRONASOL activity in several regions where opposition was strong, such as in Michaocan, Morelos, and Nueva Laguna, and was able to reverse its electoral fortunes. Yet it is not clear whether the electoral results were influenced by the curbing of inflation, the renewal of economic growth, or PRONASOL.

PRONASOL was criticized as a populist tool and as a means for President Salinas to build up his personal power base. The first criticism stemmed from the president's tactics, such as using the proceeds from the privatization of the national airline to provide electricity to 500,000 homes in the poorest regions. Populist or not, he cleverly combined salesmanship with the philosophy underlying orthodox economic reform: get the state out of production and into service provision. Inasmuch as PRONASOL is generating support for a new government approach to providing social services and for a new channel to communicate with both central and local governments, the program is contributing to poverty alleviation and to institutional development. It is difficult, therefore, to criticize the government for reaping the rewards of a good program, as happens in most countries. Yet where PRONA-SOL is re-enforcing traditional clientelistic structures controlled by the PRI, its potential to contribute to local capacity building is being severely curtailed. The building of local capacity through PRONASOL, rather than the PRI, may be a very effective means to undermine the party's authoritarian structure and monopoly control. Finally, given the size and range of activities, and the divergent records of PRONASOL programs, it is difficult to draw conclusions about their performance.

Another issue is the future of PRONASOL, given its institutional autonomy and its close connection with Salinas. The creation of Secretariat of Social Development (Sedesol) in 1992 as an umbrella agency to coordinate and direct PRONASOL activities indicated some government desire to institutionalize the program more permanently. The Zedillo government continued to place a fair amount of importance on the program, given the negative impact of the 1994 peso crisis on employment and living standards. Yet fiscal constraints also dictated a narrowing of the program's mandate.

Sub-Saharan Africa: Social Funds and Social Action Programs

The Africa cases in the study—Senegal and Zambia—provide an interesting contrast in how they reached the poor, capacity-building, and sustaining adjustments. Two kinds of approaches to safety nets are examined here. One is the social fund mechanism. The other is social action programs (SAPs). Compared with social funds, SAPs tend to have closer institutional links with the existing public sector bureaucracy, cover a broader range of activities, and are not necessarily demand-driven. In general, they have been less successful than social funds, mainly because their objectives were never clearly defined at the outset.

Senegal

In Senegal adjustment has progressed at a slow pace for more than a decade, and the political system has remained a relatively stable, if limited, democracy. Certain groups, such as civil servants and university students, had far more political weight and effective representation in the governing party than did the majority of society—the urban and rural poor, many of whom were illiterate. The first major attempt to compensate the losers from adjustment was the Délégation a l'Insertion et le Reinsertion a l'Emploi (DIRE), set up in 1987. Funded by the United States Agency for International Development (USAID), the World Bank, and the government of Senegal, the DIRE provided credits of up to $50,000 to civil servants who had retired voluntarily (the deflates) and university graduates who had previously worked in the civil service (the maitrisards) to start their own businesses. Because of a lack of training and follow-up, and the prevalence of clientelism in the disbursement of loans, the DIRE had a very poor record in terms of repayment and mortality of enterprises (32 percent). In addition, because the program's budget was administered through the public treasury, approximately $3 million was lost or "filtered" in the process. The beneficiaries were a relatively privileged group, and the projects funded included bookstores and travel agencies in central Dakar. In short, an enormous amount of resources for a country as poor as Senegal were squandered on privileged groups.

DIRE's poor record resulted in its gradual fading. Despite the program's initial high visibility, its effects on the political sustainability of adjustment were minimal: the program's image limited its impact on groups other than direct beneficiaries. Meanwhile, the program had little impact on poverty alleviation.

After a wave of civil unrest in February 1988, the government made another attempt to address the social costs of adjustment. It established the AGETIP program in conjunction with the World Bank. The AGETIP was influenced by the success of Bolivia's ESF, and it was also set up as an independent agency with a private sector director, in sharp contrast to the DIRE. The AGETIP responded to proposals from municipalities for labor-intensive infrastructure projects. In terms of efficiency and number of projects completed, the AGETIP has been remarkably successful. From its inception in 1990 to the end of 1991, the program implemented more than 100 projects and created more than 11,000 temporary jobs, primarily for unskilled urban youth. It has even been cited as a model for reforming the Senegalese public sector.

Yet the AGETIP is also influenced by politics. There is no arguing about reaching the poor and needy groups in Senegal, nor is there a cooperative relationship between the government and NGOs, which are the only organizations with extensive links to the poor. The AGETIP does not use poverty criteria to allocate its projects. In addition, as the opposition boycotted the 1990 municipal elections, the only proposals that the AGETIP funds are those from mayors of the governing party. While in some cases such proposals are directly related to poverty reduction, such as installing sewerage and water facilities, in others they may be pet projects of the mayor, such as renovating the town hotel. On the other hand, the agency does employ primarily its target group, unskilled youth, usually at below-market wages.

Because the AGETIP does not work with NGOs, it has very weak links to the poorest groups. There is a widespread popular perception that the AGETIP is "of the system" or a tool of the governing party. Thus its impact on the political sustainability of adjustment—at least among groups other than the governing party—has been limited. Its record on poverty alleviation is mixed: while it has provided a large number of temporary jobs and sorely needed infrastructure in poor areas, weak beneficiary participation has limited its potential in terms of project sustainability and capacity building.

In Senegal the debate over poverty has been subordinate to the interests of politically vocal groups. The slow pace of reform has given these groups much more opportunity to protect their privileged positions within the system. Meanwhile, the limited nature of political participation has generated a great deal of suspicion of government-sponsored initiatives—undoubtedly hampering the potential impact of the AGETIP.

Zambia

Zambia stands in sharp contrast to Senegal. Adjustment in Zambia was postponed for years under the United National Independence Party (UNIP) government, and many state benefits were linked to party membership. But the October 31, 1991 elections ushered in dramatic political change. Frederick Chiluba and the Movement for Multi-Party Democracy (MMD), which campaigned on a proadjustment platform, took more than 75 percent of the vote. Taking office, the government began to implement an economic strategy that favored free markets and made reaching the poorest and most vulnerable groups a priority. Because of the dramatic political change, groups that traditionally had privileged access to state resources found their influence reduced substantially. This shift allowed the government to focus its efforts on the poorest people. The sustainability of these changes will depend on the coherence of the MMD coalition and on how well previously marginalized groups can exercise an effective political voice.

The price policy for maize meal is telling. The heavily subsidized price of maize—which consumed more than 15 percent of government revenue—had been a political Achilles' heel for the Kaunda government. Repeated attempts to raise the price resulted in food riots—and even a coup attempt in 1990. The coupon system, intended to provide cheaper maize to poor groups, had become a tool of the UNIP party. Thus many of the poor were marginalized from the system and had to pay three to four times the official price of maize on the black market. When the Chiluba government liberalized the price of maize in December 1991—keeping subsidies on roller meal (the coarse grind that only the poorest eat)—there was no popular unrest. This calm resulted largely because the government publicly explained the measures and the need to allocate scarce resources to the most vulnerable groups. This policy differed greatly from that of the Kaunda government, which usually announced and carried out measures overnight. In addition, the Kaunda government was much more dependent for political support on entrenched interest groups with a stake in state subsidies. The dramatic political change and the pace of reform undermined the influence of these groups and allowed for greater focus on the poor.

Another telling contrast arises between SAPs under the two regimes. The Kaunda government's SAP was set up in 1990 as a catch-all social assistance program. The SAP was extremely slow getting off the ground, and it ultimately delivered few tangible social benefits. It was cumbersome because of its diffuse design and objectives, and blatant government attempts to manipulate it for political purposes. In contrast, the Social Recovery Fund (SRF) and Microprojects Unit (MPU) programs in Zambia, funded by the World Bank and the European Community, and run out of the government's National Development Planning Office, are good examples of programs that reach the needy rather than the privileged. The SRF and MPU, influenced by the ESF, respond to proposals from community organizations, mostly for renovation of infrastructure.[15] The programs require community contributions in cash or in labor. They have been successful in revitalizing the self-help spirit in many communities and in reaching remote areas long neglected by the state. While the programs were very small-scale during the Kaunda years, they grew substantially under the Chiluba government.

By giving communities contact with and a stake in a government poverty alleviation program, the SRF and MPU approach may enhance the political sustainability of economic reform and create a basis of support among previously marginalized but numerically significant groups.[16] In addition, its demand-based nature inherently encourages such groups to exercise their political voice—a choice unprecedented in Zambia, where a one-party state dominated for several decades. A significant drawback, however, is the small scale of the programs relative to the extensive poverty in Zambia (approximately 70 percent of the population lives below the poverty line). This gap prevents the programs from serving as a widespread safety net. A more positive element, however, which highlights the importance of the demonstrative effects of demand-based programs, is that the community contribution approach was incorporated on a much larger scale in the government's drought relief program. This program relied on food for work, provided relief on a major scale, and delivered services in a nonpartisan manner during the height of a severe drought in 1992–93.[17]

Safety Net Issues in Transition Economies

Safety net issues, particularly their political implications, vary tremendously in Eastern Europe and East Asia.[18] In the newly democratized and politically fragile countries of Eastern Europe, addressing safety net issues in the immediate term has particular political salience. East Asia places far less political urgency on safety net issues. Thus governments can focus more attention on reforming and creating longer-term social welfare institutions. With the exception of Mongolia, political reform in East Asia lags far behind economic reform. Also, in East Asia economic reform has entailed much less dislocation of the labor force. In Eastern Europe, in contrast, until short-term social welfare concerns are addressed, it is unlikely that any political consensus will develop on how to reform the region's extensive, but financially unsustainable social welfare institutions.

In Eastern Europe economic distortions and the predominance of the heavily industrial and state-owned sector of the economy left policymakers with no realistic alternatives to a big-bang approach to reform. This step included dismantling unsustainable state-owned industrial sectors and suffering severe declines in output. In most countries this approach entailed—or will entail—displacing large numbers of highly specialized workers and significant increases in poverty and unemployment. In societies that had traditionally espoused egalitarian values and supported an extensive state role in the provision of social welfare, these trends were politically explosive.

In addition to short-term safety net issues, these countries must reform their basic social welfare and social insurance systems. These systems are based on universal provision of services by the state, and they are no longer fiscally or operatively sustainable. Yet politically difficult and initially costly reforms of pension and health systems, for example, will be impossible until governments are able to alleviate public anxiety over increasing poverty and unemployment, and generate at least minimal societal consensus in favor of reform.

The implementation of short-term safety nets to protect the poor and vulnerable has become as much a political as an economic necessity in many countries. For example, pensioners and laid off or soon to be laid off public sector workers, who tend to be organized in politically powerful trade unions, have become major political opponents of reform. Their needs dominate the debate on social welfare, often at the expense of poorer and less vocal groups. As in other countries, the most vocal and organized groups are not necessarily the poorest and most vulnerable. This fact forces difficult choices for resource-strapped governments. Families with many children, for example, tend to form a much higher proportion of the poor than either pensioners or laid off workers, but families are rarely organized politically.[19] Political sustainability and poverty concerns will frame these choices. While this issue applies to many countries, it is particularly salient in this region because public sector unions are particularly well-organized and control strategic economic sectors.

Poland

In January 1990, soon after its inauguration, the first noncommunist government in Poland launched a dramatic, Bolivia-style stabilization and adjustment program. The program successfully stabilized hyperinflation. Yet political uncertainty soon stalled structural reforms, as several attempts to maintain a coherent government coalition in Parliament failed. Reforms such as privatization of state industrial conglomerates have been postponed. This delay has created an unsustainable drain on the state budget. The longer such reforms are postponed, the greater will be the anxiety about their potential social costs. Such anxiety increases political opposition to the adjustment program, despite the absence of any viable alternatives. This possibility was demonstrated by the December 1995 presidential elections: Lech Walesa was defeated by former communist Alexander Kwasniewski.

The rapidly increasing budget deficit makes it unviable for the government to maintain the current social welfare system. The system is based on universal free access to all benefits. Even prior to the collapse of public finances, the system was characterized by its poor quality services, unequal access, growing system of "informal" payments for services, and skewed incentive system. Among other negative effects, the incentive structure promotes premature retirement and excessive use of specialized care and emergency and hospital services. Such abuse creates dramatic shortages. Government insolvency coupled with the need to protect the poor and unemployed (whose numbers will increase in the future) dictate an immediate revamping of the social welfare system.

Proposed reform of the health and social security systems would guarantee basic health care and social security insurance for those in need. It would also introduce private providers and choice of services for those who could afford them. Such reform would alleviate the financial burden on the government and enhance service quality by introducing competition. At the same time government resources would be targeted to providing a safety net for the increasing number of poor and unemployed. Unemployment prior to 1990 in Poland was hidden by the maintenance of excess workers on government and industrial payrolls. But it now stands at roughly 15 percent and poverty at 14.4 percent of the population.[20] There is a clear need for programs that are more extensive than unemployment insurance. In Poland an effort across sectors, such as a social fund or Chilean-style public works, would be an ideal mechanism for improving employment and infrastructure, while giving impetus to municipal government development. Unfortunately, the political debate on the safety net lags far behind the proposals for reform, centering on emotional criticisms of government proposals rather than on realistic alternatives.

At the popular level there is widespread ignorance—and anxiety— about future social welfare. This problem stems from the incoherent debate and the government's past failure to explain the ongoing reform process to the public. Populist opposition movements have been quick to capitalize on this anxiety. By the summer of 1992, failure to adequately address the safety net issue and anxiety about the potential social costs of reform led to a series of industrial strikes. They virtually paralyzed the government, forcing it to make safety nets a priority. In September 1992 the government announced a social pact on the future of state enterprises. The pact was to be negotiated with unions and the private sector. While the government's new attempt to communicate its proposals to the public and to incorporate popular participation were first steps toward a realistic treatment of safety net and poverty issues, they were too little too late. The Suchocka government received a vote of no confidence in May 1993 because of the opposition's concern about the social costs of reform. The government's subsequent replacement with a coalition of former communists was a major setback for reform.

The delivery mechanisms for new forms of social assistance are severely underdeveloped. Elected local governments were only recently constituted, yet they have been given primary responsibility for providing benefits to the poor and unemployed. There are a host of unresolved issues about the nature of benefits, their delivery and financing, and about eligible beneficiaries. Without progress, the appeal of right- and left-wing strains of authoritarian populists has begun to rise. This surge is based on latent fears about social welfare, as was demonstrated by the 1995 election of a former communist. Failure to resolve the poverty and safety net issues threatens to derail the economic reform process and jeopardizes the democratic transition. Poland can learn a great deal from Latin American experiences with social funds, public works programs, and other safety nets. Attention to safety net issues is particularly important in the former socialist economies because democracy is very new, public understanding of market economics is very low, and anxiety about its social costs is very high.

Ukraine

Ukraine has launched one of the most recent efforts at macroeconomic reform in the former socialist economies. There are few places in the world where the need for reform is more evident; there are also few places where the political constraints are greater. Since independence in 1991, Ukraine's economy has been in a downward free-fall. This trend is in part due to the major economic downturn in Russia—Ukraine's most important trading partner. But, more, it is a result of incoherent macroeconomic management. Economic policy since independence has been politically driven in a context where democratic institutions are novel and fragile, and politicians are inexperienced and still committed to centrally planned economics (see Dabrowski 1994).

In 1993 Ukraine had an inflation rate of 4,735 percent—the highest of any country in the world not at war. The average wage deteriorated 80 percent between November 1991 and March 1994, and GDP declined 38 percent in 1990–93. The most recent manifestation of this decline was the outbreak of cholera in mid-1994. Poverty is increasing. Comprehensive data for 1993 are not available, but given inflation and wage trends, and benefits indexed to the minimum wage, it is evident that elderly pensioners on fixed incomes and families with many children are at risk. While estimates of the poverty headcount ratio for 1992 range from 12 percent to 29.35 percent, they are likely to be far too low when the latest trends are taken into account.[21] Social welfare and social insurance systems, meanwhile, are based on universal benefits. These benefits are administered through the state enterprise system, and they are for the most part insolvent. Thus the social systems are ill-equipped to cope

with increasing poverty and unemployment levels. Government transfers in 1992, for example, had a regressive effect on overall income distribution (Kakwani 1995). To date, the relatively widescale availability of
microplots in the Ukraine and an increasing reliance on self-production
for food have served as a safety net for many poor.

Reform attempts since independence have been stop-and-go in
character. While the collapse in production and the high inflation rate
are due to unsustainable macroeconomic distortions (such as a budget
deficit of 36 percent of GDP in 1992), most of the public, as well as the
nation's politicians attribute the collapse to market reforms.[22]

The extent and severity of Ukraine's economic crisis should come as
no surprise, given the unstable nature of the country's political institutions. Also, a central planning mentality is still pervasive at all levels.
There is no clear division of responsibilities between the executive and
the legislature, for example, and authority over the budget and credit
expansion is unclear. As a result, inflation has been driven primarily by
expansion of the fiscal deficit and expansion of credit by the semi-inde-
pendent central bank, the National Bank of Ukraine (NBU), although
there have been some attempts at monetary restraint.[23] Political instability and increases in the money supply are strongly correlated. The
executive often tries to restrain credit expansion in the early half of the
year, but a few months later Parliament completes its budgetary review
and dramatically increases the deficit.[24] In addition, the public has little understanding of the fiscal crisis. This knowledge gap is exacerbated by the government, which continues to provide public services virtually free of charge, despite the obvious inflationary implications.
Public services such as buses and telephones continue to operate for
free, for example, because the coins that are used as payment have
become worthless with hyperinflation. Electricity and fuel, meanwhile,
are heavily subsidized—and are in extremely short supply.

Meanwhile, the pension system is completely insolvent. Its implicit
debt, not accounting for new entrants into the system, is more than 200
percent of GDP—putting it among the highest such debts in the world
(Kane and Morissot 1993). The state also continues to provide "solutions" to the crisis. The Employment Fund, for example, subsidizes
worker retraining in state enterprises without any clear indication of
future demand for the skills the enterprises are providing. The payroll
tax, from which the Employment Fund's activities are funded, is the
highest in the world.

In other countries in transition a public sense of the economic crisis
has been a key factor in enabling the implementation of difficult
reforms. In Ukraine there is a clear need for a public relations and education campaign. People must be educated about the implications of
further postponing reform and about market economics.

October 1994 marked a turning point for Ukraine. Newly elected President Kuchma introduced a coherent stabilization and adjustment program. The program had the firm backing of the international community, the World Bank and the International Monetary Fund in particular. President Kuchma made a major effort to sell the plan to the Parliament and the public. He presented it as the only solution at a time of dire national crisis. He said that the alternative to rapid and dramatic reform was for Ukraine to fall permanently behind the rest of the world. He called for dialogue with the relevant actors, such as state enterprise unions and business associations. He also called for the implementation of targeted social assistance programs to protect the poor and vulnerable, whom he correctly identified as elderly pensioners and families with many children.

The Parliament's initial reactions toward the reform package were favorable, and it approved the plan by a vote of 231 to 54 on October 19 (Intelnews 1994). But support soon dissipated as the social costs of the needed price liberalization policies became evident. The socialist and communist parties, which hold a majority of the seats in Parliament, immediately began to criticize the plan as "wild west capitalism," which would impoverish the masses and make Ukraine subservient to international institutions. Unions had initially agreed to a six-month moratorium on strikes, but they broke that agreement, beginning with a prolonged strike in one of the most strategic industries: coal mining.

With the backing of external donors, the government raised allowances and other supplements, such as housing for those with less than a minimum income or less than a minimum pension, as a safety net. The number of eligible people was expected to increase as real incomes eroded further with price rises. From a technical standpoint this was a good short-term safety net strategy: the allowance system functions reasonably well, and targeting it is the only financially viable way of making allowances large enough to protect the poor.

Yet there is clearly a need for a more visible safety net, for political reasons and as a means to cope with increasing numbers of long-term unemployed. A social fund would be a visible means of providing necessary income relief and socially useful infrastructure; it would play an even more important role in encouraging autonomous community initiatives and stimulating local institutional development. Meanwhile, public works employment could be administered through such a fund or through the Employment Fund. The Employment Fund already has a legal mandate to implement public works. To date, it has acted only on a small scale, mainly because of lack of experience. Participants have been primarily women and unemployed youth, indicating that more skilled workers are finding better opportunities in the informal sector. It also indicates that public works would be a good means to target needy and vulnerable groups, and people who can not find alternative employment. These efforts could be funded by the Employment Fund's current budget surplus, which has been losing value because of inflation. Only recently was the fund placed in an interest-bearing account.

The political sustainability of reform in Ukraine hinges on the government's ability to communicate and sell the reform to the public, especially to assuage fears about its social costs (as well as protect the truly needy). More visible social assistance programs, such as those implemented in many of the above case studies, could be an important part of this process. The political moment is both opportune and critical for such an effort.

East Asia

The main social welfare issues in East Asia differ markedly from those in Eastern Europe. In East Asia the state-owned industrial sector is much smaller relative to the overall economy, and the agrarian sector is large, fairly unequal, and labor-intensive. Thus the primary concern in the transition has been the development of the private economy, beginning with reform and productivity increases in the agrarian sector. In addition, the East Asian economies began from much lower levels of income and state social service provision.

Reforms have created pockets of poverty and increased inequality, particularly in Mongolia, where the state's role in social welfare provision was the most extensive. Yet, in general, reform and the resulting increases in economic growth and agricultural productivity have been welfare-enhancing for most of the population, including many of the rural poor (Thomas and Wang 1994). In all three cases studied here—China, Mongolia, and Vietnam—reforms began in the agricultural sector. Reform of state-owned industries proceeded at different paces in the three countries, but in all they affect a small percentage of workers, who were privileged relative to the rest of the labor force. Of the three countries, only Mongolia has introduced widescale political liberalization along with economic reform. Thus the political salience of social welfare issues related to reform is much lower in East Asia, particularly in Vietnam and China, than in most Eastern Europe transition economies.

Yet East Asia needs effective safety nets for vulnerable groups—female-headed households in Mongolia (see Subbarao and Ezemenari 1995); single and elderly pensioners, and the very poor in rural Vietnam; and the aging rural population in China. More generally, widespread poverty remains a major concern. In part, poverty will be eased by sustained growth, but growth must be complemented with more broadly based and equitable social services and social insurance systems, in addition to safety nets. In the longer term the major social welfare issue is the creation of effective institutions to protect social welfare and provide social insurance in both public and private sectors of the economy. There are public systems in all three countries, but they serve only a small proportion of the labor force, and they are administratively fragmented and financially unsustainable. The minimal coverage of these systems suggests that the political obstacles to reforming them are far less formidable than those in the universal Eastern European schemes.

Politics of Safety Nets: Some Generalizations

Temporary social assistance programs implemented during economic reform can reduce poverty and help to sustain economic reform and transition. They are also much less likely to arouse political opposition than more obvious, long-term asset transfers, such as land reform. Such transfers are rarely attempted in the context of economic reform.[25] Yet the success of such programs hinges on, among other things, transparency and securing the participation of the poor, thereby enhancing their economic potential and political influence. A program's ability to perform in such a manner on a large scale depends on available resources, institutional structure, and commitment from the highest levels to insulate it from partisan pressures—a commitment present in Bolivia, not fully clear in Mexico, and clearly missing in Peru. In the countries where these conditions were absent, targeting, cost-effectiveness, the impact of the programs on incentives, the manner and speed of implementation, and, ultimately, program sustainability were affected more strongly by politics. Such conditions force greater trade-offs between political objectives and poverty reduction objectives.

To a certain extent the political leadership in Bolivia was the exception rather than the rule. But even there, the ESF was not able to reach the poorest. Indications are that other demand-based programs, such as the AGETIP in Senegal and the PRONASOL program in Mexico, have not been able to either (Moguel 1990). In some countries, such as Senegal, the authoritarian and clientelist nature of the party and local government structures serve as additional constraints to reaching the poorest sectors.

There is no empirically established link between democracy and serving the poor, however. Even in democracies the poor usually lack a political voice in addition to resources. Ironically, of the cases covered here the Pinochet regime had the most success in targeting the poorest groups. Presumably, the regime could target successfully because it did not have the political constraints of a democratic regime, namely, having to answer to the more vocal middle class. On the other hand, a broader view of poverty reduction would include the poor's participation in designing their own solutions. Such a view might place less value on the ability to target the poorest compared with the program's ability to incorporate the participation of disadvantaged groups, even if they are not the poorest. Meanwhile, raising beneficiary participation may enhance their political voice and their economic potential, and therefore increase the likelihood that resource shifts in their direction are politically sustainable. Many projects, such as new schools or health posts, also have indirect positive effects on poorer groups that do not participate in project design. And reaching the poorest groups may require a separate set of policies from those used to reach the rest of the poor.[26] Targeting can entail high costs in terms of time and resources. In this light the success or failure of demand-based programs hinges more on their ability to generate autonomous grass roots participation than on reaching the poorest groups.

Institutional autonomy and positioning of social assistance programs are issues in many countries. On the one hand, autonomy allows for rapid, transparent action that bypasses public sector bureaucratic procedures (which are often costly and time-consuming), reduces administrative costs, and directly channels benefits to the poor. On the other hand, there is the issue of longevity of extra-institutional social assistance programs; neither their budgets nor their operating procedures have any permanent guarantees. If such programs are considered short-term measures during periods of adjustment or recovery, then institutional autonomy is less of a concern. If they are considered longer-term complements to social sector policies, then it is usually necessary to establish institutional links.

Institutional development plays a key role in determining the appropriate kind of program and its delivery mechanism. Chile and Costa Rica, for example, both had a tradition of efficient public social sectors and strong propoor political parties; these countries could implement safety net policies through existing public sector institutions. In Bolivia, on the other hand, such institutions were notoriously weak, and the only means to launch a widescale effort with relative speed was to bypass them altogether.

The ability of governments to communicate their reform policies has an important impact on how they are received politically, as the cases of Peru and Zambia demonstrate. This same ability may facilitate redirecting resources to the poor. This was clearly the case in Zambia. The contrasting case of Poland demonstrates how the failure to communicate can result in political stalemate and heightened popular anxiety.

Notes

1. This chapter draws from Graham (1992, 1995). At relevant places, the contributions from Marc, Graham, Schacter, and Schmidt (1995), Milanovic (forthcoming), Kakwani (1995), and Subbarao and Ezemenari (1995) are acknowledged.

2. A caveat must be mentioned: several nondemocratic regimes, such as Chile and Indonesia, have some of the best records at implementing propoor policies. This is the case if propoor policies are narrowly defined as basic service provision, but not if they are more broadly defined as fostering the independent capacity-building initiatives that are integral to long-term poverty reduction (Stewart and van der Geest 1994).

3. Even in authoritarian Chile, an active and very effective public relations campaign—in support of so-called "capitalism popular"—was used to generate public support for the privatization of the social security system, which was initially an extremely controversial policy measure, but now has relatively widespread support.

4. For discussion of the political constraints to targeting without including the participation of beneficiaries, see Gelbach and Pritchett (1995).

5. For more details on this case, see Graham (1992) or Jorgensen, Grosh, and Schacter (1992).

6. The ESF's successor, the Fundo Investment Sociale (FIS), attempted to affect the social sector ministries more directly by requiring all projects to go to the ministries prior to approval. If the ministries delayed for more than a week, however, they forfeited their right to have input on project decisions.

7. The "neutral" political effects of demand-based funds also depend on an executive commitment to allow actors of diverse political bents to compete freely for projects. This was clearly the case with the ESF. In Sucre, for example, the largest recipient of ESF funds for health projects was an NGO affiliated with the Marxist left—hardly a supporter of the "neoliberal" Paz Estenssoro government (Graham 1992).

8. Tin miners were granted relatively generous one-shot severance payments when they were laid off.

9. It is somewhat difficult to accurately quantify PRONASOL's budget, as some money may have been diverted from what would previously have been social sector spending. See Dresser (1991) and Golden (1992).

10. Administrative costs were approximately 5 percent of total costs.

11. The framework for the PRONASOL program is detailed in his Ph.D. dissertation. For details, see Grayson (1991).

12. Dresser (1991:15). Community labor and programs to encourage children to go to school have been implemented in Mexico for decades. See Knight (1992).

13. For details on these relations, see Fox (1992) and Craig (1992).

14. A case in point is the withholding of benefits from the *tortivales* program from 48 Mexico City municipalities where the opposition was particularly active (Dresser 1991). For details see Fox (1992) and Craig (1992).

15. The proposals must go through local governments to prevent duplication and to ensure that they are in line with local government priorities. To prevent bureaucratic lags, however, the proposals are simultaneously sent directly to the MPU. Thus if a viable proposal seems to be unfairly held up in or denied by the local government, the MPU is able to follow up on it.

16. As in the case of most demand-based programs, communities participate on a voluntary basis. The project includes a promotion department, which informs communities about the program and provides some initial assistance with formulating proposals. To ensure that projects do not conflict with local government priorities, communities must also get approval from local governments during the course of submitting a proposal. And in considering proposals, the program seeks to attain a regional and provincial balance.

17. The food-for-work program was extended beyond the crisis period. At that point partisan political objectives seemed to override those of encouraging community contribution and participation, and the program began to operate far less effectively (Graham 1995).

18. Here, Eastern Europe refers to the European states of the former Soviet Union, not those of Central Asia.

19. See Milanovic (forthcoming). In contrast, as Leszek Balcerowicz stated in his presentation describing the situation in Poland at the November conference in Prague, "pensioners have a great deal of time to organize."

20. Some estimates for poverty in Poland, even by the same author, are higher and place the headcount ratio at 26 percent. The lower estimate uses the minimum pension as the poverty line, the higher one a poverty line of $4 per day, which is much higher than the World Bank's $1-per-day definition of poverty across countries. For details on Poland, see Milanovic (1994).

21. For details on the lower estimate, see Milanovic (1994) and Kakwani (1995). Kakwani uses the 29 percent figure to estimate that 16.88 percent of the people were ultrapoor in 1992.

22. For an account of economic "myths" that are pervasive in the public psyche, see Kaufmann (1994).

23. But absent fiscal restraint, these have been ineffective. As in many countries of the former Soviet Union, the central bank is independent of the executive but subordinate to the Parliament.

24. For details see Dabrowski (1994).

25. This point has been raised by Nelson (1992) and by Haggard (1991).

26. Participatory strategies are likely to have difficulty reaching the poorest of the poor. The constraints they face often range from hunger to mental illness and drug addiction (Lipton 1988).

9
Choosing and Designing Programs

Social assistance and poverty-targeted programs have had varying degrees of success in different countries. Many countries are attempting to reform existing poverty-targeted programs in response to changing economic and political conditions. Others are introducing new programs. The results of this study confirm that, aside from appropriate program choice, program design and delivery are key to successfully and efficiently reaching the poor. Seven principal lessons emerge from cross-country experience:

- The design and delivery of a program can significantly alter its outcome in favor of the poor and particular subsets of the poor who are often inadequately served by some safety nets (poor women, for example). Countries as diverse as Bangladesh, Jamaica, and Mongolia have adopted innovative designs, delivery mechanisms, and administrative procedures to stimulate participation of the poor. But in regions where the poor are overrepresented, direct poverty-targeted programs alone may not reduce the severity of poverty.
- Maintaining low program costs (as a percentage of the total budget) ensures a program's sustainability. Fiscal imperatives vary by regions. They are of paramount importance in transition countries because of the severity of fiscal contractions there. But it is important not to dilute critical transfers (family assistance and social assistance) in attempt to reduce fiscal deficits. It is also important to ensure that maintaining core safety net transfers does not induce changes that are harmful to the poor, especially in sectors that are critical for long-term poverty reduction, such as primary health care and education. For the countries in transition the critical challenge is to avoid pressures from established lobbies (such as pensioners) that are cornering a larger share of a smaller (transfer) cake at the expense of the new poor (such as the working poor, children, and single-parent families with many children). Transparency (moving from off-budget to on-budget) and decentralization are good in

theory, but the danger that protecting the poor may become nobody's business is very real. This danger is already apparent in relatively poorer countries of Eastern Europe and the former Soviet Union, where the responsibility for social assistance is being transferred to local authorities who have scant resources.

- In all programs generally, and in credit programs particularly, keeping transaction costs low is important in order to avoid eroding the net value of transfers. Thus credit programs that have attempted to subsidize interest rates have not been successful because they have led to market distortions—resulting in higher transaction costs for the borrower.

- On- and off-budget housing and energy subsidies in Eastern Europe and the former Soviet Union, and open general subsidies in Africa, Asia, and Latin America have proven unsustainable, apart from being inefficient and distortionary. Targeting, within the boundaries of political feasibility, is critical. Some countries have resorted to targeting these transfers, especially in Eastern Europe and the former Soviet Union. But the targeting mechanism adopted has not always been appropriate to the country and the type of program. Also, in most cases the choice of a particular targeting mechanism has not sufficiently accounted for the size of the target group (relative to the total population) and the information constraints.

- Universal food subsidies are fiscally unsustainable and distortionary. Targeting, therefore, is necessary for sustainable and cost-effective programs. While self-targeted approaches are politically more acceptable, country experiences point to other ways of targeting that tie the transfer to an obligation from recipients without excessive increases in transaction costs.

- All social assistance transfers generate incentive costs. It is often difficult to measure these costs empirically. Yet it is important to be aware of the behavioral changes triggered by transfer programs that raise programs' real economic costs. The best way to minimize incentive costs is to keep the amount of transfers modest.

- The political environment and opposing interests of various political coalitions ultimately determine programs' political acceptance and continuity. The poor may actually lose from too much fine tuning in targeting. In certain countries self-targeted approaches may be more cost-effective than finely targeted approaches, even if the former may not prevent leakage completely.

In addition to the above the book showed that in most countries the choice of programs was closely tied to two factors: the type of programs already existing and fiscal constraints. Also, program choice based solely on these two factors (without considering the nature of poverty and other country-specific constraints) led to inefficient design and delivery.

A Framework for Choosing among Programs

Three factors are key to the choice of programs: the extent and nature of poverty, the mix of existing programs, and country-specific constraints or conditions, including growth prospects, policy reforms, and socioeconomic and infrastructure constraints.

The Extent and Nature of Poverty

A clear understanding of the nature of poverty is usually the starting point for choosing a new program or revamping an existing one. Several questions must be addressed. Is poverty a permanent, structural problem (chronic poverty) or a temporary problem of insufficient income (transient poverty)? Which types of households are likely to be chronically poor or transient-poor, and why? Estimates of the depth and severity of poverty provide useful information for the type of program chosen.[1]

Characteristics unique to the poor also inform program choice. These traits include income and expenditure characteristics, income sources and variability, and the pattern of asset ownership; labor market characteristics; demographic characteristics, including the correlation of poverty with gender, age, fertility, and household composition; the geographic or ethnic concentration of the poor; and indicators of living standards, such as the poor's mortality, nutritional status, and literacy, and the extent of the poor's access to social services.

The nature of poverty should determine the objectives to be sought from programs. Three primary target groups and objectives are:

- For those who are able to work but whose incomes are low and irregular: income and consumption smoothing in slack seasons, or more regular livelihood creation.
- For those who are unable to provide for themselves through work (such as the handicapped): long-term assistance.
- For those capable of earning adequate incomes, but cannot earn temporarily because of shocks (such as economic reform or transition): short-term assistance, public works, and/or income generation programs.

Experience with Existing Programs

The choice of a program usually depends on a country's historical circumstances. Rarely is a social assistance program chosen in a vacuum. Most often, the country has made previous attempts to address poverty among specific groups or in the country as a whole.

Some countries are seeking to reform social protection systems—often because of increasing fiscal pressure and renewed concerns about social equity. In some cases programs that once functioned effectively no longer meet increased needs or changed country conditions. It is imperative that program choice is based on an evaluation of existing programs, their cost, and their effectiveness in reaching the poor.

Previous experience with social assistance and poverty interventions can either help or hinder effective program choice and design. For example, countries that have inherited extensive systems of old-age assistance may find that their elderly are relatively well-protected, but their children are vulnerable to poverty. Reforming this system might be difficult because the elderly form a strong lobby and may not be willing to see their entitlements reduced. Sometimes, there are common misperceptions about poverty that may not be supported by a poverty profile. Programs designed in response to misconceived public opinion would fail to reach the truly disadvantaged.

Country-Specific Constraints or Conditions

Country-specific constraints or conditions strongly influence the choice of program. These variables include infrastructure constraints; administrative constraints, including the capacity to identify, reach,

Table 9.1. Stylized Illustrations of Poverty, Country Conditions, and Program Choice

Who are the poor?	Why are they poor?
Rural landless and small holders, unorganized labor (poverty predominantly rural), urban poor.	Low agricultural productivity, high income variability, low education and skills, lack of assets.
Smallholders, urban poor, and unemployed.	Low agricultural productivity, inadequate rural credit, low education and skills.
Urban working poor, old and infirm without support, orphans and disabled children.	Economic shock (transition), sharp contraction of economic activity, contraction of public social protection expenditures.
Young families with children.	Younger workers have less seniority and less pay, demographic profile of the population tilted in favor of young families.
Women.	Discrimination in the labor market, child care responsibilities, discrimination in educational opportunities, problems with access to credit.

and monitor beneficiaries, the strength of institutions, and delivery mechanisms; political constraints; and macroeconomic conditions and the associated fiscal constraints.

An important country characteristic is the buoyancy of private safety nets (informal, interfamily, and intrafamily transfers). Such informal transfers are found not only in low-income countries in Asia and Africa, but also in some economies in transition.

If properly chosen, programs can complement economic growth and informal transfers. If not properly chosen and designed, programs can exacerbate country-specific constraints, crowd out growth-promoting investments and private safety nets, and make long-term escape from poverty difficult. Thus it is important to relate program choice to desired objectives and the nature of poverty, with a clear understanding of the potential constraints and trade-offs.

Using hypothetical country situations, we can outline the most desirable program choices (table 9.1). For example, in countries with a high incidence of rural poverty, where it is difficult to separate needy from nonneedy households, cash transfers will be infeasible both in terms of targeting and fiscal sustainability. Many African countries fall into this category. In this situation programs that feature a work

Country conditions	Program choice
Inadequate infrastructure—physical (roads), social (schools), and financial (banks or other formal credit agencies). High level of malnutrition, widespread rural poverty, and food insecurity.	Public works at market wages for unskilled labor, targeted nutrition programs in both rural and urban areas, carefully designed food transfers.
Economic reform is in progress, farm markets and urban industry being deregulated, exchange rate reform is in progress.	Urban employment programs, targeted food transfers, credit-based livelihood programs, severance payments where needed.
Country under transition/shock /adjustment, high inflation, and unemployment.	Targeted cash transfers, if information base is strong. Public employment programs.
Economies in transition.	Child allowances , child care facilities, especially if family size and poverty are strongly correlated.
Sociocultural norms, slow growth, widespread poverty, a high proportion of women and children in poverty.	Microcredit for female entrepreneurs, child care facilities, social assistance for single-parent families/widows/ other sharply identified vulnerable groups.

requirement (such as public works) may be more appropriate. Cash transfers are more feasible in countries where the poor are relatively few and are easily identified and reached. Where poverty is mostly rural, income variability high, and infrastructure inadequate, public works in slack seasons are appropriate. Where poverty is concentrated among the urban poor, targeted food transfers and temporary urban employment programs (urban public works) may be necessary. In transition countries or those experiencing sudden shocks, targeted cash transfers can work only if the information base is strong enough. Where information gaps are large but poverty is strongly correlated with family size, untargeted cash transfers—such as family allowances (already prevailing in transition countries)—can be as effective as a safety net.

While these considerations enable us to broadly determine which programs are most appropriate, the issue of program design is still crucial. In focusing on design, it is useful to consider two sets of principles: those generic to all programs and those that are program-specific.

Appropriate Program Design

A few generic design principles are pertinent to all programs.

- Private transfers are pervasive in most developing countries. These transfers may not necessarily be redistributive in nature. In fact, in some countries the poor often help the poor. Nonetheless, public transfers will greatly diminish in utility if they crowd out private transfers. It is not clear how a public transfer can be designed so as not to reduce at least some private transfers. Transfers involving work requirements may be more suitable in countries with pervasive private transfers. In countries where sharing food is very common (as in Mongolia), publicly supported food transfers may not be appropriate, except for the destitute. Similarly, in some countries harnessing community support is critical for targeted food and nutrition programs.

- Behavioral responses to public transfers must be factored in when choosing and designing a program, as they may inflate the real (economic) cost of transfer programs. A public works program with a relatively high wage rate might pull participants away from market-driven (farm) activities, thus contributing to rationing—and reducing the poverty impact. Such behavioral responses can also occur even if the transfers are made in cash. A means-tested cash transfer may reduce labor supply at the margin.

- Transfer programs must deal with the problem of fungibility of money. The degree of fungibility may vary across program types.

Thus it is important to allow for the possibility that the beneficiary may not use the entire transfer for the intended purpose. Considering that households are basically rational, such a diversion of money for consumption smoothing may not be entirely inappropriate, even if the overall impact of a credit program on livelihood generation may not be fully realized.

- In most targeted programs identifying the poorest is probably a bigger problem than including the nonpoor. There is a trade-off between minimizing exclusion errors and minimizing inclusion errors. Program conditions should not be so stringent that they result in the poorest self-selecting themselves out of the program.

- Most developing countries are fiscally strapped. To this extent, transfers that complement economic growth impose a lower implicit burden on the tax payer than do others. It is useful to rank transfers in the order of their complementarity with growth-promoting activities, and pick the ones with the closest interface. In this way greater cost-effectiveness can be achieved, in addition to reducing the need for distortionary taxes.

- For some programs it is important to pretest demand. Consider what happens if this is not done for a credit-based livelihood program. If, without pretesting, credit is advanced to two poor households to start a bullock cart business in a village, and if there is already one bullock cart owner in that village earning an income slightly above the poverty threshold, the credit program would only cut into the profits of that owner. The result is a classic zero-sum game—the village will now have three households in poverty instead of two.

Country experience reviewed in previous chapters suggests that certain country-specific design features ensure that a program has a better chance of reaching the poor cost-effectively. For each of the four major groups of programs, the pros and cons, and the most desirable design features that can produce the expected outcomes are discussed below.

Cash Transfers

Without the right level of administrative capacity, any form of income-targeted social assistance is open to potential abuse. Targeting social assistance toward the poor who are identified by a standard other than income or assets reduces the need for sophisticated administration and could be effective if there is a strong correlation between poverty and the group chosen. It does, however, increase the risk of leakage and the risk of not reaching all the poor. Cross-country experience highlights the advantages and disadvantages of cash transfer programs. It also points to some general lessons regarding these programs:

- Where programs are relatively small and the poorest are easily identifiable, cash transfers are an effective means of providing poverty
relief.
- In transition economies where poverty ratios have risen to exceptionally high levels, cash social assistance has a limited role. Means
tests to limit coverage will improve program effectiveness.
- In transition countries where poverty ratios are not high, cash social
assistances is necessary, but must be targeted. If family size is
strongly correlated with poverty, it is best to target assistance to
families with children. Where the number of children in a household does not reflect its welfare position and where information
gaps are formidable, it is best to consider alternatives to cash social
assistance, rather than administer costly and often ineffective means
tests.
- Cash transfers can lead to adverse labor supply decisions.

Since destitute children are universally recognized as acceptable
poor, there is less political resistance for family assistance transfers. As
a universal benefit, family assistance provides a decent income-
smoothing mechanism. Family assistance is typically provided as a
universal benefit without consideration of family income. But then a
significant portion of program benefits go to the nonpoor. This distribution mechanism often proves to be fiscally unstable. Some countries
have attempted to income test family assistance and quickly found this
onerous. If introduced in a country with social assistance, the value of
the transfer must be sufficient to place a family with children on equal
financial footing with a childless family. The administration of family
assistance is wasted if the family still has to rely on social assistance to
bring them out of poverty.

The key lesson from cross-country experience is that this program is
most appropriate when there is a strong correlation between poverty
and family size. Where family size does not adequately reflect the
household's welfare position, it is best to target on the basis of household characteristics (in addition to income). Where information gaps
on household characteristics are pervasive, alternatives to family
allowance should be considered, in particular transfers with a work
requirement, or other programs, such as targeted nutrition
interventions.

In designing programs, the following steps might help:

- Consider all possible targeting mechanisms, such as self-assessment
and geographical targeting, and use individual assessment only if
other methods do not identify the target group correctly. The scope
for self-selection and geographical targeting must be considered
first as filters so as to circumvent the need for individual
assessment.

- When targeting by individual assessment, assets can be included among the criteria if they are verifiable. Otherwise, look for expenditure patterns that will exclude the nonpoor from the program on the basis of ownership of land, a car, or some other commodity, and inclusion of the poor on the basis of household characteristics, such as female headship.
- Consider regional variations, particularly in large countries. Urban and rural or different rural areas may warrant variations in either the poverty line or in the treatment of income and assets.
- All cash transfers can create poverty traps and give rise to difficult trade-offs. In designing programs, especially consider the administrative cost of more refined targeting relative to cost of leakage, the disincentives to work relative to the cost of leakage, the level of the poverty line relative to value of required cash transfers, and information gaps and administrative capacity.

Food Transfers

Food transfers have been by far the most popular in-kind transfer in many developing countries. Evidence from previous chapters strongly suggests that universal food transfers are not financially sustainable, although they may be politically desirable. More recently, countries are using innovative targeting means to reach the poor, while minimizing leakage. Nutrition (direct feeding and food supplementation) programs, unlike other food transfer programs, provide limited income gains. Instead, these programs are intended for easily identifiable, high-risk individuals (preschoolers and mothers). Three key lessons are derived from country experience:
- Untargeted food transfers—whatever the form—are bound to be fiscally unsustainable, and should be avoided.
- Approaches that impose an obligation on the part of the recipient (such as a labor or time requirement) are best in screening out the nonneedy. But such obligations should not be so onerous that they raise significant transaction costs.
- Though administration-intensive, food transfers targeted to women and children, along with other services (such as immunization), can be a very effective means of supporting the poor with minimal distortions, provided communities are involved and the approach is demand-driven.

The choice and design of the program can be suitably adjusted to ensure efficient targeting, while accounting for country-specific conditions and minimizing adverse incentives. For example, food stamps have been known to perpetrate disincentives to work and cause other kinds of consumption distortions at the margin. This type of program works best if its benefits are linked to some obligation. The exact nature of that obligation may differ from country to country. Good design features should incorporate these considerations.

Public Works

Public works have been adopted as an important countercyclical intervention in many countries. They usually involve a transfer, either in cash or in-kind, in exchange for labor. If they create socially useful infrastructure, public works also complement economic growth. But if provisions are not in place to ensure that quality assets are created and maintained, these programs are not cost-effective. One merit of public works is that they are flexible and could be expanded or contracted as needed. They thus have relevance in transition countries or in countries emerging from conflict. The potential for self-targeting by fixing wages no higher than those for unskilled labor makes public works an attractive option where it is not possible to identify the truly needy. But minimum wage regulations may make it impossible to fix public works wages at an appropriate level. Further, foregone earnings can reduce the overall gain from public works programs. It must be remembered that public works are essentially a temporary safety net and should never be used as a permanent escape route from poverty. Cross-country experience points to the following lessons:
- Public works have proved to be a very effective means of consumption smoothing for poor households.
- Improved targeting can be achieved through various methods: self-targeting through type of work, form of payment, and level of wage; targeting of women through piece rates, location of work, provision of daycare; and targeting of regions adversely affected by shocks (geographic targeting).
- Program wages should be close to prevailing market wages for unskilled labor to minimize labor market distortions.
- Careful attention should be given to the quality of assets created and their maintenance to improve program cost-effectiveness.

Although the design of public works programs vary a great deal across countries, depending on the mode of transfer used, duration and timing of employment, and the extent of private sector involvement, the design features contributing to the success of public works programs are fairly consistent across countries.

The most important design element is the determination of the wage rate. In addition, a number of other design features can increase the gains to the poor. Tendering discreet public employment activities to private contractors or organizers of works is certainly conducive to efficiency. It avoids much bureaucratization (especially competition between line departments), apart from ensuring that only market wages (and not above-market wages) are paid to laborers. Timing the program in the slack seasons; offering piece rates in some situations (a large family can share the work); providing task-based wage payments (especially for women, who can then dovetail their work with chores at home); and providing basic amenities to workers at work sites are some other features that may contribute to the effectiveness of these programs.

Another critical design aspect is how to minimize transaction costs for the poor. Properly enforced piece rates are one approach. Further, peer monitoring by workers themselves is important for avoiding leakage to program administrators. Encouraging grass roots pressure groups is probably the only way to prevent abuse. In a World Bank project in Mongolia a mechanism for such monitoring is built into the design of the program.

The form in which wages should be paid—cash or food—has been much debated. Food has advantages, especially during droughts, provided it is made available to workers through several different retailers (as it occurred in Botswana) and not through a government monopoly agency. Payment of wages in food brought more women to work sites in Zambia.

Credit Programs

Credit programs aim at improving the poor's access to financial resources by providing subsidized or unsubsidized loans, often without the need for collateral. Some credit programs also provide other financial services (such as savings facilities) in addition to loans. Credit programs promote self-employment through income-generating activities in the informal sector and could thus complement economic growth. They are particularly relevant in economies with high unemployment or underemployment, and where there is little scope for expanding public sector employment. They have been undertaken in response to transitional poverty resulting from economic shocks or natural disasters, and to address chronic poverty in low-growth situations. Most credit programs aim to provide an income stream over the medium term. But unlike other social assistance programs, credit programs require high, specialized levels of financial and managerial capacity. In addition, since credit is fungible, the funds may be used for purposes other than that for which they were intended. Even the most successful credit programs have had only a modest record in reaching the ultrapoor.

To maximize the participation of the poor and ensure sustainability, the design of any credit program must determine how to minimize transaction costs both for the lender and the borrower, how to reduce covariate risks, how to rationally select target groups, and how to build performance incentives for program managers. Cross-country experience suggest four key lessons:

- Reduce transaction costs for the poor by simplifying loan processing procedures to avoid delays and repeat visits. Where necessary, subsidize transaction costs, not interest rates.
- Do not rely on program-manager (bureaucrat), income-based identification of potential beneficiaries. Rather, rely on communities, NGOs, and other local groups.
- Promote saving as an integral part of the program.
- Reduce covariate risks to borrowers and lenders through group lending, small loans, repeat loans to those who promptly repay, and so on.

Conclusion

There is no formula for providing the best or most appropriate program for a particular country. This book has attempted to provide guidance on what to consider when developing more effective and efficient programs, and to point out the pitfalls to be avoided and the positive features to be enhanced. We have brought together some of the best practices and worst examples, and asked the questions: what makes programs work well and how could they be made to work even better? Passing on that experience, it is hoped, should help improve many publicly funded safety net programs all over the world.

Note

1. "Incidence" refers to the number of poor (individuals with incomes below the poverty line). "Depth" refers to the average income shortfall (from the poverty line), of those who are poor. "Severity" refers to how far the income of the poorest fall below the poverty line. This last measure accounts for the distribution of income among the poor (Lipton and Ravallion 1995). Poverty is considered "shallow" when most of the poor are clustered close to the poverty line, in which case the severity of poverty is low.

References

Abel-Smith, B. 1979. "Income Testing of In-Kind Transfers." In Garfinkel, ed., *Income-Tested Transfer Programs: The Case for and Against*. New York: Academic Press.

Acharya, S., V. P. Panwalker, A. Rea, and R. Falk. 1988. "The Employment Guarantee Scheme in Maharashtra: Impact on Male and Female Labor." Regional Research Paper. The Population Council, Bangkok.

Adelman, I., K. Subbarao, and P. Vashishta. 1985. "Some Dynamic Aspects of Rural Poverty in India." *Economic and Political Weekly* 20(39): A103–16.

Agarwal, B. 1991. "Social Security and the Family: Coping with Seasonality and Calamity in Rural India." In E. Ahmad, J. Dreze, J. Hills, and A. Sen, eds., *Social Security in Developing Countries*. Oxford: Clarendon Press.

Ahmad, E., and A. Hussain. 1991. "Social Security in China: A Historical Perspective." In E. Ahamd, J. Dreze, J. Hills, and A. Sen eds., *Social Security in Developing Countries*. Oxford: Clarendon Press.

Ahmed, A., and K. Billah. 1994. "Food for Education in Bangladesh: An Early Assessment." International Food Policy Research Institute, Washington D.C.

Ahmed, R. 1988. "Structure, Costs, and Benefits of Food Subsidies in Bangladesh." In P. Pinstrup-Andersen, ed., *Food Subsidies in Developing Countries: Costs, Benefits, and Policy Options*. Baltimore, Md.: Johns Hopkins University Press.

Ahmed, R. and C. Donovan. 1992. *Issues of Infrastructural Development: A Synthesis of the Literature*. Washington D.C.: International Food Policy Research Institute.

Ahsan, S. M., and S. Khandker. 1995. "Cost-Effectiveness of Alternative Poverty Alleviation Instruments: A Comparison of Targeting Credit and Non-Credit Programs." World Bank, Poverty and Social Policy Department, Washington, D.C.

Ainsworth, M., and M. Over. 1992. "The Economic Impact of AIDS: Shocks, Responses and Outcomes." Population, Health, and Nutrition Technical Working Paper 1. World Bank, African Technical Department, Washington, D.C.

Alderman, H. 1988. "The Twilight of Flour Rationing in Pakistan." *Food Policy* 13(3): 245–56.

———. 1991. "Food Subsidies and the Poor." In G. Psacharopoulos, ed., *Essays on Poverty, Equity, and Growth*. Oxford: Pergamon Press.

Alderman, H., and C. H. Paxson. 1992. "Do the Poor Insure?" Policy Research Working Paper 1008. World Bank, Agriculture and Rural Development Department, Washington, D.C.

Alderman, H., and J. von Braun. 1984. *The Effects of the Egyptian Food Ration and Subsidy System on Income Distribution and Consumption*. Research Report 45. Washington, D.C.: International Food Policy Research Institute.

———. 1986. "Egypt's Food Subsidy Policy: Lessons and Options." *Food Policy* 11(August): 223–37.

Alesina, A., and D. Drazen. 1991. "Why Are Stabilizations Delayed?" *American Economic Review* 81(5): 170–80.

Andorka, R. 1990a. "Models of Demographic Policy: The Hungarian Case." Paper prepared for the Conference on Population, Society and Demographic Policies for Europe, Giovanni Agnelli Foundation, Torino. April.

————. 1990b. "Pro-natalist Population Policies and Their Impact in Hungary." *Politiques de Population* 5(3): 16–24.

Atkinson, A. B., L. Rainwater, and T. M. Smeeding. 1995. *Income Distribution in OECD Countries: Evidence from the Luxembourg Income Study.* Paris: Organization for Economic Cooperation and Development.

Bahl, Roy. 1994. "Revenue Sharing in Russia." College of Business Administration Reprint Series 61. Georgia State College, Atlanta.

Bahl, Roy, and J. F. Linn. 1992. *Urban Public Finance in Developing Countries.* New York: Oxford University Press.

Bamberger, Michael, and Abdul Aziz. 1991. *The Design and Management of Sustainable Projects to Alleviate Poverty in South Asia.* Economic Development Institute Seminar Series. Washington, D.C.: World Bank.

Barnes, D. F., J. Dowd, L. Qian, K. Krutilla, and W. Hyde. 1994. "Urban Energy Transitions, Poverty, and the Environment: Understanding the Role of Urban Household Energy in Developing Countries." World Bank, Industry and Energy Department, Power Development, Efficiency, and Household Fuels Division, Washington, D.C.

Barr, Nicholas. 1992. *Income Transfers and the Social Safety Net in Russia.* Studies of Economies in Transformation No. 4. Washington, D.C.: World Bank.

————, ed. 1994. *Labor Markets and Social Policy in Central and Eastern Europe: The Transition and Beyond.* New York: Oxford University Press.

————. 1995. "On the Design of Social Safety Nets." ESP Discussion Paper Series 65. World Bank, Education and Social Policy Department, Washington, D.C.

Basu, K. 1981. "Food for Works Programs: Beyond Roads That Get Washed Away." *Economic and Political Weekly* 16(26): 112.

————. 1996. "Relief Programs: When It May Be Better to Give Food Instead of Cash." *World Development* 24(1): 91–6.

Bentall, P. H. 1990. *Ghana Feeder Roads Project: Labor-based Rehabilitation and Maintenance.* Geneva: International Labour Office.

Behrman, J., and A. B. Deolalikar. 1987. "Interhousehold Transfers in Rural India: Altruism or Exchange?" University of Pennsylvania, Department of Economics, Philadelphia.

Berg, Alan. 1987a. *Malnutrition: What Can Be Done?: Lessons from World Bank Experience.* Baltimore, Md.: Johns Hopkins University Press.

————. 1987b. "Nutrition Review." Population, Health, and Nutrition Technical Note 8721. World Bank, Population and Human Resources Department, Washington, D.C.

Bertaud, Alain, and Bertrand Renaud. 1994. *Cities without Land Markets: Lessons of the Failed Socialist Experiment.* World Bank Discussion Paper 227. Washington, D.C.: World Bank.

Bertz, William P., and Peter G. E. Stan. 1982a. "Household Composition and Interhousehold Exchange in Malaysia." *Population and Development Review* 8 (March): 92–115.

————. 1982b. "The Strategic Bequest Motive." *Journal of Political Economy* 93(December): 1045–76.

Besley, Timothy. 1990. "Means Testing versus Universal Provision in Poverty Alleviation Programmes." *Economica* 57(225): 119–29.

————. 1995. "Savings, Credit, and Insurance." In J. Behrman and T. N. Srinivasan, eds., *Handbook of Development Economics,* vol. 3. Amsterdam: North Holland.

Besley, Timothy, and Stephen Coate. 1991. "Workfare versus Welfare: Incentive Arguments for Work Requirements in Poverty Alleviation Programmes." *American Economic Review* 82(1): 249–61.

Besley, Timothy, and Ravi Kanbur. 1988. "Food Subsidies and Poverty Alleviation." *Economic Journal* 98(September): 701–19.

————. 1993. "The Principles of Targeting." In M. Lipton and J. van der Gaag, eds., *Including the Poor.* Proceedings of a Symposium Organized by the World Bank and the International Food Policy Research Institute. Washington D.C.: World Bank.

Bienen, H. S., and Mark Gersovitz. 1985. "Economic Stabilization, Conditionality, and Political Stability." *International Organization* 39(4): 729–54.

Biggs, T. S., Donald R. Snodgrass, and Pradeep Srivastava. 1990. "On Minimalist Credit Programs." Development Discussion Paper 331. Harvard University, Harvard Institute for International Development, Cambridge, Mass.

Binswanger, H. P., S. R. Khandker, and M. R. Rosenzweig. 1993. "How Infrastructure and Financial Institutions Affect Agricultural Output and Investment in India." *Journal of Development Economics* 41(2): 337–66.

Binswanger, H. P., and J. Quizon. 1984. "Distributional Consequences of Alternative Food Policies in India." Discussion Paper No. 20. World Bank, Agriculture and Rural Development Department, Research Unit, Washington, D.C.

Bird, R. 1986. *Federal Finance in Comparative Perspective.* Toronto: Canadian Tax Foundation.

Bird, R., R. D. Ebel, and C. I. Wallick. 1995. *Decentralization of the Socialist State.* Regional and Sectoral Studies. Washington, D.C.: World Bank.

Bird, R., J. I. Litvack, and M. G. Rao. 1995. "Intergovernmental Fiscal Relations and Poverty Alleviation in Vietnam." World Bank, East Asia and Pacific Country Department I, Country Operations Division, Washington, D.C.

Blackorby, C., and D. Donaldson. 1988. "Cash versus Kind, Self-selection and Efficient Transfers." *American Economic Review* 78(4): 691–700.

Bleier, M. I., and A. Chearty, eds. 1993. *How to Measure the Fiscal Deficit.* Washington, D.C.: International Monetary Fund.

Bogetic, Z., and A. L. Hillman, eds. 1995. *Financing Government in the Transition— Bulgaria: The Political Economy of Tax Policies, Tax Bases, and Tax Evasion.* Washington, D.C.: World Bank.

Braithwaite, J. 1990a. "Income Distribution and Poverty in the Soviet Republics." *Journal of Soviet Nationalities* 1(3): 158–73.

———. 1990b. "Poverty Differentials in the USSR: Implications for Social Stability." Paper prepared for Brown Bag Luncheon Seminar, Market Reform in Socialist Economies. U.S. Department of State, Economic Planning and Analysis Staff, July, Washington, D.C.

———. 1991. "The Social Safety Net in the Sovereign Republics." Paper Presented at the Twenty-Third American Association for the Advancement of Slavic Studies National Conference, November 25, Miami, Florida.

———. 1995a. "Armenia: A Poverty Profile." PSP Working Paper and Armenia Poverty Assessment Background Paper 80. World Bank, Poverty and Social Policy Department, Washington, D.C.

———. 1995b. "The Old and New Poor in Russia: Trends in Poverty." ESP Discussion Paper 57. World Bank, Education and Social Policy Department, Washington, D.C.

Braithwaite, J., and T. Heleniak. 1990. "Social Welfare in the USSR: The Income Recipient Distribution." U.S. Bureau of the Census, Center for International Research, Washington D.C.

Braverman, Avishay, and Ravi Kanbur. 1987. "Urban Bias and the Political Economy of Agricultural Price Reform." *World Development* 15(9): 1179–87.

Bruce, N., and M. Walsman. 1988. "Transfers In-Kind: Why They Can Be Efficient and Non-Paternalistic." Working Paper 532. University of California at Los Angeles, Department of Economics.

Buckley, R. M. 1988. "The Measurement and Targeting of Housing Finance Subsidies: The Case of Argentina." World Bank, Infrastructure and Urban Development Department, Policy, Planning, and Research Staff, Washington, D.C.

Buckley, R. M., D. Faulk, and L. Olajide. 1993. "Private Sector Participation, Structural Adjustment and Nigeria's New National Housing Policy: Lessons from Foreign Experience." Working Paper 5. World Bank, Transportation, Water and Urban Development Department, Urban Development Division, Washington, D.C.

Buckley, R. M., Patric H. Hendershott, and K. Villani. 1994. "Rapid Housing Privatization in Reforming Economies: Pay the Special Dividend Now." TWURD Working Paper 12. World Bank, Transportation, Water and Urban Development Department, Urban Development Division, Washington, D.C.

Butz, William P., and P. J. E. Stan. 1982. "Household Composition and Interhousehold Exchange in Malaysia." *Population and Development Review* 8(March): 92–115.

Campbell, T. 1995a. "Mendoza Provincial Program for Basic Social Infrastructure (MEN-PROSIF). Case Study: Decentralization in LAC: Policy Lessons and Best Practices." World Bank, Latin America and the Caribbean Technical Department Advisory Group, Washington, D.C.

———. 1995b. "Quasi-Matching Grants and Decentralization in Mexico." LATIE Dissemination Note. World Bank, Latin America and the Caribbean Technical Department Advisory Group, Washington, D.C.

Campbell, T., and T. Katz. 1996. "The Politics of Participation in Tijuana, Mexico: Inventing a New Style of Governance. Case Study: Decentralization in LAC: Best Practices and Policy Lessons." World Bank, Latin America and the Caribbean Technical Department Advisory Group, Washington, D.C.

Campbell, T., G. Petersen, and J. Bazark. 1991. "Decentralization to Local Government in LAC: National Strategies and Local Response in Planning, Spending and Management." LAC Regional Studies Program Report 5. World Bank, Latin America and the Caribbean Technical Department, Washington, D.C.

Carvalho, S. 1994a. *Indicators for Monitoring Poverty Reduction.* World Bank Discussion Paper 254. Washington, D.C.

———. 1994b. "Social Funds: Guidelines for the Design and Implementation." HCD Working Paper 34. World Bank, Poverty and Social Policy Department, Washington, D.C.

Chen, S., G. Datt, and M. Ravallion. 1994. "Is Poverty Increasing in the Developing World?" World Bank, Policy Research Department, Washington, D.C.

Christen, R. P., E. Rhyne, and R. C. Vogel. 1995. "Maximizing the Outreach of Microenterprise Finance: An Analysis of Successful Programs." US Agency for International Development Program and Operations Assessment Report 10. Reference PN-ABS-51. Washington, D.C.

Cleaver, K. M. 1982. "Agricultural Development Experience of Algeria, Morocco, and Tunisia: A Comparison of Strategies for Growth." World Bank Staff Working Paper 552. World Bank, Washington D.C.

Copestake, J. 1987. "Loans for Livelihoods? An Assessment of Government Sponsored Credit Schemes Designed to Promote Rural Development in India Based on Field Work Undertaken in the Madurai Region of Tamil Nadu, between September 1984 and August 1986." Credit for Rural Development in Southern Tamil Nadu, Tamil Nadu Agricultural University, India.

———. 1992. "The Integrated Rural Development Project." In B. Harris, S. Guhan, and R. Cassen, eds., *Poverty in India.* Bombay: Oxford University Press.

Cornelius, W., A. L. Craig, and J. Fox, eds. 1994. *Transforming State-Society Relations in Mexico: The National Solidarity Strategy.* San Diego, Calif.: University of California Press.

Cox, D. 1987. "Motives for Private Income Transfers." *Journal of Political Economy* 95(June): 508–46.

Cox, D., and E. Jimenez. 1989. "Private Transfers and Public Policy in Developing Countries: A Case Study for Peru." Policy Research Working Paper 345. World Bank, Policy Research Department, Washington, D.C.

———. 1990. "Achieving Social Objectives Through Private Transfers—A Review." *World Bank Research Review* 5(2): 205–18.

Cox, D., E. Jimenez, and B. Jordan. 1994. "Family Safety Nets and Economic Transition: A Study of Private Transfers in Kyrgyzstan." National Seminar in Poverty and Social

Protection in the Kyrgyz Republic, Economic Development Institute, World Bank, Washington, D.C.

Cox, D., Z. Eser, and E. Jimenez. 1995. "Family Safety Nets during Economic Transition: A Study of Interhousehold Transfers in Russia." World Bank, Policy Research Department, Washington D.C.

Craig, A. 1992. "Solidarity: Deconstructing Discourse and Practice in the Politics of Concertation." Paper presented at the University of California at San Diego workshop "Mexico's Solidarity Program: A Preliminary Assessment," February.

Dabrowski, M. 1994. "The Ukranian Way to Hyperinflation." *Communist Economies and Economic Transformation* 6(2): 115–37.

Datt, G, and M. Ravallion. 1992. "Behavioral Responses to Workfare: Evidence for Rural India." World Bank, Policy Research Department, Washington, D.C.

———. 1994. "Income Gains for the Poor from Public Works Employment: Evidence from Two Indian Villages." Living Standards Measurement Study Working Paper 100. World Bank, Policy Research Department, Washington, D.C.

Davis, Jeffrey. 1977. "The Fiscal Role of Food Subsidy Programs." IMF Staff Papers. International Monetary Fund, Washington, D.C.

de Ferranti, D. 1985. *Paying for Health Services in Developing Countries: An Overview.* Washington, D.C.: World Bank.

de Janvry, A., and K. Subbarao. 1986. *Agricultural Price and Income Distribution in India.* Oxford: Oxford University Press.

de Janvry, A., and S. Subramanian. 1985. "The Politics and Economics of Food and Nutrition Policies and Programs: An Interpretation." Paper presented at the International Food Policy Research Institute Conference on "The Political Economy of Nutritional Improvements," June 10–14, Berkeley Springs, West Virginia.

de Janvry, A., A. Fargeiz, and E. Sadoulet. 1992. "The Political Feasibility of Rural Poverty Reduction." *Journal of Development Economics* 37(November): 351–67.

Deolalikar, A.B. 1990. "Rural Services and Public Works in Developing Countries: The Role of Access to Credit, Primary Health Services, and Public Works in Poverty Alleviation." Background paper for Food and Agriculture Organization. University of Washington, Seattle.

Deolalikar, A., and R. Gaiha. 1992. "Targeting of Rural Public Works: Are Women Less likely to Participate?" School of Business Management, Delhi University, India.

Deschamps, Jean-Jacques. 1989. *Credit for the Rural Poor: The Experience in Six African Countries: Synthesis Report.* Washington D.C.: Development Alternatives, Inc.

Dev, S. M. 1992. "Poverty Alleviation Programmes: A Case Study of Maharashtra With Emphasis on the Employment Guarantee Scheme." Discussion Paper 77. Indira Gandhi Institute of Development Research, Bombay, India.

———. 1995a. "Government Interventions and Social Security for Rural Labor." *The India Journal of Labor Economics* 38(3): 419–41.

———. 1995b. "India's MEGS: Lessons from Long Experience." In J. von Braun, ed., *Employment for Poverty Reduction and Food Security.* Washington, D.C.: International Food Policy Research Institute.

Ditch, J., and H. Barnes. 1994. "Social Assistance: Coverage, Finance, and Administration." University of York, Social Policy Research Unit, York, United Kingdom.

Dresser, Denise. 1991. *Neopopulist Solutions to Neoliberal Problems: Mexico's National Solidarity Program.* Current Issues Brief Series No. 3. La Jolla, Calif.: Center for U.S.–Mexican Studies, University of California San Diego.

Dreze, J. 1989. "Social Insecurity in India." Suntory-Toyota International Centre for Economics and Related Disciplines (STICERD), London School of Economics, Development Economics Research Programme, London.

———. 1990. "Widows in Rural India." Development Economics Research Program Discussion Paper 26. London School of Economics.

Dreze, J., and Amartya Sen. 1989. *Hunger and Public Action*. Oxford: Clarendon Press.

Dreze, J., P. Lanjouw, and N. Sharma. Forthcoming. "Credit in a North Indian Village—An Empirical Investigation." In P. Lanjouw and N. Stern, eds., *A Growth of Sorts: Palanpur 1957–1993*. New York: Oxford University Press.

Echeverri-Gent, John. 1988. "Guaranteed Employment in an Indian State: The Maharashtra Experience." *Asian Survey* 28(December): 1294–310.

Economic Commission for Latin America and the Caribbean (ECLAC). 1994. *Social Panorama of Latin America*. Santiago: United Nations.

Edirisinghe, N. 1987. *The Food Stamp Scheme in Sri Lanka: Costs, Benefits, and Options for Modifications*. Research Report 58. Washington, D.C.: International Food Policy Research Institute.

Esanu, C. 1996. "Food Subsidy and Price Policies in Romania." ASAL Food Policy Background Paper Series. Romania.

Eurostat. 1993. *Digest of Statistics on Social Protection in Europe: Volume 4—Family*. Luxembourg.

Ezemenan, K. 1997. "The Link between Public and Private Interhousehold Transfers—Implications for the Design of Safety Net Programs in Developing Countries." Paper presented at the Allied Social Science Association Meetings, New Orleans, January.

Ferghany, N. 1992. "Poverty and Unemployment Profiles on the Level of Administrative Units (Kism and Markaz) by Urban-Rural Classifications and Implied Allocations of Funds." Almishkat Center for Research and Training, Giza, Egypt.

Ferge, Z. 1991. "Social Security Systems in the New Democracies of Central and Eastern Europe: Past Legacies and Possible Futures." In G.A. Cornia and S. Sipos, eds., *Children and the Transition to the Market Economy: Safety Nets and Social Policies in Central and Eastern Europe*. Hants, England: Arebury Press.

Fox, J. 1992. "The Difficult Transition from Clientelism to Citizenship: Lessons from Mexico." Paper presented at the University of California at San Diego workshop "Mexico's Solidarity Program: A Preliminary Addessment," February.

Fox, L. 1994. "Old Age Security in Transitional Economies." Policy Research Working Paper 1257. World Bank, Policy Research Department, Poverty and Human Resources Division, Washington, D.C.

Freund, C. L., and C. I. Wallich. 1995. "Raising Household Energy Prices in Poland: Who Gains? Who Loses?" Policy Research Working Paper 1495. World Bank, Europe and Central Asia Country Department II, Office of the Director, Washington, D.C.

Gaiha, R. 1991. "Poverty Alleviation Programmes in Rural India: An Assessment." *Development and Change* 22(January): 117–54.

———. 1993. *Design of Poverty Alleviation Strategies in Rural Areas*. Economic and Social Development Paper 115. Rome, Italy: Food and Agriculture Organization of the United Nations.

———. 1995a. "How Dependent Are the Rural Poor on the Employment Guarantee Scheme in India?" University of Delhi, Faculty of Management Studies, India.

———. 1995b. "Wages, Participation, and Targeting—The Case of the Employment Guarantee Scheme in India." University of Delhi, Faculty of Management Studies, India.

Garcia, M. 1988. "Food Subsidies in the Philippines: Preliminary Results." In P. Pinstrup-Andersen, ed., *Food Subsidies in Developing Countries: Costs, Benefits, and Policy Options*. Baltimore, Md.: Johns Hopkins University Press.

Garcia, M., and P. Pinstrup-Andersen. 1987. "The Pilot Food Price Subsidy Scheme in the Philippines: Its Impact on Income, Food Consumption, and Nutritional Status." International Food Policy Research Report 61. Washington, D.C.

Garfinkel, I. 1979. *Income-Tested Transfer Programs: The Case For and Against*. New York: Academic Press.

Gaude, J., A. Guichaona, B. Martens, and S. Miller. 1987. "Rural Development and Labour-Intensive Schemes: Impact Studies of Some Pilot Programmes." *International Labour Review* 126(4): 423–46.

Gaude, J., and S. Miller, eds. 1992. "Productive Employment for the Poor." *International Labour Review* 131(1): 1–137.

Gelback, J., and L. Pritchett. 1995. "Does More for the Poor Mean Less for the Poor? The Politics of Tagging." Policy Research Working Paper 1523. World Bank, Policy Research Department, Washington, D.C.

Gertler, P., and J. van der Gaag. 1988. *The Willingness to Pay for Medical Care: Evidence from Two Developing Countries.* Washington D.C.: World Bank.

Getubig, I.P., M. Y. Johari, and A. M. K. Thas, eds. 1993. *Overcoming Poverty through Credit: The Asian Experience in Replicating the Grameen Bank Approach.* Kuala Lumpur, Malaysia: Asian and Pacific Development Centre, and Sabah, Malaysia: Institute for Development Studies.

Gill, I., and A. Dar. 1994. "Labor Market Policies and Interventions for Sustainable Employment Growth." World Bank, Education and Social Policy Department, Washington, D.C.

Gill, I., E. Jimenez, and Z. Shalitz. 1991 "Targeting Consumer Subsidies for Poverty Alleviation: A Survey and a Primer of Basic Theory." World Bank, Country Economic Department, Public Economics Division, Washington, D.C.

Glaessner, P., Kye Woo Lee, Anna Maria Sant'Anna, and Jean-Jacques de St. Antoine. 1994. *Poverty Alleviation and Social Investment Funds: The Latin American Experience.* World Bank Discussion Paper 261. Washington, D.C.: World Bank.

Glewwe, P. and Oussama Kanaan. 1989. "Targeting Assistance to the Poor Using Household Survey Data." World Bank, Population and Human Resources Department, Washington, D.C.

Golden, T. 1992. "Mexico's Leader Cautiously Backs Some Big Chances." *The New York Times* November 2, 1992, page A3.

Graham, C. 1992. "The Politics of Protecting the Poor During Adjustment. Bolivia's Emergency Social Fund." *World Development* 20(9): 1233–51.

———. 1995. "Strategies for Addressing Other Social Costs of Market Reforms: Lessons for Transitioning Economies in East Asia and Eastern Europe." World Bank, Education and Social Policy Department, Washington, D.C.

Gray, D. 1995. *Reforming the Energy Sector in Transition Economies.* World Bank Discussion Paper 296. Washington, D.C.: World Bank.

Grayson, G. 1991. "Mexico's New Politics. Building Sewers, Reaping Votes." *Commonweal* 118(October 25): 612–14.

Griffith, G. 1987. "Missing the Poorest: Participant Identification by a Rural Development Agency in Gujarat." Institute of Development Studies Discussion Paper 230. Sussex, United Kingdom.

Grootaert, C. 1995. "Poverty and Social Transfers in Poland." Policy Research Working Paper 1440. World Bank, Policy Research Department, Washington, D.C.

Grosh, M. 1992. "The Jamaican Food Stamp Programme: A Case Study in Targeting." *Food Policy* 17(1): 23–40.

———. 1994. *Administering Targeted Social Programs in Latin America: From Platitudes to Practice.* World Bank Regional and Sectoral Studies Series. Washington, D.C.: World Bank.

Grosh, M., and J. Baker. 1995. "Proxy Means Tests for Targeting Social Programs: Simulations and Speculation." Living Standards Measurement Study Working Paper 118. Policy Research Department, World Bank, Washington, D.C.

Gurgand, M., G. Pederson, and J. Yaron. 1994. *Outreach and Sustainability of Six Rural Finance Institutions in Sub-Saharan Africa.* World Bank Discussion Paper 248. Washington, D.C.: World Bank.

Haggard, S. 1991. "Markets, Poverty Alleviation, and Income Distribution: An Assessment of Neoliberal Claims." *Ethics and International Affairs* 5.

Hasan, M. 1992. "The Effect of Subsidy Reduction on Food Consumption and Its Impact on Vulnerable Groups." Cairo University, Faculty of Medicine, Cairo, Egypt.

Heaver, Richard. 1989. *Improving Family Planning, Health and Nutrition in India: Experience from Some World Bank-Assisted Programs.* World Bank Discussion Paper 59. Washington, D.C.: World Bank.

Hicks, N. 1994. "Ecuador: Replacing the LPG Subsidy with a Targeted Program." World Bank, Latin America and the Caribbean Country Department III, Washington, D.C.

Holt, S. 1991. "The Role of Institutions in Poverty Reduction." Policy Research Working Paper 627. Background paper for *World Development Report 1990.* World Bank, Washington, D.C.

Hope, E., and B. Singh. 1995. "Energy Price Increases in Developing Countries: Case Studies of Colombia, Ghana, Indonesia, Malaysia, Turkey, and Zimbabwe." Policy Research Working Paper 1442. World Bank, Policy Research Department, Public Economics Division, Washington, D.C.

Horton, S. 1992. "Unit Costs, Cost-Effectiveness and Financing of Nutrition Interventions." Policy Research Working Paper 952. World Bank, Policy Research Department, Washington D.C.

Hossain, M., 1988. "Credit for Alleviation of Rural Poverty: The Grameen Bank in Bangladesh." Research Report 65. International Food Policy Research Institute in collaboration with Bangladesh Institute of Development Studies, Washington, D.C.

India, Ministry of Rural Development. 1995. "Progress Report on Anti-Poverty Programs." Delhi.

Intelnews. 1994. Kiev. October 20.

IFPRI (International Food Policy Research Institute). 1994. *Options for Targeting Food Interventions in Bangladesh.* Washington, D.C.

ILO (International Labour Organization). 1991. *The Cost of Social Security, 1984–1986.* Geneva: International Labour Office.

Jehle, G.A. 1994. "Zakat and Inequality: Some Evidence from Pakistan." *Review of Income and Wealth* 40(2): 205–15.

Jha, Shikha. 1992. "Consumer Subsidies in India: Is Targeting Effective?" *Development and Change* 23(4): 101–28.

———. 1995. "Foodgrains Price and Distribution Policies in India: Performance, Problems and Prospects." *Asia-Pacific Development Journal* of the United Nations Economic and Social Commission for Asia and the Pacific 2: 45–63.

Jimenez, Emmanuel. 1993. "Cash Versus In-Kind Transfers." Lecture Notes, EDI Seminar on Labor Market and the Social Safety Net in the Former Soviet Union/CIS Countries. World Bank, Washington, D.C.

Johnson, G. E., and W. E. Whitelaw. 1974. "Urban-Rural Income Transfer in Kenya: An Estimated-Remittances Function." *Economic Development and Cultural Change* 22(3): 473–79.

Jorgensen, Steen, Margaret Grosh, and Marc Schacter, eds. 1992. *Bolivia's Answer to Poverty, Economic Crisis and Adjustment: The Emergency Social Fund.* Washington, D.C.: World Bank.

Kakwani, N. 1995. "Income Inequality, Welfare and Poverty: An Illustration Using Ukrainian Data." Policy Research Working Paper 1411. World Bank, Policy Research Department, Washington, D.C.

Kakwani, N., and K. Subbarao. 1990. "Rural Poverty and Its Alleviation in India." *Economic and Political Weekly* 25(March 31): A2–A16.

Kamerman, S. B., and A. J. Kahn. 1988. "Social Policy and Children in the United States and Europe." In J. L. Palmer, T. Smeeding, and B. B. Torrey, eds., *The Vulnerable.* Washington, D.C.: Urban Institute Press.

Kanbur, R., M. Keen, and M. Tuomala. 1994. "Labor Supply and Targeting in Poverty Alleviation Programs." *The World Bank Economic Review* 8(May):191–211.

Kane, C. and J. Morissot. 1993. "Who Would Vote for Inflation in Brazil?" Policy Research Working Paper 1183. World Bank, Latin America and the Caribbean Country Department I, Washington D.C.

Kaufman, D. 1982. "Social Interaction as a Strategy for Economic Survival Among the Urban Poor: Theory and Evidence." Ph.D. dissertation, Harvard University, Department of Economics, Cambridge, Mass.

———. 1994. "The Train and Disseminate Approach to Public Education: An Application to Ukraine." World Bank Resident Mission, Kiev, Ukraine.

Kaufman, D., and D. L. Lindauer. 1986. "A Model of Income Transfers for the Urban Poor." *Journal of Development Economics* 22(2): 337–50.

Keare, D., and S. Parris. 1982. "Evaluation of Shelter Programs for the Urban Poor: Principal Findings." World Bank Staff Working Paper 547. World Bank, Urban Development and Rural Development Department, Washington, D.C.

Kennedy, E. T., and H. Alderman. 1987. "Comparative Analyses of Nutritional Effectiveness of Food Subsidies and Other Food-Related Interventions." International Food Policy Research Institute and Joint WHO-UNICEF Nutrition Support Programme, Washington D.C.

Khadiagala, L. 1995. "Social Funds: Strengths, Weaknesses, and Conditions for Success." ESP Discussion Paper 52. World Bank, Education and Social Policy Department, Washington, D.C.

Khandker, S., B. Khalily, and Z. Khan. 1994a. "Sustainability of a Government-Targeted Credit Program: The Bangladesh Rural Development Board's Rural Development–12 Project in Bangladesh." World Bank, Poverty and Social Policy Department, Washington, D.C.

———. 1994b. "Sustainability of Grameen Bank: What Do We Know?" World Bank, Poverty and Social Policy Department, Washington, D.C.

———. 1995. *Grameen Bank: Performance and Sustainability.* World Bank Discussion Paper 306. Washington, D.C.: World Bank.

Knight, A. 1992. "Solidarity: Historical Continuities and Contemporary Implications." Paper presented at the University of California at San Diego workshop "Mexico's Solidarity Program: A Preliminary Assessment," February.

Knowles, J. C., and Richard Anker. 1981. "An Analysis of Income Transfers in a Developing Country: The Case of Kenya." *Journal of Development Economics* 8(April): 205–26.

Korten, F. and R. Siy. 1988. "Transforming a Bureaucracy: The Experience of the Philippine National Irrigation Administration." West Hartford, Connecticut: Kumarian Press.

Kouwenaar, A. 1988. *A Basic Needs Policy Model: A General Equilibrium Analysis with Special Reference to Ecuador.* Contributions to Economic Analysis No. 174. Amsterdam: North-Holland.

Krumm, K., B. Milanovic, and M. Walton. 1995. "Transfers and the Transition from Socialism: Key Trade-offs." World Bank, Europe and Central Asia Regional Office and Policy Research Department, Washington, D.C.

Kwon, S. 1993. *Social Policy in Korea: Challenges and Responses.* Research Monograph 93-01. Seoul: Korea Development Institute.

———. 1995. "The Role of Public and Private Transfers to Vulnerable Groups: Experiences of the East Asian Countries." World Bank, Education and Social Policy Department, Washington, D.C.

Lipton, M. 1977. *Why Poor People Stay Poor.* Canberra: Australian National University Press.

———. 1988. *The Poor and the Poorest.* World Bank Discussion Paper 25. Washington, D.C.: World Bank.

———. 1995. "IILS Contract: Successes in Antipoverty." University of Sussex, School of African and Asian Studies, Brighton, United Kingdom.

Lipton, M., and M. Ravallion. 1995. "Poverty and Policy." In J. Behrman and T.N. Srinivasan, eds., *Handbook of Development Economics.* vol 3. Amsterdam: Elsevier Science.

Macedo, R. 1987. "The Mistargeting of Social Programs in Brazil: The Federal Health and Nutrition Programs." University of Sao Paolo, Brazil.

Macrae, J., and A. B. Zwi. 1992. "Food as an Instrument of War in Contemporary African Famines: A Review of the Evidence." *Disasters: The Journal of Disaster Studies and Management* 16(12): 299–321.

Majeres, J. 1993. "Implementation of Employment Programmes: Key Issues and Options." International Food Policy Research Institute International Policy Workshop Paper. International Labour Office, Geneva.

Marc, A., C. Graham, M. Schacter, and M. Schmidt. 1995. *Social Action Programs and Social Funds: A Review of Design and Implementation in Sub-Saharan Africa.* World Bank Discussion Paper 274. Washington, D.C.: World Bank.

Martens, B. 1989. *Economic Development that Lasts: Labor-intensive Projects in Nepal and Tanzania.* Geneva: International Labour Office.

Mateus, A. 1984 "Targeting Food Subsidies for the Needy: The Use of Cost-Benefit Analysis and Institutional Design." World Bank Staff Working Paper 617. World Bank, Washington D.C.

McCleary, W. 1991. "The Earmarking of Government Revenue: A Review of Some World Bank Experience." *The World Bank Research Observer* 6(1): 81–104.

Mesa-Lago, C. 1990. "Economic and Financial Aspects of Social Security in Latin America and the Caribbean: Tendencies, Problems and Alternatives for the Year 2000." Discussion Paper, World Bank, Latin America and the Caribbean Technical Department, Washington, D.C.

———. 1993. "Safety Nets and Social Funds to Alleviate Poverty: Performance, Problems, and Policy Options." United Nations Conference on Trade and Development (UNCTAD), Geneva.

———. 1994. *Changing Social Security in Latin America.* Boulder: Lynne Rienner Publishers, Inc.

Milanovic, B. 1992a. "Distributional Impact of Cash and In-Kind Social Transfers in Eastern Europe and Russia." Policy Research Working Paper 1054. World Bank, Policy Research Department, Washington, D.C.

———. 1992b. "Income Distribution in Late Socialism: Poland, Hungary, Czechoslovakia, Yugoslavia and Bulgaria Compared." World Bank, Country Economic Department, Washington, D.C.

———. 1994. "Poverty in Transition." World Bank, Policy Research Department, Washington, D.C.

———. 1995a. "Poverty, Inequality and Social Policy in Transition Economies." Policy Research Working Paper 1530. World Bank, Policy Research Department, Washington, D.C.

———. 1995b. "Social Assistance and Higher Utility Prices." Office Memorandum. World Bank, Policy Research Department, Washington, D.C.

———. Forthcoming. *Poverty in Transition Economies.* Washington, D. C.: World Bank.

Milimo, J. T., and C. A. Njobvu. 1993. "Report on the Beneficiary Assessment Study, Phase I." University of Zambia, Lusaka.

Miller, B.D., and C. Stone. 1987. "Household Expenditure Effects of the Jamaican Food Stamp Programme." Staff Paper 36. Syracuse University, Metropolitan Studies Program, Jamaica Tax Structure Examination Project, Syracuse, New York.

Mitchell, Donald. 1996. "Food Subsidies in Ukraine." World Bank, Country Economics Department, Washington, D.C.

Moguel, J. 1990. "National Solidarity Program Fails to Help the Very Poor." *Voices of Mexico* 15 (October-December): 15–16.

Moser, C. 1993. "Urban Social Policy and Poverty Reduction." TWURD Working Paper 10. World Bank, Transportation, Water and Urban Development Department, Urban Development Division, Washington, D.C.

Musgrove, P. 1989. *Fighting Malnutrition.* World Bank Discussion Paper 60. Washington, D.C.: World Bank,

———. 1991. "Feeding Latin America's Children, An Analytical Survey of Food Programs." Regional Studies Series Report 11. World Bank, Latin America and the Caribbean Technical Department, Washington, D.C.

Mutua, K. 1995a. "The Experience of the Kenya Rural Enterprise Program (K-REP) in Developing Effective Micro Credit Schemes." Occasional Paper. Kenya Rural Enterprise Programme, Nairobi.

———. 1995b. "K-REPS Credit Operations: A Comparative Analysis of Systems." Occasional Paper, Kenya Rural Enterprise Programme, Nairobi.

Nagle, B., and S. Ghose, 1990. "Community Participation in World Bank Supported Projects." World Bank, Washington, D.C.

Narayan, D., 1995. *The Contribution of People's Participation: Evidence from 121 Rural Water Supply Projects.* Environmentally Sustainable Development Occasional Paper 1. Washington, D.C.: World Bank.

Narayana, N. S. S., K. S. Parikh, and T. N. Srinivasan. 1988. "Rural Works Programs in India: Costs and Benefits." *Journal of Development Economics* 29(2): 131–56.

Nelson, J. 1992. "Poverty, Equity, and the Politics of Economic Adjustment." In S. Haggard and B. Kaufmann, eds., *The Politics of Economic Adjustment.* Princeton: Princeton University Press.

Nichols, A. L., and R. Zeckhauser. 1982. "Targeting Transfers through Restrictions on Recipients." *American Economic Review Papers and Proceedings* 72(May): 372–77.

North, D. 1990. "Institutions, Institutional Change and Economic Performance." New York: Cambridge University Press.

OED (Operations Evaluation Department). 1986. "Pakistan Aga Khan Rural Support Program Interim Evaluation." Report 6562-PAK. World Bank, Operations Evaluation Department, Washington, D.C.

———. 1995. "The Social Impact of Adjustment Operations." Report 14776. World Bank, Operations Evaluation Department, Washington, D.C.

Pakistan, Planning and Development Division. 1993. "Pakistan: Social Action Programme (SAP)—Implementation Plans of Key Reforms." Karachi.

Persaud, T. 1991. "Chile's Housing Subsidy Program: Preliminary Indications of Results." Dissemination Note. World Bank, Latin America and the Caribbean Technical Department. Washington, D.C.

———. 1992. "Housing Delivery System and the Urban Poor: A Comparison Among Six Latin American Countries." World Bank, Latin America and the Caribbean Technical Department, Infrastructure and Energy Division, Washington, D.C.

Pfeffermann, G., and C. Griffin. 1989. "Nutrition and Health Programs in Latin America: Targeting Social Expenditures." World Bank and International Centre for Economic Growth, Washington D.C. and Panama City.

Pinstrup-Andersen, P. 1988a. "Assuring Food Security and Adequate Nutrition for the Poor." In D. E. Bell, and M. R. Reich, eds., *Health, Nutrition, and Economic Crises: Approaches to Policy in the Third World.* Dover, Mass.: Auburn House Publishing Company.

———, ed. 1988b. *Food Subsidies in Developing Countries.* Baltimore, Md.: Johns Hopkins University Press.

Pitt, Mark M., and S.R. Khandker. 1996. *Household and Intrahousehold Impact of the Grameen Bank and Similar Targeted Credit Programs in Bangladesh.* World Bank Discussion Paper 320. Washington, D.C.: World Bank.

Platteau, J. P. 1991. "Traditional Systems of Social Security and Hunger Insurance: Past Achievements and Modern Challenges." In E. Ahmad, J. Dreze, J. Hills, and A. Sen, eds., *Social Security in Developing Countries*. Oxford: Clarendon Press.

Psacharopoulos, G., ed. 1993. *Essays on Poverty, Equity and Growth*. Oxford: Pergamon Press.

Pulley, R. V. 1989. *Making the Poor Creditworthy: A Case Study of the Integrated Rural Development Program in India*. World Bank Discussion Paper 58. Washington, D.C.: World Bank.

Radhakrishna, R., S. Indrakant, C. Ravi, and K. Subbarao. 1996. "India's Public Distribution System: A National and International Perspective." World Bank, Poverty and Social Policy Department, Washington, D.C.

Ranji, M. and P. Salgado. 1989. "Report on Fiscal Aspects of the Public Sector Restructuring Project." Colombo, Sri Lanka.

Ranney, Christine K., and John E. Kushman. 1987. "Cash Equivalence, Welfare Stigma, and Food Stamps." *Southern Economic Journal* 53(April): 1011–27.

Ravallion, M. 1989. "Land-Contingent Poverty Alleviation Schemes." *World Development* 17(8): 1223–33.

———. 1991. "Reaching the Rural Poor through Public Employment: Arguments, Evidence, and Lessons from South Asia." *World Bank Research Observer* 6(2): 153–75.

Ravallion, M., and Kalvin Chao. 1989. "Targeted Policies for Poverty Alleviation under Imperfect Information: Algorithms and Applications." *Journal of Policy Modelling* 11: 213–24.

Ravallion, M., Gaurav Datt, and Shubham Chaudhuri. 1993. "Does Maharashtra's Employment Guarantee Scheme Guarantee Employment?" *Economic Development and Cultural Change* 41(2): 251–75.

Ravallion, M., and L. Dearden. 1988. "Social Security in a 'Moral' Economy: An Empirical Analysis for Java." *Review of Economics and Statistics* 70(February): 36–44.

Rempell, Henry, and Richard A. Lobdell. 1978. "The Role of Urban-to-Rural Remittances in Rural Development." *Journal of Development Studies* 14(April): 324–41.

Renaud, B. 1991. *Housing Reform in Socialist Economies*. World Bank Discussion Paper 125. Washington, D.C.: World Bank.

Sahn, D. and H. Alderman. 1995. "The Effect of Food Subsidies on Labor Supply in Sri Lanka." In D. van de Walle and K. Nead, eds., *Public Spending and the Poor*. Baltimore, Md.: Johns Hopkins University Press.

Salamin, J., and M. Floro. 1993. "Hungary in the 1980's: A Review of National and Urban Level Economic Reforms." TWURD Working Paper 2. World Bank, Transportation, Water and Urban Development Department, Urban Development Division, Washington, D.C.

Schneider, R. R. 1984. "A Framework for Analyzing Food Subsidies." International Monetary Fund, Fiscal Affairs Department, Washington D.C.

Schubert, B., and G. Balzer. 1990. *Social Security Systems in Developing Countries: Transfers as a Social Policy Option for Securing the Survival of the Destitute*. Eschborn: Deutsche Gesellschaft für Technische Zusammenarbeit (GTZ).

Selden, T. M., and M. J. Wasylenko. 1995. "Measuring the Distributional Effects of Public Education in Peru." In D. van de Walle and K. Nead, eds., *Public Spending and the Poor: Theory and Evidence*. Baltimore, Md.: Johns Hopkins University Press.

Selowsky, M. 1979. "Target Group-Oriented Food Programs: Cost Effectiveness Comparisons." *American Journal of Agricultural Economics* 61(5): 988–94.

Serageldin, I., and P. Landell-Mills, eds. 1994. *Overcoming Global Hunger*. ESD Proceedings Series 3. Washington, D.C.: World Bank.

Sen, Amartya. 1981. *Poverty and Famines*. Oxford: Clarendon Press.

———. 1990. "Levels of Poverty: Policy and Change." World Bank Staff Working Paper 401. World Bank, Washington, D.C.

Shekar, M. 1994. "The Tamil Nadu Integrated Nutrition Project (TINP-1) Revisited: An Evaluation Perspective." World Bank, Operations Evaluation Department, Washington, D.C.

Silverman, A. 1993. "Municipal Funds in Rural Southern Mexico: Supporting Participatory Rural Development." World Bank, Washington, D.C.

Singh, I. 1978. "Rural Works Programs in South Asia: A Note." Studies in Employment and Rural Development 48. World Bank, Development Policy Staff, Employment and Rural Development Division, Washington, D.C.

Sipos, S. 1994. "Income Transfers: Family Support and Poverty Relief." In Nicholas Barr, ed., *Labor Markets and Social Policy in Central and Eastern Europe: The Transition and Beyond*. Washington, D.C. and London: World Bank and London School of Economics.

Smeeding, T., B. B. Torrey, and M. Rein. 1988. "Patterns of Income and Poverty: The Economic Status of Children and the Elderly in Eight Countries." In J. L. Palmer, T. Smeeding, and B. B. Torrey, eds., *The Vulnerable*. Washington, D.C.: Urban Institute Press.

Squire, L. 1991. "Introduction: Poverty and Adjustment in the 1980s." *The World Bank Economic Review* 5(2): 177–85.

Stark, O., J. Edward Taylor, and Shlomo Yitzhaki. 1988. "Migration, Remittances, and Inequality: A Sensitivity Analysis Using the Extended Gini Index." *Journal of Development Studies* 28(May): 309–22.

Stewart, F., and W. van der Geest. 1994. "Adjustment and Social Funds: Political Panacea or Effective Poverty Reduction." Working Paper, International Labour Organization, Geneva.

Stock, E. A. 1996. "The Problems Facing Labor-based Road Programs and What to Do About Them: Evidence from Ghana." Sub-Saharan Africa Transport Policy Program Working Paper 24. World Bank, Washington, D.C.

Stock, E. A., and J. de Veen. 1996. "Expanding Labor-based Methods in Road Programs." World Bank, Africa Region, Technical Department, Environmentally Sustainable Division, Washington, D.C.

Struyk, R., and J. Daniell. 1995. "Housing Privatization in Russia." *The Economics of Transition* 3(2): 197–214.

Subbarao, K. 1985. "Regional Variations in the Impact of Anti-Poverty Programs." *Economic and Political Weekly* (October 26) 20(43): 1829–34.

———. 1989. *Improving Nutrition in India: Policies and Programs and their Impacts*. World Bank Discussion Paper 49. Washington, D.C.: World Bank.

———. 1993. "Interventions to Fill Nutrition Gaps at the Household Level: A Review of India's Experience." In B. Harris, S. Gahan, and R. H. Cassen, eds., *Poverty in India: Research and Policy*. Bombay: Oxford Chicago Press.

———. 1995. "Safety Nets and Poverty-Targeted Programs in Tanzania." World Bank, Poverty and Social Policy Department, Washington, D.C.

———. 1997. "Public Works As An Anti-Poverty Program: An Overview of Cross-Country Experience." Paper presented at the Allied Social Science Association Meetings, New Orleans, January 3–5.

Subbarao, K., and K. Ezemenari. 1995. "Transition, Poverty and Social Assistance in Mongolia." ESP Discussion Paper 55. World Bank, Education and Social Policy Department, Washington, D.C.

———. 1997. "Social Assistance Cash Transfers and Poverty Relief: Economies in Transition in a Global Contest." World Bank, Poverty, Gender, and Public Sector Management Department, Washington, D.C.

Subbarao, K., and K. Mehra. 1995. "Social Assistance and the Poor in Romania." ESP Discussion Paper 66. World Bank, Education and Social Policy Department, Washington, D.C.

Subbarao, K., and K. Rudra. 1996. "Protecting the Poor in a High Growth Economy: Effectiveness of Poverty-Targeted Programs in Thailand." World Bank, Poverty and Social Policy Department, Washington, D.C.

Subbarao, K., A. Ahmed, and T. Teklu. 1995. *Philippines Social Safety Net Programs:*

Targeting, Cost Effectiveness and Options for Reform. Discussion Paper 317. Washington, D.C.: World Bank.

Subbarao, K., J. Braithwaite, and J. Jalan. 1995. "Protecting the Poor During Adjustment and Transitions." Human Capital Development and Operations Policy Working Paper 58. World Bank, Poverty and Social Policy Department, Washington, D.C.

Tanzi, V. 1995. "Fiscal Federalism and Decentralization: A Review of Some Efficiency and Macroeconomic Aspects." Paper presented for the World Bank's Annual Bank Conference on Development Economics, Washington, D.C.,May 1-2.

Teklu, T. 1994a. "Labor-Intensive Rural Roads in Kenya, Tanzania, and Botswana: Some Evidence on Design and Practice." International Food Policy Research Institute, Washington, D.C.

————. 1994b. "Minor Roads Program in Kenya: Potential for Short-Term Poverty Reduction Through Asset Creation." International Food Policy Research Institute, Washington, D.C.

————. 1995a. "Employment Programs for Food Security in Sub-Saharan Africa." 2020 Brief 28. International Food Policy Research Institute, Washington, D.C.

————. 1995b. "Labor-Intensive Public Works: The Experience of Botswana and Tanzania." In J. von Braun, ed., *Employment for Poverty Reduction and Food Security.* Washington, D.C.: International Food Policy Research Institute.

Thomas, V., and Y. Wang. 1994. "Asian Socialist and Non-Socialist Transition Experiences." Paper presented at the Asia Foundation Project Comparing Transitions in East Asia and Eastern Europe, Prague, December 2–3.

Tolley, George S. 1991. *Urban Housing Reform in China: An Economic Analysis.* World Bank Discussion Paper 123. Washington, D.C.: World Bank.

Tuck, L., and K. Lindert. 1996. *From Universal Food Subsidies to a Self-Targeted Program. A Case Study in Tunisian Reform.* World Bank Discussion Paper 381. Washington, D.C.: World Bank.

UNICEF. 1995. "Monitoring Economic and Social Welfare Indicators in Central and Eastern European Countries." Trans Monee Database. Economic and Social Policies Research Programme, International Child Development Centre, Florence, Italy.

van de Walle, D., and K. Nead. 1995. *Public Spending and the Poor: Theory and Evidence.* Baltimore, Md.: Johns Hopkins University Press.

van de Walle, D., M. Ravallion, and M. Gautam. 1994. "How Well Does the Social Safety Net Work? The Incidence of Cash Benefits in Hungary, 1987–89." Living Standards Measurement Study Working Paper 102. World Bank, Policy Research Department, Washington, D.C.

van Domelen, Julie. 1992. "Working with Non-Governmental Organizations." In S. Jorgensen, M. Grosh, and M. Schacter, eds., *Bolivia's Answer to Poverty, Economic Crisis, and Adjustment: The Emergency Social Fund.* Washington, D.C.: World Bank.

Vivian, J. 1994. "Social Safety Nets and Adjustment in Developing Countries." United Nations Research Institute for Social Development (UNRISD), Geneva.

von Braun, Joachim. 1989. "Social Security in Sub-Saharan Africa: Reflections on Policy Challenges." Development Economics Research Programme Discussion Paper 22. London School of Economics and Political Science.

von Braun, Joachim, T. Teklu, and Patrick Webb, eds., 1992. "Labour-Intensive Public Works for Food Security in Africa: Past Experience and Future Potential." *International Labour Review* 131(1): 19–33.

Walker, Bridget M., and Gabriel L. Dava. 1994. "The Social Dimensions of Adjustment (SDA) Initiative in Mozambique." One World Action, London.

Webb, A., K. Y. Lee, and A. San't Anna. 1995. *The Participation of Nongovernmental Organizations in Poverty Alleviation: A Case Study of the Honduras Social Investment Fund Project.* World Bank Discussion Paper 295. Washington, D.C.: World Bank.

Weitzman, M. L. 1977. "Is the Price System or Rationing More Effective in Getting a Commodity to Those who Need it Most?" *Bell Journal of Economics* 8(2): 517–24.

Wijga, A. 1983. "The Nutritional Impact of Food-for-Work Programmes." Netherlands Universities Foundation for International Cooperation, Wageningen, The Netherlands.

World Bank. 1983. "Bangladesh: Selected Issues in Rural Employment." Report 4292-BD. South Asia Programs Department, Washington, D.C.

———. 1989a. "Domestic Energy Pricing Policies." Industry and Energy Working Paper, Energy Series Paper 13. Industry and Energy Department, Washington, D.C.

———. 1989b. *Feeding Latin America's Children*. Latin American and the Caribbean Region Internal Discussion Paper. Washington, D.C.

———. 1989c. "Senegal: Public Works and Employment Project." Report 8032. Africa Region, Sahelian Department, Infrastructure Division, Washington, D.C.

———. 1990a. *Morocco: Reaching the Disadvantaged: Social Expenditure Priorities in the 1990s*. Washington, D.C.

———. 1990b. *Pakistan: A Profile of Poverty*. Report 8848. Country Operations Division, Washington, D.C.

———. 1991a. *America's Children: Survey of Food Programs*. Washington, D.C.

———. 1991b. *Democratic and Popular Republic of Algeria: Consumer Price Subsidy Reform*. Washington, D.C.

———. 1991c. *Nepal: Poverty and Incomes*. Washington, D.C.

———. 1991d. "Staff Appraisal Report: Burkino Faso Public Works and Employment Project." Report 9535-BUR. Africa Region, Sahelian Department, Infrastructure Operations Division, Washington, D.C.

———. 1991e. "Staff Appraisal Report: Republic of Niger Public Works and Employment Project." Report 9032-NIR. Africa Region, Sahelian Department, Infrastructure Operations Division, Washington, D.C.

———. 1992a. *Bolivia Emergency Social Fund II*. Project Completion Report 11471. Washington, D.C.

———. 1992b. "Conference on Public Expenditures and the Poor: Incidence and Targeting." June 17–19, Washington D.C.

———. 1992c. "Memorandum and Recommendation of the President of the International Development Association to the Executive Directors on a Proposed Credit in an Amount Equivalent to SDR 109.5 Million to the Republic of Zimbabwe for an Emergency Drought Recovery and Mitigation Project." Report P-5819-ZIM. Washington, D.C.

———. 1992d. "Memorandum and Recommendation of the President of the International Development Association to the Executive Directors on a Proposed Credit in the Amount Equivalent to US$20 Million to the Republic of Mali for a Public Works and Capacity Building Project." Report P-5742-MLI. Washington, D.C.

———. 1992e. *Senegal Second Public Works and Employment Project*. Staff Appraisal Report 10421. Africa Region, Sahelian Department, Infrastructure Division, Washington, D.C.

———. 1993a. *Ethiopia: Toward Poverty Alleviation and a Social Action Program*. Washington D.C.

———. 1993b. *The Gambia: An Assessment of Poverty*. Washington, D.C.

———. 1993c. *Housing—Enabling Markets to Work with Technical Supplements*. World Bank Policy Paper. Washington, D.C.

———. 1993d. *Indonesia: Public Expenditures and the Poor*. Washington D.C.

———. 1993e. *Latvia: The Transition to a Market Economy*. World Bank Country Study. Washington, D.C.

———. 1993f. *Mali: Assessment of Living Conditions*. Washington, D.C.

———. 1993g. "Memorandum and Recommendation of the President of the International Development Association to the Executive Directors on a Proposed Credit in the Amount Equivalent to SDR $7.9 Million to the Republic of the Gambia for a Public Works and Capacity Building Project." Report P-6092-GM. Washington, D.C.

————. 1993h. *Poland: Income Support and the Social Safety Net during the Transition.* World Bank Country Study. Washington, D.C.

————. 1993i. "Project Completion Report Republic of Ghana: Priority Works Project (Credit 1874-GH)." Africa Regional Office, Country Department IV, Infrastructure Division, Washington, D.C.

————. 1993j. *Ukraine: The Social Sectors during Transition.* World Bank Country Study. Washington, D.C.

————. 1993k. "Uruguay Poverty Assessment: Public Social Expenditures and Their Impact on the Income Distribution." Latin America and the Caribbean Region, Washington, D.C.

————. 1993l. *Uzbekistan: An Agenda for Economic Reform.* World Bank Country Study. Washington, D.C.

————. 1994a. *Averting the Old Age Crisis: Policy Options for a Graying World.* New York: Oxford University Press.

————. 1994b. *Colombia Poverty Assessment.* Washington, D.C.

————. 1994c. *Ecuador: Energy Pricing, Subsidies and Interfuel Substitution.* Report 11798-EC. Energy Sector Management Assistance Programme, Latin America and the Caribbean Region, Washington, D.C.

————. 1994d. *Hashemite Kingdom of Jordan: Poverty Assessment.* Washington, D.C.

————. 1994e. *Honduras Country Economic Memorandum/Poverty Assessment.* Washington, D.C.

————. 1994f. *Honduras Social Investment Fund.* Project Completion Report 13573. Latin America and the Caribbean Region, Washington, D.C.

————. 1994g. *Honduras Social Investment Fund.* Mid-term Review. Washington, D.C.

————. 1994h. *Honduras Social Investment Fund.* Project Performance Audit Report 13839-HO. Latin America and the Caribbean Region, Washington, D.C.

————. 1994i. *Indonesia: Stability, Growth and Equity in Repelita VI.* Washington, D.C.

————. 1994j. *Kingdom of Morocco: Poverty, Adjustment, and Growth.* Volumes I and II. Washington, D.C.

————. 1994k. "Kyrgyz Republic Economic Report." Report 12942. Washington, D.C.

————. 1994l. "Mauritania Poverty Assessment." Report 12182-MAU. Africa Region, Sahelian Department, Country Operations Division, Washington, D.C.

————. 1994m. "Memorandum and Recommendation of the President of the International Development Association to the Executive Directors on a Proposed Credit in the Amount Equivalent to SDR 12.4 Million to the Republic of Chad for a Public Works and Capacity Building Project." Report P-6211-CD, Washington, D.C.

————. 1994n. "Memorandum and Recommendation of the President of the International Development Association to the Executive Directors on a Proposed Supplemental Credit in the Amount Equivalent to SDR 6.8 Million to the Republic of Chad for the Social Development Action Project." Report P-6309-CD. Washington, D.C.

————. 1994o. "Memorandum and Recommendation of the President of the International Development Association to the Executive Directors on a Proposed Supplemental Credit in the Amount Equivalent to SDR 6.9 Million to the Republic of Mali for a Public Works and Capacity Building Project." Report P-6285-MLI. Washington, D.C.

————. 1994p. "Memorandum and Recommendation of the President of the International Development Association to the Executive Directors on a Proposed Supplemental Credit in the Amount Equivalent to SDR 6.9 Million to the Republic of Niger for a Public Works and Employment Project." Report P-6283-NIR. Washington, D.C.

————. 1994q. *Moldova: Moving to a Market Economy.* World Bank Country Study. Washington, D.C.

————. 1994r. "Russia: Social Protection During Transition and Beyond." Report 11748-RU, Vol. II. Europe and Central Asia Region Country Department III, Human Resources Division, Washington, D.C.

————. 1994s. *Statistical Handbook 1994. States of the Former USSR. Studies of Economies in Transformation No. 10.* Washington, D.C.

————. 1994t. *Ukbekistan (Adjusting Social Protection).* Washington, D.C.

————. 1994u. *Zambia: Poverty Assessment.* Washington, D.C.

————. 1995a. *Hungary: Structural Reforms for Sustainable Growth.* Washington, D.C.

————. 1995b. *The Kyrgyz Republic Poverty Assessment and Strategy.* Volume 1 (Main Report) and Volume 2 (Statistical Annex). Washington, D.C.

————. 1995c. "Memorandum and Recommendation of the President of the International Development Association to the Executive Directors on a Proposed Credit in the Amount Equivalent to US$40.0 Million to the Republic of Madagascar for a Social Fund II Project." Report P-6635-MAG. Washington, D.C.

————. 1995d. "Performance Audit Report: Honduras Social Investment Fund Projects I and II (Credits 2212-HO and 2401-HO)." Report 13839-HO. Washington, D.C.

————. 1995e. "Philippines: Selected Social Safety Net Programs: Targeting, Cost-Effectiveness and Options for Reform." Report 13921-PH. East Asia and Pacific Region Country Department I, Human Resources Operations Division, Washington, D.C.

————. 1995f. "Poverty in Russia: An Assessment." Report 14110-RU. Europe and Central Asia Country Department III, Human Resources Division, Washington, D.C.

————. 1995g. "Chile: Second Housing Sector Project." Project Completion Report 13769. Latin America and the Caribbean Region, Washington, D.C.

————. 1995h. "Project Preparation Mission, Egypt Social Fund for Development II." Middle East and North Africa Region, Washington, D.C.

————. 1995i. "Republic of Madagascar Social Fund II Project." Staff Appraisal Report 14489-MAG. Sub-Saharan Africa Region, Washington, D.C.

————. 1995j. "Republic of Tunisia: From Universal Food Subsidies to a Self-Targeted Program." Report 14596. Middle East and North Africa Country Department I, Washington, D.C.

————. 1995k. *Social Indicators of Development.* Washington, D.C.

————. 1995l. *Sri Lanka: Poverty Assessment.* Washington, D.C.

————. 1995m. *World Development Report 1995: Workers in an Integrating World.* New York: Oxford University Press.

————. 1995n. *Understanding Poverty in Poland.* A World Bank Country Study. Washington, D.C.

————. 1996. "Pakistan—First, Second, and Third Income Generating Projects for Refugee Areas." Operations Evaluation Department, Washington, D.C.

Yaron, Jacob. 1992a. *Assessing Development Finance Institutions: A Public Interest Analysis.* World Bank Discussion Paper 174. Washington, D.C.: World Bank.

————. 1992b. *Successful Rural Finance Institutions.* World Bank Discussion Paper 150. Washington, D.C.: World Bank.

————. 1994. "What Makes Rural Finance Institutions Successful?" *The World Bank Research Observer* 9(1): 49–70.

Directions in Development

Begun in 1994, this series contains short essays, written for a general audience, often to summarize published or forthcoming books or to highlight current development issues.

Africa's Management in the 1990s and Beyond: Reconciling Indigenous and Transplanted Institutions

Building Human Capital for Better Lives

Class Action: Improving School Performance in the Developing World through Better Health and Nutrition

Decentralization of Education: Community Financing

Decentralization of Education: Politics and Consensus

Decentralization of Education: Teacher Management

Deep Crises and Reform: What Have We Learned?

Early Child Development: Investing in the Future

Financing Health Care in Sub-Saharan Africa through User Fees and Insurance

Global Capital Supply and Demand: Is There Enough to Go Around?

Implementing Projects for the Poor: What Has Been Learned?

Improving Early Childhood Development: An Integrated Program for the Philippines

India's Family Welfare Program: Moving to a Reproductive and Child Health Approach (with a separate supplement)

Investing in People: The World Bank in Action

Managing Commodity Booms — and Busts

Meeting the Infrastructure Challenge in Latin America and the Caribbean

Monitoring the Learning Outcomes of Education Systems

MIGA: The First Five Years and Future Challenges

Nurturing Development: Aid and Cooperation in Today's Changing World

Nutrition in Zimbabwe: An Update

Poverty Reduction in South Asia: Promoting Participation of the Poor

Private and Public Initiatives: Working Together for Health and Education

Private Sector Participation in Water Supply and Sanitation in Latin America

Reversing the Spiral: The Population, Agriculture, and Environment Nexus in Sub-Saharan Africa (with a separate supplement)

A Strategy for Managing Water in the Middle East and North Africa

Taxing Bads by Taxing Goods: Pollution Control with Presumptive Charges

Toward Sustainable Management of Water Resources

Trade Performance and Policy in the New Independent States

The Transition from War to Peace in Sub-Saharan Africa

Unshackling the Private Sector: A Latin American Story

The Uruguay Round: Widening and Deepening the World Trading System